REVOLUTIONARY
FRENCH COOKING

DANIEL GALMICHE

DUNCAN BAIRD PUBLISHERS

LONDON

REVOLUTIONARY FRENCH COOKING
Daniel Galmiche

First published in the USA and Canada in 2014
by Duncan Baird Publishers, an imprint of
Watkins Publishing Limited
PO Box 883, Oxford OX1 9PL, England

A member of Osprey Group

Osprey Publishing
PO Box 3985
New York, NY 10185-3985
Tel: 212 753 4402
Email: info@ospreypublishing.com

Publisher: Grace Cheetham
Editors: Nicola Graimes and Wendy Hobson
Americanizer: Beverly Le Blanc
Art Direction and Design: Manisha Patel
Cover Design: Georgina Hewitt
Commissioned Photography: Yuki Sugiura
Food Stylists: Daniel Galmiche with Aya Nishimura
Prop Stylist: Wei Tang
Production: Uzma Taj

ISBN: 978-1-84899-212-2

10 9 8 7 6 5 4 3 2 1

Typeset in Eurostile
Color reproduction by PDQ, UK
Printed in China

Publisher's note
While every care has been taken in compiling the recipes for
this book, Watkins Publishing Limited, or any other persons who
have been involved in working on this publication, cannot accept
responsibility for any errors or omissions, inadvertent or not, that
might be found in the recipes or text, nor for any problems that
might arise as a result of preparing one of these recipes. If you are
pregnant or breastfeeding or have any special dietary requirements
or medical conditions, it is advisable to consult a medical
professional before following any of the recipes contained in this
book. Ill or elderly people, babies, young children and women who
are pregnant or breastfeeding should avoid recipes containing
raw meat or fish or uncooked eggs.

Notes on the recipes
Unless otherwise stated:
• Use free-range eggs and poultry
• Use extra-large eggs and medium fruit and vegetables
• Use fresh ingredients, including herbs and chilies
• 1 tsp. = 5ml   1 tbsp. = 15ml   1 cup = 240ml
• Cooking containers specified by dimensions are measured
length x width x height

Watkins Publishing is supporting the Woodland Trust, the UK's
leading woodland conservation charity, by funding tree-planting
initiatives and woodland maintenance.

www.dbp.co.uk

Contents

24 LIBERTÉ

Classic dishes released from the constraints of traditional French cooking

82 EGALITÉ

Democratic recipes that elevate humble ingredients to starring roles

150 FRATERNITÉ

Dishes that bring innovation and style to classic combinations of ingredients

Dedication

This book is dedicated to two very special and important people—my wife, Claire, and my son, Antoine. Without them in my life, and their tremendous support, I would not be able to do what I do. They both love food, they have endless patience and they are fun to be with. They also understand what I do for living, which makes it so much easier for me when I am so often at work. So this cookbook is for you guys, with all my love—always.

Foreword

Daniel's new cookbook is well named, because we're in the midst of a cooking revolution, especially here in Britain, where Daniel and I both cook. A few years ago some colleagues and I published a statement describing this revolution under the headings "excellence," "openness" and "integrity." Daniel, naturally, has categorized it under *"liberté*," *"égalité"* and *"fraternité*," but he identifies many of the same characteristics as typical of modern cuisine: respect for both tradition and innovation; enthusiasm and curiosity about the whole gamut of ingredients; and a determination to pursue excellence, but also to demystify cooking.

Such sentiments are typical of Daniel. His cooking style is different from mine, but when I first met him I immediately recognized a kindred spirit —warm, energetic and completely caught up in the romance of cooking and the pleasures of the table. So, when he became head chef at Cliveden, which is just a short drive from the Fat Duck, we would meet up regularly for a coffee and a chat about every aspect of cuisine.

Sadly, the ever-increasing pressures on our time mean we aren't able to do this any more. But in the pages that follow you'll get a taste of what it's like to hang out with Daniel, and experience his brilliant cooking and infectious enthusiasm for anything to do with food.

Vive la révolution!

Heston Blumenthal

Introduction

I could almost have started this book with a story:

> *Once upon a time in Franche-Comté, a young boy was walking through the kitchen at his great-aunt's house. Suddenly he stopped in his stride, looked up and shouted,*
>
> *"When I grow up, I want to be a cuisinier." He was five years old. At that time, nobody thought anything about it and life went on as usual. But, some time later …*

… that young boy did, indeed, become a chef. And I am sure you know who I am talking about!

I have always enjoyed my profession and, after many years, I still love it. It's challenging, exciting and fun. It gives me the chance to work with some fabulous people—dedicated, knowledgable and hard-working—some with considerable experience and others young and eager to learn and experiment, always keen to try new techniques, new produce, new ideas.

Back to my roots
But that is moving ahead. From as long ago as I can remember, I was surrounded by gourmands. Food was very important in our house and I learned all the time from my mom—for I watched her constantly. Mom was passionate about food, always testing, asking me what I thought, or calling Dad to make him try this sauce or that new dish. She went to so much trouble to cook for all of us and was always totally focused. She hated it when something wasn't right, even to the point of starting again from scratch if it was for the Christmas dinner, or another special day, and she was not happy with the dish.

The style of cooking reflected the classic cuisine of France, but even more it followed the traditional style of Franche-Comté. All the time, we followed the seasons and enjoyed the freshest produce at its best. Dad used to hunt, so Mom cooked whatever was in season, with fresh vegetables from our garden and fruit from the orchard. To this day, my favorite dish is *gibelotte de lapin*, farm rabbit casserole—always a delight.

When I was fifteen, I went to catering college for a year, and after that I began a three-year apprenticeship to learn the skills of my craft. That was really hard work, with the long hours, strict discipline and so much to learn. You had to stay focused every moment, which was very tiring at times. But that is something that never changes in a good kitchen. Dedication, focus, discipline and passion are vital if you want to be a good chef, and if you want to be successful.

When I qualified, I clearly remember the first day I started work. It was in the Luxeuil-les-Bains Hotel, in Beausite. The chef just put three large boxes of spinach leaves in front of me, showed me how he wanted them prepared and off I went. And, I've never looked back. I loved cooking from the start, even though it was tough—like cleaning the stove and replacing the coal early in the morning, in winter, when I was being punished for not coming up to scratch. Luckily for me, though, that was the last winter before the coal-fired stove was replaced with a modern version.

When I finally emerged into the culinary world of France, I was imbued with the classic principles of French cuisine and I applied them rigorously. I strove for perfection in everything and honed my skills and experience in restaurants in France, Britain, Singapore and Portugal, among other places. Having settled in Britain in 1986, I gained a Michelin star in four different restaurants, and then was finally appointed executive head chef at The Vineyard in 2009.

French brasserie cooking

If I felt very fortunate to have advanced my career to such a level, I felt even more so in 2010 when I was offered the opportunity to publish my first book. As soon as we set to work on my *French Brasserie Cookbook*, I knew exactly what I wanted the concept to be and what I wanted the recipes to look like. This book would represent my childhood memories of cooking: using the seasons, featuring local specialties, the grandmother way. I wanted it to be totally French, very regional and to paint a picture of the way we cooked in my home in Franche-Comté.

Setting the idea in a broader context, I had always believed that brasserie cooking had developed from that very same style of home cooking, but that the link hadn't been made completely, and when I researched the idea I found it to be true. So the project not only allowed me to revisit so many of the recipes from my childhood, but also gave me the chance to learn so much more about where brasserie food originally came from, when it was created and why it has become so popular.

It is difficult to describe the emotions when you actually hold your first book in your hands. And what I love in particular is all the positive feedback. It pleases me enormously that you are out there cooking my recipes and enjoying them, so, please, do continue to cook—and to tell me all about your successes.

Looking back ... looking forward

When I started to think about a new book, I decided a complete change of perspective was needed. *French Brasserie Cookbook* was a book focused on my roots in French cooking, looking back to recapture the past traditions of my childhood, with some modern twists along the way, of course. But things have changed in cooking in France, as they have in countries all around the world, and I wanted to reflect those changes. This book, I decided, would have its gaze fixed firmly on the future.

It used to be the case that classic French cuisine was *the* cuisine—everything else was just cooking. French food stood alone as establishing the principles of how to cook: the ingredients, the methods, the presentation. Absolute rules were laid down on how you would make each recipe and chefs never strayed from those rules—there was one way to make a particular dish and that was the only way to do it. French style and technique set the benchmark for all cooking; it did not just consider itself superior, it was in a class of its own and, while some might have begrudged its eminence, most people agreed.

The rumblings of discontent

Slowly and surely, however, things began to change in the world of food and cooking. People began to travel farther afield and try new ingredients and new flavors they then wanted to reproduce when they got home. As restaurants became more varied and accessible, an increasing number of people took advantage of the opportunity to dine out, and to experiment with new flavors and styles. The culinary public was becoming more knowledgeable and more sophisticated.

At that time, many ingredients that are now so easy to find in any supermarket were only available to the privileged few living in major cities. It seems strange now that it was not so long ago that sun-dried tomatoes, balsamic vinegar, pistachio nuts and even crème fraîche—to name just a few—were difficult to come by! Subsequently, however, supermarket chains began to change, too, broadening their scope and offering some of these new, "exotic" ingredients.

Man the barricades

And so the real revolution began. Quietly at first, but gaining increasing momentum, both chefs in restaurants and cooks at home began to experiment. They started to wonder if they could make dishes they enjoyed on vacation—even if they adapted them to suit the ingredients available—

and it worked. Cooks tried different international cuisines and learned from them, mixing European with Asian, or African with Caribbean. They took full advantage of the exciting options in supermarkets and cooking became a playground for freedom and experimentation. And didn't we love it!

Many home cooks were spending more money on excellent-quality food, taking more time in the kitchen, especially at weekends, cooking for themselves or entertaining friends. Looking to expand their knowledge and broaden their skills, they absorbed recipes, techniques and ideas as fast as they could from the new food magazines and the flood of cooking shows on TV. Their kitchen shelves displayed a selection of excellent cookbooks in which chefs shared their recipes, complete with beautiful photographs to illustrate the final results.

Blowing with these winds of change was another gust of fresh air: the move toward lighter, healthier foods with lower fat and less sugar.

The winner emerges

Emerging from this revolution came the less prescriptive, more eclectic style that is how we cook today. French cuisine first lost its unique status, then fell out of favor and began to fade into the background. Did we really need all that cream and those heavy sauces? Why should there be just one right way to make a dish when it could be delicious made in different, often simpler, ways? Why did cooking have to be so time-consuming if quicker techniques gave the same results? Why should cooks feel under pressure to do everything "right" by the book, when cooking was meant to be fun? French cuisine was dismissed as outmoded—we had moved on.

The foundations remain

Meanwhile, I was enjoying this new way of cooking for a more modern, knowledgeable, relaxed audience, but I never abandoned my roots in classic French cooking. At The Vineyard, we were introducing innovative ideas all the time, making our food lighter and more modern, trying to improve our offering and chime in with this modern zeitgeist. Our simpler techniques made cooking more fun and more accessible. Guests loved trying our taster menus and giving us their feedback on particular successes.

But just because something needs to change, it does not mean that it should be abandoned entirely. While we all need to break away from our parents and make our own way, the values and standards we have learned from them remain vitally important. We might have shaken loose from the constraints of classic French style, but the foundations remained intact: quality ingredients treated with care and respect to create a range of delicious dishes.

And that is what this book sets out to do: show you just how wonderful French food can be when used as a sound and secure foundation on which to build. I have taken the best of French style and given it new twists and innovative touches that rejuvenate and energize this fabulous cuisine.

Liberté, égalité, fraternité

So, what are we trying to achieve here? Having established the concept for this new book, it seemed only logical to use the motto of the French Revolution to define its heart: *liberté, égalité, fraternité*. The three main chapters of the book bring a unique slant to modern French cooking. Each original recipe uses an unusual marriage of flavors with unexpected twists and surprises, plus I even let you in on some professional secrets.

Liberté showcases recipes that have been released from the shackles of traditional French cooking, replacing complex traditional French techniques with simpler ones and bringing fresh, new ideas to the table. One I particularly like is a beautiful pork shoulder steak, a dish that seems so simple but is made sublime with the innovation of fresh cabbage, still crunchy and full of flavor, cooked with fresh chili and gingerroot to give it strength, and drizzled with honey to lift the dish (see page 50).

Egalité brings democracy to the recipes by elevating humble ingredients to take the starring roles. Ingredients like the common Jerusalem artichoke become the basis for an imaginative recipe rather than being a scarcely noticed side dish—witness my Jerusalem Artichoke Velouté with Truffle Oil and Chive Cream (see page 97).

Fraternité celebrates traditional brotherhoods by creating dishes that bring innovation and style to classic combinations of ingredients. My Chocolate, Chili and Lemongrass Tart (see page 208), for example, beautifully illustrates this chapter of the book.

In each of these chapters, I have used ideas we have been developing in our restaurant to make sure they are right up to date. That did raise the issue of whether they were too complicated for home cooks, or perhaps needed professional equipment that home cooks did not have, so I also thought about how easy the food would be to make at home. Recipes that are too daunting to attempt would have no place in my book! So, I adapted the techniques to make sure any competent cook would be able to recreate them without any problems. You won't need expensive, professional equipment. You will need a reasonably well-equipped kitchen, however, including kitchen scales, a few small tools like a thermometer and a timer, a good blender, a steamer and a wok (we are going to use that for your smoking ingredients—how exciting is that?), but nothing out of the ordinary. Mind you, I do not promise all the recipes are simple, because some are not, but they are all achievable—and they all have a very interesting twist. Just follow the methods carefully and enjoy both cooking and eating the food.

Beyond the barricades

Hopefully you will agree we have thrown open the door to a whole new range of interesting opportunities for home cooks to expand their repertoire and test their culinary skills.

I think you are going to really enjoy cooking the recipes in this book; they are different, entertaining and fun. I know every chef says the same, but I am confident I am right! And the fact my friend Heston Blumenthal has written the foreword for this book (as he did for my first book) is, for me, very flattering and humbling, and makes me think that he, too, likes the way I have presented these recipes for you. Because, trust me, Heston is no stranger to this type of cooking, as he has proved so many times.

Holding my *French Brasserie Cookbook* was a dream come true for me. Now another dream has come true, because, if you are reading this, you are holding my second book in your hands. Enjoy!

BASIC RECIPES

In this chapter, you will find a few basic recipes that are essentials in many of my dishes, like a homemade stock and a salad dressing. Plus, I've selected some recipes that are perfect to serve with the main courses in this book. Complex dishes are complemented most effectively by the simplest accompaniments, and if they are carefully created using the best ingredients, then you really cannot go wrong.

Chicken Stock

MAKES 2 quarts
PREPARATION TIME 10 minutes,
   plus at least 1 hour cooling
COOKING TIME 2 to 2½ hours

4½ pounds chicken wings or bones,
   or 2 chicken carcasses
1 thyme sprig
2 carrots, peeled and halved
   lengthwise
1 small handful parsley stems
1 small onion, unpeeled and halved
6 black peppercorns

1 Put all the ingredients in a large, heavy-bottomed saucepan over high heat. Add 4 quarts cold water and bring to a boil, then skim off any foam that rises to the surface. Turn the heat down to low and leave the stock to simmer, uncovered, 2 to 2½ hours until the liquid reduces by half.

2 Remove the pan from the heat and pass the stock through a strainer, using a ladle to help you, then leave it to cool at least 1 hour.

3 If you want to freeze the stock, divide the cool stock into small plastic tubs with lids, leaving some headspace for it to expand, then pop the containers in the freezer up to 4 weeks.

Beef or Veal Stock

MAKES 2 quarts
PREPARATION TIME 15 minutes,
   plus at least 1 hour cooling
COOKING TIME 3 hours 40 minutes

2¾ pounds beef bones from roast
   beef or veal bones
2 tablespoons olive oil
1 thyme sprig
2 parsley sprigs
2 carrots, peeled and halved
   lengthwise
2 onions, peeled and quartered
1 celery stick, chopped
1 garlic bulb, unpeeled and halved
   crosswise
6 black peppercorns
2 bay leaves

1 Heat the oven to 400°F. Put the bones in a roasting pan and roast 20 minutes, stirring occasionally, or until they are golden brown. Transfer the bones to a large, heavy-bottomed saucepan, add all the remaining ingredients and cook over medium heat 10 minutes.

2 Add 4 quarts cold water and bring to a boil over high heat. Skim off any foam that rises to the surface, then turn the heat down to low and simmer, uncovered, 1 hour.

3 Top up the water to the previous level, then return to a boil and simmer 2 hours longer, or until the liquid reduces by half. Remove the pan from the heat and pass the stock through a strainer, using a ladle to help you, then leave it to cool at least 1 hour.

4 If you want to freeze the stock, divide the cool stock into small plastic tubs with lids, leaving some headspace for it to expand, then pop the containers in the freezer up to 4 weeks.

NOTE AND VARIATION
Using Beef Stock: Most chefs use veal jus rather than beef stock, because it can be too strong. Use the bones from your Sunday joint to make a good stock, or substitute a store-bought veal jus.
For Lamb Stock: Use lamb bones instead of beef bones and make as above. Leave the stock to cool, then chill. Lift off the layer of fat from the surface, then use or freeze as above.

Fish Stock

MAKES 2 quarts
PREPARATION TIME 10 minutes, plus
  30 minutes soaking and at least
  1 hour cooling
COOKING TIME 2¼ to 2¾ hours

2¾ pounds fresh fish bones,
  flesh removed
1 small handful parsley stems
1 onion, unpeeled and quartered
1 thyme sprig
1 celery stick, halved
6 black peppercorns

1 Put the fish bones in a large bowl, cover with cold water and leave to soak 10 minutes, then rinse thoroughly, using a strainer. Repeat this process three more times.

2 Put the bones in a large, heavy-bottomed saucepan with all the remaining ingredients and cover with 4 quarts cold water. Bring to a boil over high heat, then skim off any foam that rises to the surface. Turn the heat down to low and leave the stock to simmer, uncovered, 2 to 2½ hours until the liquid reduces by half.

3 Remove the pan from the heat and pass the stock through a strainer, using a ladle to help you, then leave it to cool at least 1 hour.

4 If you want to freeze the stock, divide the cool stock into small plastic tubs with lids, leaving some headspace for it to expand, then pop the containers in the freezer up to 4 weeks.

Vegetable Stock

MAKES 1½ quarts
PREPARATION TIME 15 minutes,
  plus at least 1 hour cooling
COOKING TIME 2¼ hours

2 tablespoons olive oil
1 celery stick, chopped
1 thyme sprig
1 scallion, chopped
1 handful parsley stems, chopped
1 garlic clove
2 carrots, peeled and halved
  lengthwise
2 new potatoes, halved
6 black peppercorns
2 button mushrooms, halved

1 Warm the oil in a large, heavy-bottomed saucepan over medium heat. Add all the remaining ingredients, partially cover, and cook 10 minutes. Add about 3 quarts cold water and bring to a boil over high heat, then turn the heat down to low and leave the stock to simmer, uncovered, 2 hours, or until the liquid reduces by half.

2 Remove the pan from the heat and pass the stock through a strainer, using a ladle to help you, then leave it to cool at least 1 hour.

3 If you want to freeze the stock, divide the cool stock into small plastic tubs with lids, leaving some headspace for it to expand, then pop the containers in the freezer up to 4 weeks.

Mayonnaise
with Variations

MAKES scant 1 cup
PREPARATION TIME 10 minutes

2 egg yolks
1 tablespoon French mustard
a squeeze lemon juice
⅔ cup sunflower oil or grapeseed
  oil
sea salt and freshly ground
  black pepper

1 Beat together the egg yolks and mustard in a bowl. Add a few drops of lemon juice and season with salt and pepper. Gradually drizzle in the oil, a little at a time, whisking continuously until the mayonnaise thickens.

2 For the variations, stir the additional ingredients into the mayonnaise, then whisk in 2 tablespoons hot water to help bind the ingredients.

VARIATIONS (pictured on page 14; optional)
For Chili Mayonnaise: Add 1 long red chili, seeded and finely chopped.
For Tarragon Mayonnaise: Add 1 tablespoon tarragon vinegar and 1 teaspoon chopped tarragon leaves.
For Garlic Mayonnaise: Add 2 finely chopped garlic cloves.

French Dressing

MAKES about ⅔ cup
PREPARATION TIME 5 minutes

2 teaspoons Dijon mustard
2 tablespoons white balsamic
  vinegar
¼ cup olive oil or sunflower oil
¼ cup extra virgin olive oil
  or sunflower oil
sea salt and freshly ground
  black pepper

1 Whisk together the mustard, vinegar and 2 tablespoons water in a small bowl, then whisk in the olive oil and extra virgin olive oil until you have a very thick, glossy liquid.

2 Season with salt and pepper to taste before drizzling over salads.

Croutons

SERVES 4
PREPARATION TIME 5 minutes
COOKING TIME 5 minutes

2 tablespoons unsalted butter
2 tablespoons olive oil
2 small slices sourdough bread,
  crusts removed and cut into
  ½-inch cubes
sea salt and freshly ground
  black pepper

You can cut the bread into whatever size or shape croutons you like, just make sure you cook them until they are golden brown on each side, without letting them burn.

1 Melt the butter with the oil in a large skillet over medium heat. When the butter is foaming, add the cubes of bread and fry 45 to 60 seconds on each side until they are golden brown.

2 Drain the croutons on paper towels and season with salt and pepper.

Reduced Balsamic Vinegar

MAKES about 4 tablespoons
COOKING TIME 12 minutes

½ cup balsamic vinegar

1 Pour the vinegar into a small sauté pan or skillet over medium heat and bring to a simmer.

2 Turn the heat down to low and simmer 10 minutes, or until the liquid reduces by half and is thick and syrupy.

Belgian Endive and Radish Salad

SERVES 4
PREPARATION TIME 10 minutes

2 large heads Belgian endive, halved lengthwise and leaves separated
12 radishes, thinly sliced
3 tablespoons chopped parsley leaves
1 tablespoon Chardonnay vinegar
3 tablespoons extra virgin olive oil
sea salt and freshly ground black pepper

1 Toss the Belgian endive leaves, radishes and parsley together in a bowl.

2 Whisk together the Chardonnay vinegar and oil in a small bowl and season with salt and pepper. Drizzle the dressing over the leaves and toss together to combine.

Tomato and Deep-fried Caper Salad

SERVES 4
PREPARATION TIME 10 minutes
COOKING TIME 1 minute

4 large beefsteak tomatoes, thinly sliced
1 red onion, very thinly sliced
3½oz baby capers in a jar
⅔ cup vegetable oil
½ cup extra virgin olive oil
1 tablespoon sherry vinegar
1 small handful basil leaves, torn
sea salt and freshly ground black pepper

1 Put the tomatoes and red onion on a serving plate and season with salt and pepper. Open the jar of capers, strain off 2 tablespoons of the liquid and leave to one side. Take out half the capers and pat them dry very carefully on paper towels.

2 Put the vegetable oil in a small saucepan over medium heat until just shimmering. Be careful not to overheat the oil—it must not be smoking but needs to be hot enough to fry the capers. Carefully add the dry capers to the hot oil and fry 30 seconds, or until they are nice and crisp. Again, make sure you don't leave them frying for too long, because they just need to be crisp. Drain the capers on paper towels.

3 To make the dressing, whisk together the reserved caper liquid, the extra virgin olive oil and sherry vinegar, then pour it over the tomatoes. Scatter the deep-fried capers over the top, then finish with freshly torn basil leaves.

Creamed Mashed Potatoes with Horseradish

SERVES 4
PREPARATION TIME 30 minutes
COOKING TIME 55 minutes

2¼ pounds Idaho potatoes, unpeeled
¾ cup plus 2 tablespons whole milk
¾ cup plus 2 tablespons
  heavy cream
2 garlic cloves, sliced
1-inch piece horseradish, peeled,
  or 2 teaspoons wasabi paste
sea salt and freshly ground
  black pepper

1 Put the potatoes in a large saucepan, cover with cold water and add a pinch of salt. Bring to a boil over high heat, then turn the heat down to low, partially cover with a lid and leave to simmer 30 to 40 minutes, or until they are cooked through.

2 Meanwhile, heat the oven to 400°F. Drain the potatoes, then put them in a roasting pan and roast 10 minutes. Remove the pan from the oven and as soon as the potatoes are cool enough to handle, peel them and pass them through a strainer, using a ladle to help you, or through a food mill into a bowl. Cover the bowl and leave to one side but do not let the potatoes become cold or they will be gluey when they are mashed.

3 Put the milk, cream and garlic in a saucepan over medium heat and bring to a boil. Pour half the mixture into the potatoes and mix well, then gradually add the remaining liquid, stirring all the time. Season with salt and pepper to taste, then grate 2 teaspoons of the horseradish directly over the mash so you get all the juices. Alternatively, sprinkle with the wasabi paste. Serve hot.

Rutabaga Boulangère

SERVES 4
PREPARATION TIME 15 minutes,
  plus making the stock
COOKING TIME 55 minutes

a little butter, for greasing
2 large rutabagas, about 1¼ pounds
  each, peeled and cut into
  ¼-inch slices
2 large white onions, sliced
2 garlic cloves, finely chopped
2 thyme sprigs, leaves picked
2¼ cups Chicken Stock (see
  page 16)
sea salt and freshly ground
  black pepper

1 Heat the oven to 400°F and lightly butter a shallow baking dish large enough to hold about 1½ quarts liquid. Bring a large saucepan of salted water to a boil. Add the rutabaga and boil 4 to 5 minutes, then drain and spread out on a clean dish towel to dry. Leave to cool slightly before building your *boulangère*.

2 Spread a layer of rutabaga in the bottom of the prepared dish, followed by a layer of the onions and a sprinkling of garlic and thyme leaves. Season with a little salt and pepper. Repeat with as many layers as will fit in the dish, but finish with a layer of rutabaga. Press down lightly.

3 Put the stock in a saucepan over medium heat and warm slightly, then pour it over the *boulangère*. The stock should not cover the top layer of rutabaga, because the rutabaga will sink down slightly as it cooks.

4 Bake 45 to 50 minutes, then check to see that the rutabaga is tender when pierced with the tip of a knife. If not, return the dish to the oven 5 minutes longer, then check again until the knife slides easily into the rutabaga. Serve hot.

Thai-style Pilaf Rice

SERVES 4
PREPARATION TIME 10 minutes,
  plus making the stock
COOKING TIME 25 minutes

4 tablespoons olive oil
1 large onion, diced
1½-inch piece gingerroot, peeled
  and diced
1 long red chili, seeded and
  finely chopped
1 lemongrass stalk, split lengthwise
1 cup basmati rice
1¾ cups Vegetable Stock (see
  page 16)
3 tablespoons unsalted butter, diced
grated zest and juice of 1 lime
sea salt and freshly ground
  black pepper

1 Heat the oven to 300°F. Heat an ovenproof skillet over medium heat. Add the oil and onion and fry 3 minutes, or until the onion is just soft, then add the ginger, chili and lemongrass and fry 3 minutes longer, or until all the flavorings are soft, but not colored.

2 Turn the heat down to low and add the rice. Fold it in gently, then leave it to sweat 3 to 4 minutes. Add the stock, turn the heat up and bring to a simmer. Season with salt and pepper, dot the butter over the top of the rice, then cover with a *cartouche* (see page 218) or a lid and transfer to the oven 12 to 14 minutes.

3 Check to see if the rice is tender and the liquid is absorbed. If the rice is not quite tender, return it to the oven 5 minutes longer, then check again. Remove the *cartouche* and discard the lemongrass, then season the rice with the grated lime zest and juice and salt and pepper to taste. Serve hot.

Tomato Coulis

MAKES 3½ cups
PREPARATION TIME 20 minutes
COOKING TIME 40 minutes

12 ripe tomatoes
2 tablespoons olive oil
1 red chili, seeded and chopped
10 ounces roasted peppers from
  a jar, drained and finely chopped
1 small shallot, finely chopped
⅓ cup strawberries, hulled
4 garlic cloves, crushed
a pinch sugar
a pinch smoked paprika
4 tablespoons white balsamic
  vinegar
2 large basil leaves
sea salt and freshly ground
  black pepper

1 With a sharp knife, cut a small cross on the bottom of each tomato, then put them in a heatproof bowl and cover with boiling water. Leave 30 seconds, then lift them out with a slotted spoon and put them in a bowl of ice water. Lift the tomatoes out, then peel off and discard the skins. Cut the tomatoes into quarters, remove and discard the seeds, then roughly chop the flesh.

2 Heat a sauté pan over high heat. Add the tomatoes, oil, chili, peppers, shallot, strawberries and garlic. Turn the heat down to low and sweat 4 to 5 minutes until all the ingredients are soft.

3 Add the sugar and paprika, then stir in the vinegar and deglaze the pan by stirring to remove any caramelized bits stuck to the bottom. Cover with a *cartouche* (see page 218) or a lid and cook over low heat 30 to 35 minutes until you have a very soft puree.

4 Transfer the puree to a blender, add the basil and blitz to a fine puree, or use a hand-blender. Pass the puree through a fine strainer, using a ladle to help you, into a bowl, then season with salt and pepper to taste.

Savory Piecrust Dough

MAKES enough for an 11¼-inch pan
PREPARATION TIME 15 minutes, plus
   2 hours chilling

1 stick unsalted butter, at room
   temperature and roughly chopped
2 cups all-purpose flour, plus extra
   for dusting
a pinch salt
1 egg yolk
3 tablespoons milk or water

1 Put the butter, flour and salt in a mixing bowl and rub together with your fingertips until you have a crumbly, powdery texture. Add the egg yolk and milk and continue working the dough until the ingredients are combined and the texture is smooth. Turn out the dough onto a lightly floured countertop and knead 1 to 2 minutes until silky smooth.

2 When the dough is ready, either wrap it in a clean dish towel or put it on a plate, cover with a clean dish towel and leave in the refrigerator 2 hours before using—this relaxes the dough and make it easier to use.

Sweet Piecrust Dough

MAKES enough for an 8-inch pan
PREPARATION TIME 10 minutes, plus
   20 minutes chilling

grated zest of ½ blood orange
6 tablespoons unsalted butter, soft
a pinch salt
½ cup confectioner's sugar
¼ cup very finely ground
   blanched almonds
1 egg
1⅓ cups plus 1 tablespoon
   all-purpose flour

1 Beat together the orange zest, butter, salt, sugar, ground almonds and egg in a bowl until light and fluffy, then sift in the flour and fold through. As soon as the dough is formed, stop! You don't want to work this dough at all.

2 Wrap the dough in plastic wrap and put in the refrigerator 20 minutes, then bake as directed in the recipe.

Beurre Noisette

MAKES ½ cup
COOKING TIME 5 minutes

1 stick unsalted butter
2 teaspoons lemon juice
sea salt and freshly ground
   black pepper

1 Heat a skillet over medium-high heat. Add the butter and cook it a few minutes until it turns a nutty golden brown.

2 Add the lemon juice and swirl to combine, then remove the pan from the heat immediately. Season with salt and pepper.

Chili Crème Anglaise

MAKES 5¼ cups
PREPARATION TIME 20 minutes, plus
  30 minutes infusing and at least
  1 hour chilling
COOKING TIME 15 minutes

1 quart whole milk
1 long red chili, halved lengthwise
  and seeded
1 vanilla bean, halved lengthwise and
  seeds scraped out
8 egg yolks
1 cup sugar

1 Put the milk in a saucepan over low heat. Add the chili and vanilla seeds. Whisk, then throw in the vanilla bean as well. Bring to a boil, then remove the pan from the heat, cover with plastic wrap and leave to infuse at room temperature 30 minutes.

2 Meanwhile, whisk together the egg yolks and sugar in a large bowl. Strain the chili-infused milk through a fine strainer onto the egg yolk mixture and mix well, then pour it back into the pan. Put over medium heat and simmer 5 to 8 minutes, stirring continuously (otherwise you will get scrambled eggs!) until the mixture starts to thicken. You will be able to tell when the crème anglaise is ready if you run two fingers down the back of the spoon and the two lines don't immediately join. If the custard does start to scramble, don't panic—you can rescue it by pouring the mixture into a food processor and blitzing it until it regains a smooth, thick texture.

3 Strain the sauce once more into a clean bowl and mix a few minutes to cool the custard, then put it in the refrigerator to chill at least 1 hour. It will keep in a covered container in the refrigerator about a week.

Real Vanilla Ice Cream

SERVES 4
PREPARATION TIME 10 minutes, plus
  20 minutes infusing and at least
  3 hours freezing
COOKING TIME 10 minutes

½ cup whole milk
1 vanilla bean, split and seeds
  scraped out
3 egg yolks
¾ cup plus 2 tablespoons
  heavy cream

1 First make a sabayon (see page 218). Put the milk, vanilla bean and seeds in a saucepan over low heat and bring just to a simmer. Remove the pan from the heat, cover with a lid and leave the milk to infuse 20 minutes. Remove the vanilla bean, wash and pat it dry with paper towels. (You can then add the bean to a jar of sugar to make your own vanilla sugar.)

2 Whisk together the egg yolks and warm milk in a heatproof bowl set over a saucepan of gently simmering water, making sure the bottom of the bowl does not touch the water. Heat 5 to 8 minutes, stirring continuously, until the custard thickens. Remove the pan from the heat and whisk continuously until the mixture cools completely.

3 Whip the cream until it forms soft peaks, then fold it into the custard. Pour the mixture into a 2¼-cup freezerproof container. Cover with plastic wrap and put in the freezer at least 3 hours until firm.

LIBERTÉ

Classic dishes released from the constraints of traditional French cooking

It is not easy to describe what we mean by "*liberté*" in cooking, especially for me, because I have been classically trained and there are boundaries I have been taught not to cross. But I have found myself trying more and more new ideas and techniques that improve the taste, the flavor, the texture and the lightness of dishes.

And it is those dishes, generally very traditional French recipes, that I have released from the shackles of classical techniques and modernized to share with you in this chapter, for example Beef Carpaccio with Beef Tartare and Wasabi Cream (see page 30). But, despite any changes, it is important to retain the essence of a dish, whatever you combine it with The best dishes need spontaneity, flexibility and that liberty of expression on the plate.

Chicken and Lemongrass Broth

My mother never let anything go to waste. She always made use of everything, so if we had a roast chicken she would keep the carcass and use it to make the base of a beautiful clear soup, then add extras, such as vegetables, herbs and lentils. I have always enjoyed making broths at home, and here I've added a new twist with fragrant lemongrass and lime zest. To make a more substantial soup, you can add cooked rice or lentils to the broth and heat through thoroughly before ladling it over the chicken.

SERVES 4
PREPARATION TIME 30 minutes
COOKING TIME 2 hours

FOR THE BROTH BASE
1 tablespoon olive oil
1 small chicken, about 2¼ pounds total weight
2 carrots, peeled and roughly chopped
1 lemongrass stalk, bruised
3 thyme sprigs
1 small bunch cilantro, leaves picked and stems reserved

FOR THE CHICKEN AND LEMONGRASS BROTH
2 large carrots, peeled and quartered lengthwise
3 lemongrass stalks, 2 bruised, 1 peeled
2 thyme sprigs
finely grated zest of 1 lime
2 tablespoons extra virgin olive oil
sea salt and freshly ground black pepper

1 To make the broth base, heat a large Dutch oven or skillet over medium heat. Add the olive oil and chicken and seal the chicken 3 to 4 minutes on each side until just starting to turn light golden brown. Add the chopped carrots, lemongrass stalk, thyme and half the cilantro stems and cook 5 minutes longer, or until the chicken is brown all over and the vegetables just colored.

2 Transfer the chicken and vegetables to a large, deep saucepan, cover with about 2 quarts cold water and bring to a boil over high heat, skimming off any foam that rises to the surface, which will help keep the soup clear. Add the quartered carrots, the bruised lemongrass, the thyme and the remaining cilantro stems. Return the liquid to a simmer, then turn the heat down to very low, cover the pan with a lid and simmer 1¼ to 1½ hours until the chicken is very tender and starts to fall apart.

3 Carefully remove the chicken from the pan and leave to one side to cool slightly. Strain the vegetable broth into a clean pan, reserving the solids, and return the broth to a low heat. Simmer, uncovered, 10 to 15 minutes until the broth reduces by one-third and is full of flavor.

4 Meanwhile, carefully lift the quartered carrots out of the strainer, discarding the rest of the solids. Finely chop the carrots and put in deep soup bowls. When the chicken is cool enough to handle, remove and discard the skin, then pull the chicken meat off the bones and tear it into pieces. Add the chicken and a pinch salt and pepper to the soup bowls, then scatter the cilantro leaves over. Sprinkle the lime zest over and drizzle with the extra virgin olive oil.

5 Remove the tough outer leaves, top and root from the remaining lemongrass stem, then slice very thinly and add to the bowls. By now, the broth should be ready, so simply add a couple of ladlefuls to each bowl before serving.

Coriander and Star Anise Pork Rillettes

In my first book, the *French Brasserie Cookbook*, I included a recipe for a classic duck rillettes, but in this book I wanted to bring a different and more modern character to this popular dish by replacing the herbs with spices, including star anise. It brings an exotic, yet delicate, scent that goes perfectly with the pork. Use the whole spice rather than ground, because the latter just doesn't have the same depth of flavor.

SERVES 4
PREPARATION TIME 10 minutes, plus 6 to 12 hours marinating and at least 24 hours chilling
COOKING TIME 4 hours

2 pounds 10 ounces boneless Boston butt, diced
¼ cup sea salt
2 teaspoons coriander seeds
2 star anise
6⅔ cups goose fat
leaves from 2 cilantro sprigs
freshly ground black pepper
toast or warm crusty bread, to serve

1 Put the pork, salt, half the coriander seeds and 1 star anise in a large bowl and season with pepper. Turn everything until combined, then cover the bowl with plastic wrap and leave to marinate in the refrigerator 6 to 12 hours. The longer you leave the pork to marinate, the better the flavor will be.

2 After the pork has marinated, heat the oven to 275°F. Rinse the marinade off the pork, reserving the star anise, then pat the pork dry with paper towels.

3 Melt the goose fat in a large Dutch oven over low heat. Add the pork and turn until it is well coated, then transfer the pot to the oven and cook, uncovered, 4 hours, or until the meat falls apart when prodded with a fork. Strain the pork through a fine strainer, then put it into a bowl, leaving the fat to one side. Shred the pork using two forks, then add about ½ cup of the cooking fat to moisten.

4 Transfer the shredded pork to a sealable jar or small earthenware dish and press down lightly. Pour enough of the cooking fat over the top to cover the pork and seal it, then add the reserved star anise and scatter with the remaining coriander seeds and cilantro leaves. (Any remaining goose fat can be put in a jar and kept for other uses, such as roasting potatoes.) Cover the jar or dish with a lid or parchment paper and chill at least 24 hours before serving to let the flavors mingle. Serve the rillettes with warm crusty bread.

Beef Carpaccio with **Beef Tartare** and **Wasabi Cream**

The dish carpaccio was first created in 1950 by Giuseppe Cipriani for the Comtesse Amalia Mocenigo, who had been advised by her doctor she should eat her meat raw. At the same time, works by the famous fifteenth-century painter, Vittore Carpaccio, were being exhibited. His paintings almost always contained large areas of red in varying tones, and this reminded Cipriani of meat, and so he gave his dish the name carpaccio. Although other meats and fish, particularly tuna, can be used for carpaccio, this dish is made with succulent beef tenderloin. I have given it a modern twist by serving it with a piquant wasabi cream accompanied by beef tartare seasoned with capers and shallot, and some tiny, delicate croutons, fresh chives and arugula.

SERVES 4

PREPARATION TIME 25 minutes, plus 2 to 3 hours freezing and making the croutons

12 ounces beef tenderloin, trimmed
3 tablespoons olive oil
¾ cup plus 2 tablespoons whipping cream
1 teaspoon wasabi paste
3 tablespoons finely snipped chives
3 tablespoons very finely diced Croutons (see page 18)
sea salt and freshly ground black pepper
1 handful arugula leaves, to serve

FOR THE TARTARE

2 teaspoons finely chopped shallot
1 teaspoon chopped parsley leaves
1 teaspoon tomato ketchup
1 teaspoon chopped capers
1½ teaspoons olive oil
5 ounces beef tenderloin, trimmed and very finely chopped

1 To make the carpaccio, lay two pieces of plastic wrap, 12 x 8 inches each, on top of each other to form one sheet of plastic wrap. Put the beef tenderloin in the middle and drizzle with 1 tablespoon of the oil, then wrap the beef in the plastic wrap to form a tight cylinder. Put it in the freezer 2 to 3 hours until it is firm but still slightly soft when pressed.

2 Meanwhile, prepare the tartare. Mix the shallot, parsley, tomato ketchup and capers in a bowl, then drizzle in the remaining oil, stirring continuously. Finally, stir in the chopped beef and season with salt and pepper to taste. Cover the bowl with plastic wrap and chill until ready to serve.

3 Just before serving, gently whisk together the cream and wasabi paste in a bowl until soft peaks form. Cover with plastic wrap and leave at room temperature.

4 Take the beef out of the freezer and remove the plastic wrap. Using a very sharp knife, cut it into very thin slices and arrange on serving plates, spreading the slices out. Work quickly, because the beef will soon thaw and it is much easier to work with them when still slightly frozen.

5 Season with salt and pepper to taste, sprinkle with the chives, croutons and a drizzle of oil, and serve with the tartare, wasabi cream and fresh arugula leaves.

Scallops with Cauliflower Puree and Hazelnut Dressing

This noble shellfish is delicate and sweet, and simply needs sealing briefly in butter and olive oil before serving. Try to find scallops in the shell, but if you can't, you can use prepared or frozen scallops. The apple lends a fresh crispness to the dish and offers a wonderful contrast to the softness of the scallops and the cauliflower puree. Enjoy with a glass of Condrieu or Viognier.

SERVES 4
PREPARATION TIME 20 minutes
COOKING TIME 45 minutes

1 cauliflower, leaves and stem
   removed, cut into large florets
7 tablespoons unsalted butter
2 tablespoons olive oil
12 scallops, rinsed
¼-inch slice crisp green eating
   apple, unpeeled, cut into thin strips
sea salt and freshly ground
   black pepper

FOR THE HAZELNUT DRESSING
1 teaspoon hazelnut oil
2 teaspoons extra virgin olive oil
1 teaspoon white balsamic vinegar
½ teaspoon finely chopped
   celery leaves

1 Bring a large saucepan of salted water to a boil over high heat. Meanwhile, cut 2 of the large cauliflower florets into 12 mini florets, about ½ inch each. When the water is boiling, add the large cauliflower florets and boil 7 to 8 minutes until they are very soft when pierced with a knife. Drain them well and pat them dry with paper towels.

2 Melt 5 tablespoons of the butter and half the olive oil in a large sauté pan over medium-low heat. Add the cooked cauliflower and fry about 30 minutes, stirring occasionally, until the cauliflower is very soft (actually overcooked) and golden brown. Keep the heat medium-low and take care not to burn the butter or the cauliflower.

3 Meanwhile, make the hazelnut dressing. Whisk together the hazelnut oil, extra virgin olive oil and white balsamic vinegar in a bowl until just emulsified. Bring a small saucepan of salted water to a boil, add the small cauliflower florets and boil 2 minutes, or until just tender. Drain and refresh under cold running water, then pat dry and add to the dressing.

4 Put the cooked cauliflower in a blender with 2 tablespoons hot water and blitz to a fine, smooth puree. Add a little extra hot water if the puree is coarse or very thick. Season with salt and pepper to taste, then pass the puree through a fine strainer, using a ladle to help you, into a small, clean saucepan. Cover the pan with a lid and keep warm.

5 Remove the roes from the scallops, trim off any tough flesh and remove any veins, then season with salt and pepper. Melt half the remaining butter with the oil in a nonstick skillet over medium heat. When the butter is a hazelnut color, add half the scallops and cook 1½ to 2 minutes, depending on their size, until light golden. Turn the scallops over and cook 1 minute longer, then remove them from the pan, put on paper towels and keep warm. Repeat with the remaining oil and butter to cook the remaining scallops.

6 Add the celery leaves to the dressing. Top the cauliflower puree with the the scallops, then drizzle with the dressing. Scatter the florets over the top and finish with the apple strips to serve.

Poached Oysters with **Cucumber Fricassee**

In France, oysters are massively popular. Here, I've served them with lightly cooked cucumber, which, although it is best known as a salad vegetable, is delicious prepared this way—its fresh taste and crisp texture complements the oysters perfectly and tastes superb with brown bread.

SERVES 4
PREPARATION TIME 35 minutes
COOKING TIME 15 minutes

16 oysters in the shell
Fish Stock (see page 17; optional)
1 tablespoon gin
2 tablespoons unsalted butter
1 small cucumber, peeled, seeded
  and cut into 2-inch pieces, thinly
  sliced lengthwise into julienne
  strips
4 tablespoons plain Greek yogurt
  or crème fraîche
leaves from 4 watercress sprigs,
  roughly chopped
finely grated zest of 1 lime
sea salt and freshly ground
  black pepper

1 To open the oysters, put them flat-side up, one at a time, on a clean, folded dish towel. Holding the rounded side of the shell in your hand, insert the tip of an oyster knife into the top edge and wiggle it slightly from side to side, at the same time as pushing it in a little farther. As you twist the knife, the top half of the shell should pop open. Lift off the top shell carefully and discard it, keeping the oyster, juices and bottom half of the shell. Strain the juices into a bowl, adding enough fish stock to make up to 1 cup liquid, if necessary. Push the knife under the oysters to separate them from the shells, then leave them to one side. Bring a saucepan of water to a boil over high heat. Add the bottom shells and return to a boil, then remove the pan from the heat, strain the liquid and put the shells on a dish towel to dry. Leave to one side until required.

2 Divide the juice-stock liquid between two small saucepans, ideally one shallow and the other slightly deeper. Bring the liquid in the shallow pan to a boil, then turn the heat down to low and simmer a few minutes until the liquid reduces by three-quarters and is syrupy. Add the gin, return to a simmer and simmer 5 to 7 minutes until it is syrupy again. Remove the pan from the heat, cover with a lid and leave to one side.

3 Meanwhile, melt the butter in a skillet over medium heat. When the butter is foaming, add the cucumber and fry 1 to 2 minutes until just light golden, but still crisp. Season with salt and pepper to taste, then tip onto a dish towel to drain. Spoon into the cleaned oyster shells.

4 Bring the second pan containing the juices and stock to a boil. Turn the heat down to low, add the oysters, cover the pan with a lid and simmer 2 to 3 minutes until they are just cooked. Check that they are ready by pressing very lightly with your finger—there should be a little resistance, but you don't want them to be firm. Discard the cooking liquid, then spoon the oysters on top of the cucumber in the shells.

5 If the reduced liquid has become cold, gently warm it up again. Whisk in the yogurt, taking care not to overheat it or it will separate. Add the watercress, then remove the pan from the heat and stir the leaves through. Season the sauce with pepper to taste, then spoon over the oysters and sprinkle with the lime zest before serving.

Provençal Salad with **Zucchini Flower Tempura**

SERVES 4
PREPARATION TIME 25 minutes,
   plus 30 minutes marinating
   and 5 minutes chilling
COOKING TIME 25 minutes

1 zucchini, cut lengthwise into long,
   thin strips
2 tablespoons olive oil
a pinch fresh edible lavender flowers
   or rosemary flowers
1 tablespoon white balsamic vinegar
2 tablespoons extra virgin olive oil
juice of ½ lemon
6 purple baby artichokes or bottled
   artichokes in oil, drained
2 thick slices pancetta, about
   1½ ounces total weight, cut
   into lardons
1 small handful arugula leaves
1 small handful baby red chard
   leaves
½ white onion, thinly sliced
6 yellow cherry tomatoes, halved
   crosswise or quartered
2 tablespoons ripe olives, pitted and
   roughly chopped
sea salt and freshly ground
   black pepper

**FOR THE ZUCCHINI FLOWER TEMPURA
   BATTER**
sunflower oil, for deep-frying
2 eggs
1 cup cold sparkling or still water
2 tablespoons cornstarch
1¼ cups all-purpose flour
a pinch salt
1 teaspoon lemon juice
8 zucchini flowers with the small
   zucchini attached

1 Mix the zucchini with ½ teaspoon of the olive oil and half the lavender flowers, then season with salt and pepper. Cover with plastic wrap and leave to marinate in the refrigerator about 30 minutes. Whisk together the balsamic vinegar and extra virgin olive oil in a bowl until just combined, then season with a little salt and pepper. Leave to one side.

2 Meanwhile, prepare the baby artichokes, if using fresh. Fill a large bowl with water and stir in the lemon juice. Remove and discard the outer leaves from the first artichoke and cut off the top. Trim and peel the stem, then cut the artichoke into quarters lengthwise. Cut out and discard the choke (the "furry" middle) and put the artichoke in the lemon water to stop it discoloring. Repeat with the other artichokes, then drain them and pat them dry.

3 Heat a large skillet over medium heat. Add 1 tablespoon of the olive oil and the artichokes and cook 8 to 10 minutes, turning them over occasionally, until just tender. Transfer them to a plate and leave to one side. Add the remaining olive oil and the lardons to the skillet and fry 3 minutes, or until golden brown and crisp. Drain the lardons on paper towels and leave to one side.

4 Heat a ridged griddle pan over high heat until very hot. Add the zucchini slices and griddle 10 seconds on each side, or until just colored in places. Transfer them to a plate and leave to one side.

5 To make the tempura batter, pour in enough sunflower oil to fill a deep-fat fryer or deep, wide saucepan by two-thirds. Heat the oil to 325°F, or until a cube of bread browns in 40 seconds. While the oil is heating, prepare the batter. Beat together the eggs and water in a large bowl until foamy. Sift the cornstarch and flour over the top and gently mix with a pair of chopsticks until the batter is just combined. It doesn't matter if the batter is slightly lumpy, because it's important not to overwhisk it. Stir in the salt, lemon juice and a handful ice cubes, cover the bowl with plastic wrap and leave the batter to rest in the refrigerator 5 minutes. Dip the zucchini flowers and zucchini, one at a time, into the batter, then put them straight into the hot oil. Deep-fry 2 minutes, then flip them over and fry 2 minutes longer, or until the batter is crisp, but not colored. Drain the fried flowers on paper towels and season with a pinch salt.

6 Top the arugula and chard with the artichokes, zucchini, onion, tomatoes and olives. Drizzle the dressing over the salad and add the lardons. Toss to combine, then put the zucchini flowers on top and serve immediately while the batter is still crisp.

Tomato Confit, Chili and Lemon Thyme Tartlets

These classic tarts represent, for me, all I love about the Mediterranean, such as the climate, the colors, the heat, the scents and the goodness of the fresh local and seasonal ingredients. My new additions of tomato confit, chili and lemon thyme give a freshness and great depth of flavor. You can also top the tartlets with a few peppery arugula leaves.

SERVES 4
PREPARATION TIME 20 minutes
COOKING TIME 2 hours 20 minutes

8 large, vine-ripened plum tomatoes, cut into ½-inch round slices, with the ends discarded
4 tablespoons olive oil
leaves from 6 lemon thyme sprigs
13 ounces rolled puff pastry dough, thawed if frozen
6 vine-ripened tomatoes
1 garlic clove, unpeeled but lightly crushed
1 white onion, finely chopped
2 long red chilies, seeded and finely chopped
3 tablespoons extra virgin olive oil, plus extra for drizzling
sea salt and freshly ground black pepper
Belgian Endive and Radish Salad (see page 19), to serve

1 Heat the oven to 300°F and line a baking sheet with parchment paper. Put the sliced tomatoes on the prepared baking sheet, drizzle with half the olive oil, scatter one-third of the lemon thyme over and season with salt. Bake 2 hours, turning the tomatoes once, until they are dry and wrinkly. If they don't look quite ready, return them to the oven 30 minutes longer, then check once more. Leave them to one side on the baking sheet.

2 Turn the oven up to 350°F. Cut the dough into 4 circles, each about 4 inches in diameter, then prick each circle all over with a fork. Put the dough circles on a cookie sheet, cover with a sheet or parchment paper and put a second cookie sheet on top. Put the dough circles, sandwiched between the cookie sheets, in the oven 10 to 12 minutes until they are golden brown and baked through. Carefully lift off the top cookie sheet and leave the pastry circles to cool.

3 Meanwhile, with a sharp knife, cut a small cross on the bottom of each of the remaining tomatoes, then put them in a heatproof bowl and cover with boiling water. Leave 30 seconds, then lift them out with a slotted spoon and put into a bowl of ice water. Lift the tomatoes out, then peel off and discard the skins. Cut the tomatoes into quarters and remove and discard the seeds, then roughly chop the flesh.

4 Heat a sauté pan over medium heat. Add the remaining olive oil and the chopped tomatoes and cook a few minutes to release the tomato juices. Add the garlic, onion and chilies, turn the heat down to medium-low and cook 20 to 30 minutes until thick and very soft. Stir once in a while to make sure the tomato mixture doesn't catch or stick to the bottom of the pan. Season with salt and pepper to taste, then add another one-third of the lemon thyme and the extra virgin olive oil.

5 To assemble the tartlets, divide the chopped tomato mixture between the pastry circles and spread it over the tops with the back of a spoon. Lay the slices of tomato confit on top, overlapping them slightly. Drizzle with a little extra virgin olive oil and scatter the remaining lemon thyme over. Return the tartlets to the oven 5 to 8 minutes longer to warm through. Serve the tartlets warm with a Belgian endive and radish salad.

Semolina Gnocchi with **Almond Crumb**

Gnocchi is a kind of dumpling made with potato or semolina, and the name comes from the Italian word *nocchio* meaning "knot in the wood," which I find very charming. You will see I've changed the shape slightly to make the gnocchi easier to roll and I also deep-fry them to give a crisp, golden outside. The carrot juice dressing is great and so is the crunchy almond topping.

SERVES 4
PREPARATION TIME 20 minutes, plus 10 minutes cooling
COOKING TIME 30 minutes

2 cups almond milk
1⅓ cups extra-fine semolina, plus extra for dusting
3½ tablespoons unsalted butter, soft
3 tablespoons finely grated Parmesan cheese
1 teaspoon sunflower oil, plus extra for deep-frying
⅔ cup blanched almonds
1½ ounces stale sourdough bread, torn into small pieces
1 garlic clove, finely chopped
1 tablespoon roughly chopped chervil, or dill or chives, plus extra to serve
2½ cups carrot juice
sea salt and freshly ground black pepper

1 Pour the almond milk into a large saucepan and bring to a simmer over high heat, then slowly pour in the semolina. Cook about 5 minutes, stirring continuously with a spatula, until you have a thick, stiff paste. Remove the pan from the heat and season with salt and pepper, then stir in half the butter and all of the Parmesan.

2 Generously dust the countertop with semolina. Take a small ball of the mixture about 1 inch in diameter. Roll it on the countertop with the palm of your hand into a cylinder about ⅝ inch in diameter, gently pressing one end, while still rolling, to form a point. Roll again in the semolina to fully coat, then leave to one side. Repeat to make the remaining gnocchi.

3 Heat a large skillet over medium heat. Add the oil and the almonds and fry 1 to 2 minutes, shaking the pan occasionally, until they are lightly colored. Drain off any excess oil, then add the remaining butter, the bread and garlic and toss to combine. After another 1 to 2 minutes, when the butter is foaming, toss once more, then drain in a strainer. Tip the contents of the strainer onto a double layer of paper towels and leave to cool and become crunchy. Roughly chop to a crumble consistency, season with a little salt and pepper, then stir in the chervil and leave to one side.

4 Pour the carrot juice into a saucepan and cook over medium heat about 10 minutes, stirring occasionally, until it reduces by half and is slightly syrupy. Season with salt and pepper to taste.

5 Meanwhile, pour enough sunflower oil for deep-frying into a deep-fat fryer or a deep, wide saucepan and heat to 325°F, or until a cube of bread browns in 40 seconds. Add the gnocchi, a few at a time, to the hot oil and deep-fry 3 to 4 minutes, turning occasionally, until cooked all the way through and crisp and golden on the outside. Drain on paper towels and keep warm while you fry the remaining gnocchi. (You can reheat the fried gnocchi just before serving by briefly returning them to the hot oil, then draining again on paper towels.) Serve the gnocchi hot, sprinkled with the almond crumb and finished with a generous drizzle of carrot juice and a sprinkling of chervil.

Eggs en Cocotte with **Dried Mushrooms** and **Rosemary Croûtes**

I've used duck eggs to give a rich and interesting flavor to these *cocottes*, but do watch the timing so the yolks remain soft and runny. The dried mushrooms add an intense burst of flavor to the finished dish. They can be prepared up to a week in advance and kept in an airtight container.

SERVES 4
PREPARATION TIME 30 minutes,
  plus 1 hour infusing
COOKING TIME 25 minutes,
  plus 2½ hours drying

FOR THE DRIED MUSHROOMS
3 cups thinly sliced button
  mushrooms
2 egg whites, lightly beaten
1 teaspoon crushed sea salt, plus
  extra to season

FOR THE ROSMARY CROûTES
3 tablespoons olive oil
leaves from 1 rosemary sprig
8 slices day-old baguette, each
  about ⅛ inch thick

FOR THE EGGS
3 cups roughly chopped mixed wild
  mushrooms
1 teaspoon olive oil
½ small shallot, finely chopped
½ garlic clove, finely chopped
5 thyme sprigs, leaves picked from
  1 sprig
3 tablespoons unsalted butter, soft
4 duck eggs or extra-large hen eggs
1¼ cups chilled whipping cream
  (it must be straight from the
  refrigerator)
freshly ground black pepper

1 To dry the mushrooms, heat the oven to 150°F, not on a fan setting, and line a large baking sheet with parchment paper. Add the mushrooms in a single layer, brush lightly with the egg whites and sprinkle with the salt, then bake 2½ hours, or until they are dry and crisp. Remove the mushrooms from the oven and leave to cool. Blitz 2 small handfuls into a powder in a mini food processor, then leave to one side. (You can store the remaining mushrooms in a sealed container up to one week.)

2 Meanwhile, to make the croûtes, put the oil and rosemary leaves in a saucepan and heat. Remove the pan from the heat and leave to infuse 1 hour. Strain the oil through a fine strainer and discard the rosemary.

3 Turn the oven up to 275°F and line a baking sheet with parchment paper. Brush both sides of the bread slice with the rosemary-infused oil and place in the baking sheet. Cover with a second piece of parchment paper and a slightly smaller baking sheet, which fits inside the large one. This helps the bread stay flat and toast evenly. Bake 8 to 10 minutes until the slices are light golden, then leave them to cool between the baking sheets.

4 Meanwhile, bring a saucepan of water to a boil. Add the chopped wild mushrooms and return the water to a boil. Drain well, then tip the mushrooms onto paper towels and pat dry. Heat a large skillet over medium heat. Add the oil, shallot and garlic and cook 2 minutes, or until soft but not colored. Turn the heat up to high, add the mushrooms and sauté 2 minutes longer, or until just soft. Season with salt and pepper to taste, then add the thyme leaves, cover with a lid and leave to one side.

5 After the croûtes are removed from the oven, turn the oven up to 350°F. Line a small roasting pan with parchment paper and brush the insides of four ⅔-cup ramekins with the soft butter. Spoon the mushrooms into the ramekins and crack an egg into each one. Pour the cream over to just cover, season with salt and pepper and top each one with a thyme sprig. Put the ramekins in the roasting pan, pour in enough hot water to come halfway up the sides and bake 10 to 12 minutes until the tops are just set. Turn off the heat and leave in the oven 2 to 3 minutes longer, but make sure the yolks remain runny. Sprinkle with the dried mushrooms and serve with the rosemary croûtes for dipping into the egg.

DEHYDRATING FOOD

Intensity of flavor has to be the number one reason for dehydrating foods. Although, of course, it originated in ancient times as a simple, but effective, means of preserving foods through the lean winter months, now it's more about the fact that taking out the water not only means bacteria can't grow, it also produces some radical transformations, concentrating both taste, texture and goodness. Plus, it still means you don't have to waste any seasonal gluts, but can, instead, easily transform all kinds of foods into handy pantry items, from fruit strips that make a great lunchbox snack to dried mushrooms to sprinkle into a risotto to intensify the flavor.

Of course, drying food will never replace freezing, as that does a better job of retaining the taste, appearance and goodness of fresh food. But dehydrating is easy, costs virtually nothing, does not need any special equipment —and still gives you a huge range of flavorsome and densely textured treats to enjoy.

Sun-dried produce
Not surprisingly, the original dehydrator was the sun! And you'll still see fruit, vegetables or herbs spread out on cloths or wooden trays in sunny courtyards or barn roofs when you are on vacation in hotter climes. In Portugal, Spain or even Madagascar, you might come upon rows of flattened fish laid out to dry, a traditional practice as popular as salting or smoking.

Drying food in hot countries is virtually effortless. In cooler, more humid areas, it can be more challenging. If you are not careful, food can become moldy on the drying tray, so techniques have to be different. Reindeer meat in Scandinavia, for example, is pickled in salt water before being dried in the spring sunshine when the air temperature is below zero, while in Iceland, shark meat is also dried in subzero temperatures.

But commercial dehydrators don't need sunlight. They push hot air around the food to dry it quickly and conveniently whatever the weather.

At The Vineyard
In The Vineyard kitchen, as in many professional kitchens, we often use dehydrators. A subtle, sweet celery leaf sprinkled with sugar can become as transparent and fragile as glass to finish a terrine. Slices of pancetta, gently oven-crisped, then finished in the dehydrator, are perfect crumbled over a pea velouté, roasted poultry, a risotto or even roast pork. A few blanched, dried mushrooms can be blitzed to a dust to flavor soup or an egg *en cocotte* (see page 39).

Dehydrating at home
But you don't need a commercial dehydrator, and you don't need to live in the land of eternal sunshine either —though wouldn't that be nice! In our house back in France, drying ingredients was a seasonal affair. Every fall, wooden boxes lined with newspaper would appear in the boiler room, perched on the top of the boiler, and gradually be filled with our harvest of mushrooms. The boiler room was always the warmest part of the house. Not surprisingly, our dogs soon realized this and selected it as their winter bedroom—sensible creatures! That memory makes me smile, as it is so fresh in my mind.

Newspapers, by the way, are ideal for absorbing moisture from drying foods and I still use them today. I dry foods in my glass greenhouse—the sun's heat on the enclosed space dries foods like tomatoes perfectly. I also dry herbs, especially basil and tarragon, and use them to flavor oils, but I do that in the microwave. Just spread out the separate leaves on a sheet of paper towel, lay another sheet on top, then microwave on High for three or four 30-second bursts, watching carefully.

Mostly, however, I dry food in my domestic oven on a very low setting. I usually make use of the time control, then I can just leave it alone to do its own thing for long periods without interruption. It's quicker to dry food in an oven than by sun-drying or even using a dehydrator, and you only need a couple of baking sheets and a thermometer. It's true you can only make small quantities in an oven, but I think that can be an advantage. It means you can experiment with plenty of different foods and there's no risk of making the effort to dry a large quantity of something you later decide you don't like!

You can dry most foods, apart from those with a high water content, such as cucumbers, because they are likely to spoil before the process is finished. Fruit tend to become crisp more quickly than vegetables, but you can dry most things in 8 to 12 hours. Good vegetables to start with are onions, garlic and peppers. For fruit, try apples, peaches, apricots or pears.

How to dehydrate food in your oven

- Make sure your equipment, surfaces and hands are all clean.
- Only fresh, good-quality food will give the best results. Wash it, then pat it dry with paper towels.
- Prepare the food as though you were cooking it, so you might peel and core an apple, remove the pit from a plum, trim the fat off meat. Then leave them whole, or cut into thin slices or strips.
- For foods like apple that tend to go brown when cut, add 1½ teapoons vinegar or lemon juice to 1 cup of water, then dip the slices as you cut.
- Blanch hard fruit or vegetables in boiling water for a few seconds, then refresh in ice water and pat dry.
- Fruit like apples, pears, peaches and rhubarb will keep their flavor if you poach them first in a light syrup.
- You can marinate meats in olive oil and vinegar, then toss with seasonings before dehydrating.

- Put food in a single layer, not overlapping, on a lined baking sheet or a wire rack in the oven (or the racks in your hydrator). Put a drip tray under meat. Items with similar drying times can be mixed on a rack.
- Switch on the oven to 115° to 150°F or lower, depending on the recipe. If your oven doesn't go below 150°F, don't worry. Set it to its lowest temperature but leave the oven door slightly open, enough for the air to circulate and keep a constant temperature.
- Turn the tray every 30 minutes or so if you can until the food is completely dry. That will be 4 to 5 hours for beets, onions and peppers; 6 to 8 hours for garlic; 8 to 10 hours for apples, mushrooms and pears; 10 to 12 hours for apricots, peaches and potatoes.

Most dried foods will last well, so keep them in sterilized, airtight jars in a cool, dark, dry place—then you can enjoy intriguing your friends at your next dinner party.

Dehydrated Pumpkin Crisp
This makes an easy introduction to drying vegetables so do have a go at making this delicious sprinkle for your next risotto.

Start by heating the oven to 150°F and lining a large baking sheet with parchment paper. Then, simply grate the flesh of 4 ounces peeled butternut squash or pumpkin into long spaghetti-like strips straight over the baking sheet. Bake 4½ hours, turning the baking sheet halfway through. The strands will stick together in a net-like shape and become dry and crisp. Simply break them over the dish to serve. They'll keep in an airtight container for up to a month.

Follow the same recipe using strips of grated carrot or parsnip for delicious versions of the crisp. Or, why not try making a batch of each and breaking a colorful selection to finish off your dish.

Chicken Poached with **Kaffir Lime Leaves**

I love the fragrance of kaffir lime leaves as much as I like the smell of lime blossom, or even lemon or orange. When I lived in in the Algarve, in Portugal, the scent of citrus blossom was all around us from morning to night, invading our apartment and, when mixed with the breeze and the heat, was such a great fragrance. Here, the lime leaves gently lift the broth by adding a delicate scent and a refreshing flavor that goes so well with the chicken.

SERVES 4
PREPARATION TIME 10 minutes,
  plus making the stock
COOKING TIME 30 minutes

4 chicken breast halves, skin on,
  about 6 ounces each
1 tablespoon olive oil
1 thick slice fresh horseradish
6 kaffir lime leaves
5⅓ cups Chicken Stock (see
  page 16)
2 cups peeled potatoes cut into
  ½-inch dice
4½ cups thinly shredded hispi
  or other young, spring cabbage
1 small handful cilantro leaves,
  roughly chopped
sea salt

1 Put the chicken breast halves in a large saucepan and just cover with lukewarm water. Put over medium-low heat about 5 minutes and slowly bring to a simmer. Lift the chicken out of the water and drain on paper towels, then, when cool enough to handle, carefully remove the skin from each and reserve. Cover the chicken breasts with plastic wrap and leave to one side. Discard the poaching water.

2 Heat the oven to 375°F and line a baking sheet with parchment paper. Put the skin, flesh-side down, on the prepared tray and brush with the oil. Cover with a second sheet of parchment paper and a slightly smaller baking sheet, which fits inside the large sheet. This will help to keep the skin flat and let it cook evenly. Roast 10 to 12 minutes until it is golden brown and nearly crisp. If the shin isn't ready, return the baking sheets to the oven 5 minutes longer, then check again. Leave the skin to cool between the baking sheets so it crisps even more.

3 Meanwhile, to make the broth, put the horseradish, kaffir lime leaves and stock in the cleaned saucepan and bring almost to a boil over high heat. Turn the heat down to medium and simmer 10 to 12 minutes until the broth reduces by one-third, skimming off any foam that rises to the surface.

4 Add the poached chicken breasts and potato to the simmering broth and simmer 8 minutes, then add the cabbage and simmer 2 minutes longer, or until the chicken is cooked through and the cabbage is just wilted. Season with salt to taste, then scatter the cilantro leaves over.

5 Remove the chicken, lime leaves and horseradish from the broth. Leave the chicken to one side and discard the flavorings. Ladle the broth and vegetables into soup bowls. Slice the chicken breasts and put them on top, then break the crisp chicken skin into pieces and scatter over just before serving.

Chicken Pot-roasted in Cider and Paprika

I have always enjoyed the delicate flavor of smoked sweet paprika, which is milder than smoked hot paprika, but should still be used carefully. Often found in Eastern European and Spanish dishes, sweet paprika brings an original twist to this French-style chicken pot-roasted in cider.

SERVES 4
PREPARATION TIME 10 minutes, plus making the stock
COOKING TIME 1 hour

1 tablespoon olive oil
4 chicken legs
1¾ cups dry hard cider
2¼ cups Chicken Stock (see page 16)
1 teaspoon smoked sweet (mild) paprika
12 small turnips, peeled and quartered
sea salt and freshly ground black pepper
Thai-style Pilaf Rice, to serve (see page 21)

1 Heat a Dutch oven over high heat. Add the oil and the chicken legs, skin-side down, and seal them 5 to 6 minutes, turning them once, until they are brown all over. (You might need to do this in batches.) Spoon off any excess oil, then add the cider and deglaze the pot by stirring to remove any caramelized bits stuck to the bottom. Cook a few minutes until the cider reduces by half, stirring occasionally.

2 Add the stock and paprika and bring to a simmer over medium heat, then turn the heat down to low, partially cover with a lid and simmer about 15 minutes. Add the turnips, partially cover again and simmer 15 minutes longer, or until the chicken is cooked through and the turnips are tender.

3 Remove the chicken and turnips from the pot and put on separate plates. Season the chicken with salt and pepper.

4 Return the pot to a medium heat and cook 6 to 8 minutes until the sauce reduces to a glaze and you have about 2 cups. Return the chicken and turnips to the pot and heat through, spooning the sauce over them. Serve with pilaf rice.

Warm Soy-glazed Quail Salad

Szechuan peppercorns have a big, bold flavor, yet they are seldom used outside Chinese cooking. This fragrant spice works well with quail—which for me is a much underused meat—but make sure you toast it well first.

SERVES 4
PREPARATION TIME 30 minutes, plus making the croutons
COOKING TIME 40 minutes

4 quail, about 5 ounces each, gutted and cleaned
1 cup plus 2 tablepoons duck or goose fat
4 quail eggs
12 baby zucchini, sliced into thin ribbons using a vegetable peeler
leaves from 1 thyme sprig
2 tablespoons olive oil
1 tablespoon honey
2 tablespoons rice wine vinegar
1 tablespoon soy sauce
½ teaspoon Szechuan peppercorns, toasted and crushed (see page 68)
2 small or 1 large head Belgian endive, sliced crosswise
1 handful Croutons (see page 18)
1 handful flat-leaf parsley leaves, chopped
sea salt and freshly ground black pepper

1 Prepare the quail by removing the legs and breasts from each one, or ask your butcher to do this for you. Wrap each leg tightly in plastic wrap and then aluminum foil. (Leave the breasts to one side, covered.) Melt the duck fat in a saucepan over low heat until it is starting to shimmer. Add the foil-wrapped legs and return the fat to a shimmer. Cook 20 to 25 minutes until they are cooked through and tender. Remove the pan from the heat and leave the legs to one side in the fat.

2 Meanwhile, bring a small saucepan of water to a boil. Add the quail eggs and cook 2 minutes, then drain and refresh them in ice water—the yolks should still be slightly runny. Peel the eggs and leave to one side.

3 Put the zucchini ribbons in a bowl with the thyme and oil, season with salt and turn until coated. Heat a ridged griddle pan over high heat until very hot, then griddle the zucchini in batches 1 to 2 minutes, turning over once, until charred in places. Transfer to a plate, cover and keep warm.

4 Unwrap the quail legs and brush with half the honey. Heat a large skillet over high heat. Add 1 to 2 tablespoons of the duck fat from the other pan, then add the quail legs, skin-side down, and cook 2 to 3 minutes until the skin is crisp and golden brown. Transfer them to a plate, cover with foil and leave to rest while you cook the breasts.

5 Season the quail breasts with salt and pepper. Put them in the skillet, skin-side down, and cook over high heat 2 to 3 minutes until the skin starts to crisp. Turn the breasts over and cook 2 minutes longer until cooked through but still nicely moist. Transfer them to the plate with the legs. Pour the rice wine vinegar and soy sauce into the pan and deglaze by stirring to remove any caramelized bits stuck to the bottom. Stir in the Szechuan peppercorns and remaining honey and heat briefly. Before the honey starts to color, add the quail legs and turn to coat them in the honey glaze, then remove and add the breasts to the pan, skin-side down only, and glaze until they are a lovely golden color.

6 Cut the quail breasts in half diagonally, then put on top of the Belgian endive and the zucchini ribbons with the legs. Halve the quail eggs and put on top, then sprinkle with the croutons and parsley. Drizzle with any glaze left in the pan and serve immediately.

Medallions of Pork
with **Coriander** and **Garlic**

I often make this dish for myself at home, partly because it's so quick, but also as I love the mix of flavors. It's important, however, to use really good-quality meat to make sure the result is really tender. The garlic, sautéed in its skin until soft, perfectly complements the nuttiness of the crushed coriander seeds, then both combine with the buttery pork juices and fresh cilantro. All these great flavours are then served with succulent slices of pork tenderloin. Fantastic!

SERVES 4
PREPARATION TIME 5 minutes, plus making the stock and at least 1 hour marinating
COOKING TIME 15 minutes

2 boneless pork tenderloins, about 10 ounces each, trimmed and cut into 1-inch-thick slices
1 tablespoon olive oil
½ teaspoon coriander seeds, crushed
8 garlic cloves, unpeeled and lightly crushed
1 tablespoon vegetable oil
7 tablespoons unsalted butter
¾ cup plus 2 tablespoons Chicken Stock (see page 16)
1 small handful cilantro leaves, roughly chopped
sea salt and freshly ground white pepper
boiled, mashed carrot, to serve

1 Put the pork in a large dish, pour the olive oil over and sprinkle with the crushed coriander seeds. Cover with plastic wrap and leave to marinate in the refrigerator at least 1 hour until ready to use.

2 Bring a small saucepan of water to a boil over high heat. Add the garlic, then turn the heat down to low and simmer 5 minutes, or until soft, taking care to simmer and not boil, so the skins stay attached to the garlic. Lift the cloves out with a slotted spoon and drain on paper towels, then leave to one side.

3 Heat the vegetable oil with 1½ tablespoons of the butter in a large sauté pan over medium-high heat. Add the pork and when it just starts to brown, add the garlic. Cook the pork with the garlic 2 to 3 minutes on each side until both are golden brown, taking care not to burn the garlic. Remove the pork and garlic from the pan and leave to one side on a plate, covered with aluminum foil to keep warm.

4 Discard the fat in the pan, then return the pan to a medium heat, making sure it does not get too hot. Pour in the stock and deglaze the pan by stirring to remove any caramelized bits stuck to the bottom. Add the remaining butter to the pan, a little at a time, whisking to incorporate it into the sauce. When all the butter is added, add the unpeeled garlic and the resting juices from the pork and heat through.

5 Just before serving, add the fresh cilantro leaves to the sauce and season with salt and pepper to taste. Spoon the sauce over the pork and serve with mashed carrot.

Pork Steaks with **Chili–Ginger Cabbage**

Pork shoulder, or Boston butt, is a very tasty part of the pig and the small amount of fat it contains brings a lovely flavor to this dish. I think the secret to the success of this recipe, however, lies in the cabbage! I have used a hispi cabbage, also called pointed or sweetheart, which is braised in a delicious combination of chili, ginger and honey that gives it a wonderful balance of flavors.

SERVES 4
PREPARATION TIME 10 minutes
COOKING TIME 20 minutes

2 tablespoons sunflower oil
4 Boston butt steaks, about
   5 ounces each
5 tablespoons unsalted butter
1 hispi or other young, spring
   cabbage, quartered lengthwise,
   stem removed and shredded
2 long red chilies, seeded and
   finely chopped
1½-inch piece gingerroot, peeled
   and cut into julienne strips
2 tablespoons honey
1 tablespoon roughly chopped
   flat-leaf parsley leaves
2 tablespoons extra virgin olive oil
sea salt and freshly ground
   black pepper

1 Heat the oven to 275°F. Heat a large skillet over medium heat. Add the sunflower oil and the pork steaks and cook 3 to 4 minutes until they are golden brown underneath, then add 2 tablespoons of the butter, turn the pork and cook the other side until golden. Transfer the pork to a plate, cover with aluminum foil and keep warm in the oven. Leave the skillet to one side.

2 Bring a saucepan of salted water to a boil. Add the cabbage, cover the pan with a lid and return the water to a boil, then drain immediately. Return the cabbage to the pan and add 1½ of the red chilies, the ginger, honey and 2 tablespoons the remaining butter and season with salt and pepper. Cover the pan with a lid, put over very low heat and gently braise the cabbage 2 to 3 minutes until just it is tender. Remove the pan from the heat, cover and leave to one side while you finish making the sauce.

3 Return the skillet to a high heat. When the juices are bubbling, add ½ cup water and cook 2 minutes, or until it reduces by half. Reduce the heat to medium, add the remaining butter to the pan, a little at a time, whisking to incorporate it into the sauce. Add the remaining chili and half the parsley and stir through. Check the seasoning, adding more salt and pepper to taste. Remove the pork from the oven and pour any resting juices into the sauce, stirring one last time.

4 Stir the remaining parsley into the cabbage. Scoop the cabbage out of the pan with a slotted spoon into a warm bowl, making sure any residual liquid stays in the pan. Return the pan to a high heat and boil the liquid until it reduces and is slightly syrupy. Add the extra virgin olive oil, season with salt and pepper to taste, then spoon the sauce over the cabbage. Serve the pork with the buttery sauce spooned over the top and with the honey-coated cabbage.

Tomato Farci with Lamb and Lavender

In this book you'll come across a few *farci* (stuffed) dishes, because it's a very typical style of cooking in France, and in this recipe I have given the technique a modern approach. I do like lavender with lamb, so I decided instead of simply sprinkling roast lamb with lavender flowers, I would use them to flavor ground lamb, then stuff the mixture into large beefsteak tomatoes before roasting them. It's important to use lavender that hasn't been sprayed with chemicals, so try to buy from an organic source. This makes a great family dish that only needs a mixed salad to serve alongside.

SERVES 4
PREPARATION TIME: 15 minutes
COOKING TIME 35 minutes

4 beefsteak tomatoes
14 ounces ground lamb
2 edible lavender sprigs, young
  leaves only from the tips
2 to 3 tablespoons olive oil
sea salt and freshly ground
  black pepper
mixed salad, to serve

1 Heat the oven to 325°F and line a small baking dish large enough to hold the tomatoes upright with parchment paper. Cut the top off each tomato, about one-quarter of the way down, and reserve to make 4 lids. Turn the tomatoes upside-down and press to squeeze out the seeds, then discard the seeds. Scoop the flesh out of the inside of each tomato, then season the insides with salt and pepper to taste.

2 Roughly chop the tomato flesh, then mix it with the ground lamb. Add a pinch of the blue tips of the lavender, then season well with salt and pepper. Divide the lamb mixture into 4 equal portions and roughly roll each portion into a ball, then press each into a tomato shell so the filling comes a little above the top of the tomatoes. Put the reserved tomato lids on top, then put the stuffed tomatoes in the prepared baking dish.

3 Drizzle the tomatoes with the oil and bake 35 minutes, or until the lamb is cooked through. To check that the lamb is ready, insert a skewer into the middle and if it comes out clean, the meat is cooked. If not, return the dish to the oven and cook 5 minutes, then test again. Serve with a mixed salad.

Roast Rump of Lamb with Licorice

In France, as in Spain, we use licorice root quite a lot. In fact, I remember as a young boy buying licorice root and chewing it on my way to school, then keeping it in my bag during class and getting it out again to chew on my way back home—great memories! In this recipe, I use it to skewer the lamb rumps so the flavor infuses the meat while cooking, without it becoming overpowering. The lamb is also really good served with very thin strips, or "tagliatelle," of zucchini sautéed in olive oil with a little garlic and chili and finished with chopped flat-leaf parsley.

SERVES 4
PREPARATION TIME 10 minutes, plus 1 hour soaking and overnight marinating
COOKING TIME 20 minutes

1 small stick licorice root, about 4 inches long and ½ inch thick
4 small lamb rumps, about 5 ounces each
½ cup olive oil
4 teaspoons unsalted butter
¾ cup plus 2 tablespoons Lamb Stock or Chicken Stock (see page 16)
sea salt and freshly ground black pepper
steamed Swiss chard, to serve

1 Put the licorice in a small bowl of warm water and leave about 1 hour until it is soft enough to bend easily. Working from the middle of the root toward the end, peel away the outer layer, reserving the peelings. Cut the root lengthwise into quarters, leaving the long pieces to dry on a plate.

2 Put the lamb in a shallow bowl and pour the oil over, then add a generous pinch of pepper and the licorice peelings. Stir to coat, then cover each rump tightly with plastic wrap, pressing the plastic wrap directly onto the lamb so there is not any air inside. Leave to marinate in the refrigerator overnight to help tenderize the meat.

3 The next day, heat the oven to 275°F. Remove the lamb from the marinade and, using a skewer, make an incision through the middle of each piece of meat. Insert a piece of the licorice root through each of the pieces of lamb.

4 Heat an ovenproof skillet over medium-high heat. Add the lamb and cook 3 to 4 minutes on all sides, adding the butter when cooking the final side. Transfer the lamb, still in the pan, to the oven and roast 5 to 8 minutes, then turn the oven up to 350°F and roast 4 minutes longer until the lamb is cooked through, but still slightly pink in the middle. Transfer the lamb to a warm plate, cover with aluminum foil and leave to rest while you make the gravy.

5 Return the pan you cooked the lamb in to a high heat and when the juices are bubbling, add the stock and deglaze the pan by stirring to remove any caramelized bits stuck to the bottom. Cook 5 minutes, or until it is reduced by half, then add any resting juices from the lamb and season with salt and pepper to taste. Serve with steamed Swiss chard.

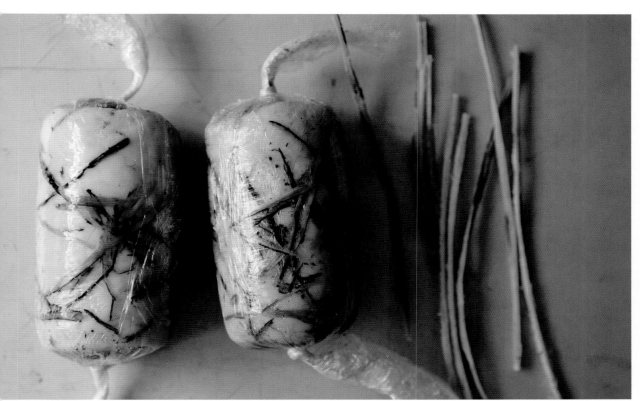

Venison Bourguignonne
with **Dark Chocolate** and **Star Anise**

Venison is a great alternative to beef in a bourguignonne, and this is a dish I like to put on the menu at The Vineyard restaurant when venison is in season, usually as the "dish of the week." My modern version of the French classic is finished with dark chocolate, providing a hint of tobacco and bark, which combines beautifully with the earthy flavor of the wild mushrooms and woody aroma of the star anise. To bring the dish together, you need to use a robust red wine, such as one from the southern Rhône region, which also has a hint of spice and chocolate. All in all, a magical combination. I like to serve this with mashed buttered rutabaga or turnip.

SERVES 4
PREPARATION TIME 20 minutes, plus making the stock and at least 3 hours marinating
COOKING TIME 2 hours 25 minutes

1¾ pounds boneless venison haunch, cut into large cubes
1 quart red wine, such as French southern Rhône
2 thyme sprigs
3 garlic cloves, crushed with the blade of a knife
1 star anise
3 tablespoons Cognac
¾ cup plus 2 tablespoons olive oil
2 tablespoons all-purpose flour
2½ cups Beef Stock (see page 16)
1 bouquet garni, made with 1 thyme sprig, 1 parsley sprig and 1 bay leaf, tied with kitchen string
2 carrots, peeled, halved lengthwise and cut into chunks
12 pearl onions or small shallots
1 ounce dark organic chocolate, 70% cocoa solids, grated
⅔ cup diced thick pancetta
2 handfuls mixed seasonal wild mushrooms, such as girolles, horn of plenty and chanterelles
1 handful flat-leaf parsley leaves, roughly chopped
sea salt and freshly ground black pepper

1 Mix together the venison, wine, thyme, garlic, star anise and Cognac in a large nonmetallic bowl. Cover with plastic wrap and leave to marinate in the refrigerator at least 3 hours. Drain the venison through a colander into a bowl, reserving the flavored marinade.

2 Heat 4 tablespoons of the oil in a large Dutch oven over medium heat. Add the venison and cook at least 20 minutes until very well colored on all sides, but not burned. Season with salt and pepper, then sprinkle in the flour and cook, stirring, 2 to 3 minutes longer until the meat is lightly coated. Add the stock and the reserved marinade and bring to a boil, skimming off any foam that rises to the surface. Add the bouquet garni, carrots and onions, turn the heat down to low, partially cover and simmer 1 hour 50 minutes, stirring occasionally, until the meat is very tender and the sauce has become rich and silky.

3 Five minutes before the venison is ready, transfer 2 ladlefuls of the sauce into a bowl. Whisk in the chocolate until it melts and is combined. Return the chocolate-flavored sauce to the pot and stir together well, then re-cover the pot and turn off the heat.

4 Heat the remaining oil in a skillet over medium heat. Add the pancetta and fry 2 to 3 minutes until it is just colored, then stir in the wild mushrooms and fry 1 to 2 minutes longer until it is just tender. Add everything to the venison and stir through. Season with salt and pepper to taste, then stir in the parsley, taking care not to break up the venison.

Pan-fried Skate Wings with Chili–Lime Butter

Skate wings are classically served with a Beurre Noisette (see page 22) and capers, but I think they go just as well with this chili- and lime-flavored butter. It's the same basic idea, but the chili brings a touch of heat and sunshine to the dish, which skate has the depth of flavor to take. Add a splash of fresh lime juice and a little garlic and you have a memorable meal.

SERVES 4
PREPARATION TIME 10 minutes
COOKING TIME 5 minutes

4 skate wings, about 5 ounces each,
    cleaned and prepared
1 tablespoon unsalted butter
1 tablespoon olive oil
1 tablespoon chopped flat-leaf
    parsley leaves
a little all-purpose flour, for dusting
boiled new potatoes, to serve

FOR THE CHILI–LIME BUTTER
1 cup plus 2 tablespoons unsalted
    butter, softened
1 red chili, seeded and finely
    chopped
1 garlic clove, crushed
finely grated zest of 1 lime
juice of ½ lime
leaves from 2 flat-leaf parsley
    sprigs, chopped
sea salt and freshly ground
    black pepper

1 To make the chili–lime butter, put the butter, chili, garlic, lime zest, lime juice and parsley in a nonmetallic bowl and season with salt and pepper. Mix together with a wooden spoon, then put 4 heaped teaspoons to one side. (The rest of the chili–lime butter can be frozen for future use. Wrap half the remaining butter in plastic wrap, roll it into a log shape and twist the ends. Repeat with the remaining butter. Wrap each log in a piece of aluminum foil and put in the freezer to firm up. You can then cut pieces off at your convenience for use on grilled, barbecued or pan-fried meats or fish.)

2 Briefly rinse the skate wings in ice-cold water, then pat dry with a clean dish towel. (Do not use paper, because it will stick.)

3 Heat one or two nonstick skillets, large enough to hold the skate wings, over medium heat. Add the unflavored butter and the oil and heat until the butter just melts. Lightly dust the skate wings with flour, shaking off any excess. Add the skate wings and fry 5 minutes, turning them over once, or until they are just golden brown. As you turn the skate wings, add the reserved chili–lime butter to the pan and spoon it over the fish. (Alternatively, cook the skate wings 1 or 2 at a time and keep them warm in the oven at 300°F while you cook the remaining skate wings.)

4 Remove the skate wings from the pan and put on serving plates. Stir the parsley into the pan, then spoon the flavored butter over the top of the skate wings. Serve with boiled new potatoes.

Mussel, Ginger and **Lemongrass Gratin**

Moules marinière is the classic way to cook mussels and a very good way at that, but mussels in a gratin with a creamy, aromatic sauce flavored with lemongrass, ginger and fresh cilantro is rather delicious, too. Mussels are very good value and easy to cook, just make sure they are very fresh and throw away any with broken shells before cooking and those that don't open once cooked. Don't forget a fresh baguette or homemade French fries to dip into the sauce—this dish wouldn't be the same without them!

SERVES 4
PREPARATION TIME 20 minutes, plus
 making the stock
COOKING TIME 20 minutes

6½ pounds mussels, rinsed
3 tablespoons unsalted butter, soft
2 tablespoons olive oil
1 large shallot, roughly chopped
2 lemongrass stalks, bruised
1½-inch piece gingerroot, peeled
 and roughly chopped
1 cup not-too-acidic or not-too-dry
 white wine, such as Riesling
 from Alsace
2 handfuls cilantro leaves, chopped
1 cup Fish Stock (see page 17)
1¾ cups whipping cream
⅓ cup grated pecorino cheese
sea salt and freshly ground
 black pepper

1 Thoroughly scrub the mussels under cold running water and rinse well. Remove the beards by pulling them toward the large part of the shell. If any of the mussels are open, tap them hard against the countertop and if they don't close, discard them.

2 Generously butter four 7-inch flameproof gratin dishes. Heat a large, deep saucepan over medium heat. Add the oil, shallot, lemongrass and ginger and fry 2 to 3 minutes until they are just soft, but not colored. Turn the heat up to high, add the wine and cook until it reduces by one-third, letting the alcohol evaporate. Add the mussels and half the cilantro leaves, cover the pan with a lid and cook about 5 minutes at the very most, shaking the pan occasionally, until all the mussels are open. Discard any that remain closed. Remove the pan from the heat and scoop all the mussels into a colander using a slotted spoon. Leave them to cool slightly before shelling. Discard the shells.

3 Spoon the shelled mussels into the prepared gratin dishes and put the dishes on a broiler tray. Strain the juices from the pan and bowl through a fine strainer into a measuring jug. Reserve 7 ounces of the liquid.

4 Meanwhile, heat the broiler to high. Pour the mussel liquid into a sauté pan and add the stock and cream. Put over low heat and bring almost to a boil, then simmer 5 minutes, or until the liquid reduces by half and is thick enough to coat the back of a wooden spoon. Season with pepper to taste and a little salt, if necessary.

5 Ladle the cream sauce over the mussels in the gratin dishes. Sprinkle the remaining cilantro over the tops, then finish with a sprinkling of cheese on each, making sure the cheese covers the cilantro so it doesn't discolor. Put the dishes under the hot broiler a minute or so until the tops are bubbling and golden brown. Serve hot.

Pan-roasted Langoustines with **Cilantro**

What makes this dish is the quality and freshness of the langoustines—make sure they are absolutely fresh and you will have a super-simple, yet very tasty, dish. The shellfish come in a fragrant butter sauce, flavored with aromatic cilantro, garlic and fresh lime juice. This is great served with buttery pilaf rice flavored with fresh ginger or just a simple salad.

SERVES 4
PREPARATION TIME 10 minutes
COOKING TIME 8 minutes

16 whole langoustines, shell on
1 teaspoon olive oil
1¼ sticks unsalted butter
2 garlic cloves, finely chopped
1 handful cilantro leaves,
  roughly chopped
1 lime, cut into wedges
Thai-style Pilaf Rice (see page 21),
  to serve

1 Heat the broiler to high. To prepare the langoustines, cut them in half lengthwise, then put cut-side down on paper towels to absorb any water. This is particularly important if the langoustines have been frozen.

2 Heat a large, nonstick skillet over high heat until it is searing hot. Add the oil and one-third of the butter and when the butter is foaming, put half the langoustines, flesh-side down, in the pan. Cook about 2 minutes, then flip them over, transfer them to a roasting tray and repeat with the remaining langoustines.

3 Melt the last of the butter in the skillet until foaming. Stir in the garlic and cilantro, then spoon straightaway over the langoustines. Put the langustines under the broiler 2 minutes, then squeeze the lime juice over the tops and serve with pilaf rice.

Ragout of Summer Vegetables with Vanilla Beurre Blanc

This is a perfect summer dish, as it's colorful, light and fresh. The vegetables only need a minimal amount of cooking before they are coated in a light butter sauce, scented with fresh vanilla seeds and thyme. One small point, however—don't over do the vanilla or you will disturb the delicately balanced flavor of the dish. This is delicious served on its own or alongside roasts.

SERVES 4
PREPARATION TIME 20 minutes, plus
  making the stock
COOKING TIME 40 minutes

½ cup podded fava beans, gray
  outer casing removed
1½ cups podded peas
½ cup halved green beans
3 ounces baby carrots, scrubbed
3 ounces baby leeks, trimmed and
  each cut into 3 pieces
3 ounces baby turnips, peeled
  and quartered
1 bunch asparagus tips
1 baby cauliflower, cut into florets
leaves from 1 thyme sprig
sea salt and freshly ground
  black pepper

FOR THE VANILLA BEURRE BLANC
2 cups Vegetable Stock (see
  page 17)
1¾ sticks unsalted butter, soft,
  cut into cubes
1 shallot, finely chopped
finely grated zest and juice of ½ lime
1 vanilla bean, split in half
  lengthwise and seeds scraped out
  (you can keep the bean for flavoring
  vanilla sugar)

1 Pour the stock for the vanilla *beurre blanc* into a small sauté pan and cook over medium-high heat 15 minutes, or until it reduces to ⅔ cup. Leave to one side.

2 Meanwhile, bring a saucepan of salted water to a boil over high heat. Add the vegetables and cook, one type at a time, 2 to 5 minutes each until just tender. Lift them out with a slotted spoon and refresh in ice water, then drain once more, tip carefully into a bowl and leave to one side. Put a lid on the pan of water and reserve for reheating the vegetables just before you are ready to serve.

3 To make the *beurre blanc*, melt 4 teaspoons of the butter in a small saucepan over medium heat. Add the shallots and fry 2 minutes until they are just soft. Stir in the lime juice, then add the reduced stock and the vanilla seeds. Bring to a simmer and simmer 5 to 8 minutes until there is slightly less than ½ cup of buttery stock.

4 Turn the heat down to very low and gradually whisk in the remaining soft butter, a few cubes at a time. Keep whisking until the butter is incorporated before adding the next batch; this stops the sauce splitting by keeping it at a constant temperature. As you are whisking, you should see a foam of tiny bubbles form on top of the mixture and when all the butter has been added, the sauce should be pale in color and light in consistency, similar to a very thin custard, and should just coat the back of the spoon. This will take 10 to 12 minutes. At this point, season with salt and pepper to taste and add the lime zest. Cover with a lid and leave to one side in a warm place.

5 Return the pan of water to a boil over high heat. Add the vegetables and cook 1 minute or so until heated through, then drain on paper towels. Serve the vegetables on plates with the vanilla *beurre blanc* spooned over the tops and sprinkled with the thyme.

Butternut Squash and **Saffron Risotto**

This is the most popular risotto we serve at The Vineyard, and I love it, too. The saffron-infused stock and mashed roasted squash seem to intensify the flavor of the risotto. If you are using carnaroli rice, my grain of choice, follow the recipe closely and keep the heat low when you add it, otherwise the rice can break down and produce a sticky risotto. You can also finish it with a sprinkling of dehydrated, crisp butternut squash along with the Parmesan cheese. A small herb salad is an ideal accompaniment.

SERVES 4
PREPARATION TIME 20 minutes, plus
   making the stock
COOKING TIME 55 minutes

1 small butternut squash, unpeeled,
   quartered lengthwise and seeded
3¾ cups Vegetable Stock (see
   page 17)
2 pinches saffron strands
1¼ sticks unsalted butter
1 onion, finely chopped
1½ cups risotto rice, such arborio
   or carnaroli
6 tablespoons freshly grated
   Parmesan cheese
2 tablespoons plain Greek yogurt
1 tablespoon snipped chives
sea salt and freshly ground
   black pepper
Dehydrated Pumpkin Crisp (see page
   41), to serve (optional)

1 Heat the oven to 315°F. Put the butternut squash in a roasting pan, cover with aluminum foil and roast 45 minutes, or until very tender.

2 When the squash has been in the oven about 30 minutes, start to make the risotto. Heat the stock and saffron in a saucepan and bring to a simmer, then turn the heat down to very low. Melt 5 tablespoons of the butter in a skillet over low heat. Add the onion and cook 3 to 4 minutes, stirring occasionally, until soft. Add the rice and mix with a wooden spoon over low heat until it is coated in the butter and onion mixture.

3 Add the hot stock to the pan, little by little, stirring continuously until the liquid is absorbed before adding more stock. Carry on adding the stock, stirring to stop it sticking, about 20 minutes until the rice has a lovely creamy texture.

4 When the squash is cooked, and while the risotto is still cooking, remove the squash from the roasting pan and leave until it is just cool enough to handle. Scoop the flesh away from the skin into a bowl and mash roughly with a fork. When the rice is almost cooked, fold in the mashed squash, the Parmesan, yogurt, chives and the remaining butter. If the risotto is a little thick, add a few more spoonfuls of stock to loosen it, then season well with salt and pepper and serve immediately with pumpkin crisp scattered over the top, if you like.

Grapefruit Gratin with **Honey–Saffron Sabayon** and **Nut Brittle**

I love all sorts of fruit—well, perhaps with the exception of durian. Here, I am using pink grapefruit, which is one of my favorites. I find it so refreshing with its own mix of sweet and sour. The combination of honey and saffron in the sabayon makes it seem really exotic, too, as well as light and frothy on top of the sharp grapefruit. It does seem as if they were all meant for each other.

SERVES 4
PREPARATION TIME 20 minutes,
  plus cooling
COOKING TIME 30 minutes

FOR THE NUT BRITTLE
½ cup superfine sugar
⅓ cup blanched or unblanched
  hazelnuts, very finely chopped

FOR THE GRAPEFRUIT AND SABAYON
a pinch saffron strands, infused
  in 4 tablespoons warm water
4 large pink grapefruit, scrubbed
  and patted dry
2 tablespoons honey
3 egg yolks

1 To make the nut brittle, line a large baking sheet with parchment paper. Heat the sugar in a dry, nonstick skillet over medium heat until the sugar melts and turns a light brown caramel and reaches 320°F on a candy thermometer. Remove the pan from the heat and stir in the hazelnuts. Return the pan to the heat until the caramel becomes liquid again, stirring to coat the nuts completely.

2 Immediately pour the hazelnut mixture into the prepared baking sheet. Cover with a second sheet of paper, then, using a rolling pin, roll into a thin, even layer about ¼ inch thick. Leave to cool and harden, then remove the paper and break into small pieces. Alternatively, put in a food processor and pulse to a coarse crumble consistency. Leave to one side.

3 To make the sabayon, heat the saffron water in a small pan over low heat until it reduces by one-third and turns dark orange in color. Pass it through a strainer into a large heatproof bowl. Leave to one side.

4 Finely grate the zest of one of the grapefruit, then peel all of them, removing the skin and white pith. Segment the grapefruit over a strainer suspended over a saucepan to catch the juices. Line a cookie sheet with a clean dish towel, then put the segments on the prepared sheet and leave to dry slightly.

5 Add the honey to the grapefruit juices and bring to a boil over medium heat, then turn the heat down to low and simmer 6 to 8 minutes until it reduces to a thick syrup. Add the syrup and egg yolks to the saffron water and mix together. Set the bowl over a saucepan of gently simmering water, making sure the bottom of the bowl does not touch the water. Beat the mixture, using an electric mixer, 8 to 10 minutes until it turns pale and thick.

6 Meanwhile, heat the broiler to high. Put the grapefruit segments in fan shapes on four flameproof serving plates. Spoon the sabayon over the tops to cover the segments, then broil briefly until light golden brown. Sprinkle with the nut brittle and serve.

Cocoa-infused French Toast with Roasted Peaches

My mom often made *pain perdu*, as we knew French toast, for me when I was growing up. It was seen as a sin to throw bread away, so any leftover bread was sliced and dipped into egg and milk and fried in butter. In this new version, the cocoa transforms this classic dish to create a stylish, modern dessert with the added elegance of roasted peaches. You can also adapt this dish and serve it with pears, apricots or plums instead of peaches, if you like, or even make it with coconut milk instead of cow milk.

SERVES 4
PREPARATION TIME 10 minutes
COOKING TIME 25 minutes

5 tablespoons unsalted butter
2 large, firm peaches, quartered and pits removed
3 tablespoons maple syrup
2 tablespoons unsweetened dark cocoa powder
¾ cup plus 2 tablespoons whole milk, slightly warm
2 eggs, lightly beaten
2 tablespoons sugar
4 x 1-inch slices *pain de campagne* or other country-style bread
2 tablespoons slivered almonds, toasted
3 tablespoons crème fraîche
1 teaspoon chopped rosemary leaves

1 Heat the oven to 350°F. Melt half the butter an ovenproof sauté pan over medium heat. When it is foaming, add the peaches and sauté 2 to 3 minutes, turning them once, until they are golden on both sides. Add 2 tablespoons of the maple syrup and turn the peaches to coat them in the syrup, then transfer them to the oven and roast 5 to 8 minutes until they are just soft. Remove the pan from the heat and leave the peaches to one side on a plate. Leave the oven on.

2 Mix half the cocoa powder with the warm milk, eggs and sugar in a wide, shallow bowl, stirring until the sugar dissolves. Leave to cool slightly, if necessary. Add 2 slices of the bread and soak both sides. Put the bread on a clean dish towel to drain slightly, then repeat with the remaining slices of bread.

3 Heat a large, nonstick skillet over medium heat. Add the remaining butter and maple syrup and, when they melt, swirl the pan until they are combined. Put the egg-soaked bread slices in the pan and fry 1 to 2 minutes on each side until they are just golden and slightly crisp, taking care they do not burn. You might need to do this in batches.

4 Put the French toast in a shallow baking sheet and top with the roasted peaches, a sprinkling of toasted almonds and a dusting of the remaining cocoa powder. Heat through in the oven 2 to 3 minutes.

5 Meanwhile, mix together the crème fraîche and rosemary. Serve the French toast and peaches with the rosemary-flavored crème fraîche.

Soft Pan-fried Pears with Cardamom and Szechuan Pepper

Ever since I lived in Southeast Asia, I've enjoyed adding Asian spices to my cooking, not only for their flavor but for their fragrance, too. Pears can take lots of different spices, especially cardamom and Szechuan pepper, yet the right quantity is critical, as too much would overwhelm the subtlety of this delicate fruit. You can use the same quantity of syrup and adjust the number of pears according to the size of the pears and your guests' appetites. This dessert goes really well with the Pistachio Madeleines (see page 75).

SERVES 4
PREPARATION TIME 10 minutes
COOKING TIME 35 minutes

1 teaspoon Szechuan peppercorns
1 cup sugar
1 teaspoon cardamom pods, lightly crushed
juice of ¼ lime
4 large or 8 small, firm pears, such as William, or Comice, peeled with the stems left on
2 tablespoons unsalted butter

1 Put the Szechuan peppercorns in a small, dry skillet over medium heat and toast 1 to 2 minutes, shaking the pan occasionally, until they are just colored and aromatic. Tip them onto a plate and crush lightly with the flat blade of a knife.

2 Bring the sugar, half the cardamom, the lime juice and 3½ cups water to a boil in a saucepan over medium heat. Stir occasionally 5 to 8 minutes until the sugar dissolves and starts to turn syrupy.

3 Add the pears to the pan with the syrup. You need to cover the pears with a *cartouche* (see page 218). Turn the heat down to very low and simmer 8 minutes, or until the pears are slightly soft. To check the pears, insert the tip of a knife into the thickest part—there should still be a little resistance. Put the pears on a clean dish towel to drain. Return the pan to the heat and simmer 8 to 10 minutes until the syrup reduces by about three-quarters.

4 Meanwhile, melt the butter in a large, nonstick skillet over medium heat. When the butter is foaming, add the pears and the remaining cardamom and cook 3 to 4 minutes, turning occasionally, until they are light golden all over.

5 Add 4 tablespoons of the reduced syrup to the pan and cook the pears 4 to 5 minutes, basting them occasionally with the syrup, until they are tender, but not mushy. Baste the pears again with the syrup and add the crushed Szechuan pepper. Serve the pears with the syrup poured over the top and any remaining syrup served separately.

Pineapple, Chili and **Lemongrass Tarte Tatin**

One of the sweetest fruits—and a particular favorite of mine—is the pineapple. This exotic fruit tastes wonderful baked in a tarte tatin in place of the traditional apples and, of course, it needs less added sugar. The confident aroma and lusciousness of the pineapple pairs remarkably well with stronger spices and flavorings, and in this recipe I have contrasted it with fragrant lemongrass and a hint of chili. You might be surprised by how successfully these two spices marry with the fruit—and with the buttery flavor of the pastry—to make a truly superb dessert. If you like, serve it with a scoop of coconut ice cream or sorbet.

SERVES 4
PREPARATION TIME 20 minutes, plus 30 minutes chilling and at least 5 minutes resting
COOKING TIME 1 hour

8 ounces puff pastry dough, thawed if frozen
all-purpose flour, for dusting
scant ½ cup superfine sugar
2 pounds 10 ounces pineapple, peeled, cored and cut into large wedges
3 tablespoons unsalted butter
1 red chili, seeded and finely chopped, plus ½ red chili, cut into strips, to serve (optional)
½ lemongrass stalk, bruised and halved lengthwise

1 Roll out the dough on a lightly floured countertop, then cut out a circle slightly larger than an 8-inch tatin pan or flameproof baking dish. Roll the dough over the rolling pin, then transfer it to a cookie sheet, cover with plastic wrap and chill in the refrigerator 30 minutes to prevent the dough shrinking during baking.

2 Meanwhile, heat the oven to 375°F. Melt the sugar slowly in the tatin pan over medium heat until it turns golden brown. Add the pineapple and cook 6 to 8 minutes, or until light golden brown. Remove the pan from the heat. Using a slotted spoon, transfer the pineapple to a plate and leave to rest 5 to 8 minutes to release the juice.

3 Stir the butter into the sugar in the pan. Sprinkle one-third of the chopped chili over the pan. Put the pineapple wedges tightly around the edge of the pan in a circle, then make smaller circles of tightly fitting pineapple within this circle until the bottom is covered and all the pineapple is used. Put the lemongrass on top of the pineapple, add the strips of chili, if you like, and bake 30 minutes.

4 Remove the pan from the oven and sprinkle another one-third of the chili over the pineapple. Put the dough on top, pushing the edges into the pan. Return the pan to the oven and bake 20 minutes longer, or until the pastry is golden brown and crisp.

5 Remove the tart from the oven and leave to cool a few minutes. Put an upside-down plate, slightly larger than the pan, on top of the tart and, holding both the plate and pan, turn the pan over to transfer the tart to the plate, right side up. Sprinkle with the remaining chili, if you like. Serve warm, removing the lemongrass and chili strips before cutting into portions.

Pineapple Beignets with **Mango Carpaccio**

In my view, pineapple is made for a *beignet*, or fritter, because its fresh, slightly sharp taste has just the right amount of acidity to cut through the rich batter coating. The thin slices of sweet mango go well with the acidity of the pineapple, too, while the piquancy of the pink peppercorns add that unusual finishing touch.

SERVES 4
PREPARATION TIME 20 minutes, plus 20 minutes cooling
COOKING 25 minutes

FOR THE MANGO CARPACCIO
1 large, semiripe mango, peeled, pitted and thinly sliced
¼ cup superfine sugar
2 pinches dried pink peppercorns

FOR THE PINEAPPLE BEIGNETS
1 small pineapple, peeled, cored, quartered lengthwise and cut into small chunks about ⅔-inch thick
1 cup all-purpose flour
2 eggs, separated
a pinch salt
½ cup beer, preferably bitter, or dry hard cider
2 tablespoons sunflower oil, plus extra for deep-frying
2 tablespoons superfine sugar, plus extra for dusting

1 To make the carpaccio, put the mango in a deep roasting pan. Put the sugar and ⅔ cup of water into a small saucepan and bring to a boil, swirling the pan occasionally, until the sugar dissolves. Pour the syrup over the mango and scatter with the peppercorns. Cover the pan with plastic wrap and leave to one side to infuse and cool.

2 Strain the mango syrup back into the washed small pan. Put the mango slices on serving plates and leave to one side. Return the peppercorns to the pan with the syrup and bring to a boil, then boil 5 minutes, or until the syrup is thick enough to coat the back of a spoon. Remove the pan from the heat and leave the syrup to cool once more.

3 To make the *beignets*, line a baking sheet with a clean dish towel and spread the pineapple out on it in a single layer. Cover with another dish towel and press down firmly to remove any liquid. Leave to dry, covered, while you prepare the batter. Mix together the flour, egg yolks, salt, beer and oil to make a thick, smooth paste. Beat together the egg whites and sugar in a separate bowl, using an electric mixer, until soft peaks form. Gently fold them into the beer batter.

4 Meanwhile, pour enough oil to deep-fry the *beignets* into a deep-fat fryer or a deep, wide saucepan and heat to 325°F, or until a cube of bread browns in 40 seconds.

5 Thread a piece of pineapple onto a long skewer and dip briefly into the batter until completely coated. Using a fork, carefully push the pineapple off the skewer into the hot oil. Repeat with the rest of the pineapple, frying about 6 pieces at a time. When the *beignets* start to float to the surface, carefully turn them over and continue to fry 4 to 5 minutes until they are golden brown and crisp. Remove them with a slotted spoon and drain on paper towels, then dust immediately with sugar. Put the *beignets* on top of the mango carpaccio, then spoon over a little of the cool syrup to serve.

Warm Chocolate Cookies with Coconut Ice Cream

When you are making chocolate cookies, the choice of chocolate is very important. Here, I have chosen chocolate with 60% pure cocoa—not overbitter, as a lot of people don't like that, but instead one that is a touch richer, with hint of tobacco leaf, bark and spices coming through to give a thoroughly modern twist. The cookies have a soft, cakelike texture.

SERVES 4
PREPARATION TIME 25 minutes, plus at least 3 hours freezing
COOKING TIME 15 minutes

FOR THE COCONUT ICE CREAM
3 egg yolks
½ cup less 1 tablespoon coconut milk
4 tablespoons toasted shredded coconut
1¾ cups heavy cream

FOR THE CHOCOLATE COOKIES
7 tablespoons unsalted butter, plus extra for greasing
5 ounces dark chocolate, 60% cocoa solids, broken into pieces
2 eggs, separated
¼ cup superfinesugar
½ cup plus 1½ tablespoons all-purpose flour
a pinch salt

1 To make the ice cream, first make a sabayon (see page 218). Whisk together the egg yolks and coconut milk in a heatproof bowl set over a saucepan of simmering water, making sure the bottom of the bowl does not touch the water. Whisk 5 to 8 minutes until it thickens. Remove the pan from the heat, add the shredded coconut and whisk continuously until the mixture cools completely.

2 Whip the cream, using an electric mixer, until soft peaks form, then fold it into the sabayon. Pour into a 1-pint freezerproof container. Cover with plastic wrap and put in the freezer at least 3 hours until firm.

3 To make the cookies, heat the oven to 425°F. Lightly grease two 12-hole mini tart pans. Melt the chocolate and butter in a small saucepan over low heat, stirring occasionally.

4 Meanwhile, beat together the egg yolks and sugar in a large mixing bowl, using an electric mixer, about 5 minutes until pale, thick and double in volume.

5 As soon as the chocolate melts, fold in the flour with a wooden spoon or spatula until they are combined. You must be very careful when doing this and work quite quickly. Pour the chocolate mixture slowly into the egg mixture and fold together.

6 Whisk the egg whites with the salt in a large, clean bowl until soft peaks form, then fold them into the chocolate mixture. Spoon the batter into the prepared tart pans, half-filling each hole, to make 12 to 18 cookies. Bake 5 to 6 minutes until they are risen and slightly firm to the touch. Remove the pan from the oven and turn out the cookies onto a wire rack to cool until just lukewarm, then serve with the coconut ice cream.

Pistachio Madeleines with Chocolate Sorbet

This makes for a perfect combination, but you might also like to serve the madeleines with vanilla ice cream or even just a delcious, ripe pear. They also go well with the strawberries on page 79, as an alternative for the lime shortbread. So many flavors seem to be made for madeleines—vanilla, cinnamon, star anise, hazelnut, orange, honey—but, for me, the one thing you certainly can't beat is when they are served warm straight out of the oven.

SERVES 4

PREPARATION TIME 30 minutes, plus overnight resting and making the *beurre noisette*

COOKING TIME 15 minutes

FOR THE CHOCOLATE SORBET
½ cup less 1 tablespoon superfine sugar
½ cup unsweetened, dark cocoa powder
4 ounces dark chocolate, 60% cocoa solids, broken into small pieces

FOR THE PISTACHIO MADELEINES
unsalted butter, for greasing
1 cup plus 2 tablespoons all-purpose flour
¾ teaspoon baking powder
2 eggs
½ cup less 1 tablespoon superfine sugar
3 tablespoons milk
4 teaspoons mild honey
⅔ cup warm Beurre Noisette (see page 22)
¼ cup pistachio nuts, toasted and chopped

1 First, prepare the madeleines. Lightly grease a 12-hole madeleine tray. Sift the flour and baking powder into a mixing bowl and leave to one side. Beat together the eggs and sugar in a large mixing bowl, using an electric mixer, about 10 minutes until the mixture is pale, thick and doubles in volume.

2 Heat the milk and honey together in a small saucepan until the honey is just melted. Fold the flour mixture into the egg mixture, then pour in the milk and honey, stirring until combined. Add the warm *beurre noisette* and mix slowly until fully incorporated, then fold in the pistachios. Spoon the mixture into the prepared madeleine tray, half-filling each hole. Cover with plastic wrap and leave to rest in the refrigerator overnight.

3 To make the sorbet, pour 1¼ cups water into a small saucepan. Mix together the sugar and cocoa powder, then add to the water and bring to a boil, whisking continuously. It's very important not to let the cocoa powder sink to the bottom of the pan and burn.

4 Put the chocolate pieces in a heatproof bowl. When the cocoa mixture has reached a boil, pour the hot liquid onto the chocolate pieces and whisk until the chocolate melts. Pass the mixture through a fine strainer into a 1-pint freezerproof container and freeze until hard.

5 When the sorbet is hard, cut the mixture into pieces and blitz in a food processor until smooth. Return to the freezer container and freeze at least 3 hours until firm.

6 The next day, heat the oven to 400°F. Bake the madeleines 5 minutes, then turn the tray around in the oven, front to back, even if you have a fan oven, and bake 5 minutes longer, or until they are light golden and slightly firm to the touch. Insert a skewer into a madeleine and if it comes out clean, they are ready. If not, bake 2 minutes longer and check again. Remove the tray from the oven and leave to cool 5 minutes, or until lukewarm before turning out and serving with the chocolate sorbet.

Orange and Tarragon Gâteau with Candied Orange

We rarely consider herbs in a dessert, and particularly in baking, but the mix of tarragon and orange works so well. I'd had an idea of using these together for a while, but didn't quite get the correct balance. So my chef and I tried and tried and finally got it right in this gâteau. It's all in the quantity—you can't be heavy-handed with the tarragon—and the end result is fantastic.

SERVES 4 to 6
PREPARATION TIME 30 minutes, plus 30 minutes cooling
COOKING TIME 30 minutes

3½ tablespoons unsalted butter, melted
1 cup very finely ground blanched almonds
⅓ cup all-purpose flour
½ teaspoon baking powder
4 egg whites, scant ½ cup
¼ cup less 1 tablespoon superfine sugar
finely grated zest and juice of 1 small orange
2 tablespoons roughly chopped tarragon leaves, plus leaves from 1 tarragon sprig, to decorate

FOR THE CANDIED ORANGE
½ cup superfine sugar
1 large unwaxed orange, cut crosswise into ¼-inch-thick slices, discarding the end slices

1 Heat the oven to 315°F. Lightly grease a deep 7-inch cake pan with a removable botton with about 1 tablespoon of the melted butter and line the bottom with parchment paper. Sift the ground almonds, flour and baking powder into a bowl and leave to one side.

2 Beat together the egg whites and sugar in a large bowl, using an electric mixer, until soft peaks form. Mix together the orange juice and remaining melted butter, then gently fold into the whisked egg whites. Gradually fold in the almond mixture, orange zest and chopped tarragon, a spoonful at a time, until incorporated.

3 Pour the batter into the prepared cake pan and smooth the top. Bake 18 to 20 minutes until the cake is risen and golden. Check that the cake is baked by inserting a skewer into the deepest part. If it comes out clean, it is baked. If not, bake 2 to 3 minutes longer and check again. Remove the pan from the oven and leave the cake to cool 5 minutes on a wire rack before turning out, removing the paper and returning it to the wire rack, bottom-side up, to cool completely.

4 Meanwhile, make the candied orange. Line a baking sheet with parchment paper. Pour ⅔ cup water into a saucepan and stir in the sugar. Heat over high heat until the sugar dissolves and the liquid becomes slightly syrupy. At the same time, put the orange slices in a small saucepan and just cover with water. Bring to a boil over high heat, then discard the water. Repeat this again with fresh water. Drain the oranges again, add them to the pan containing the syrup and bring to a simmer. Simmer 5 minutes longer, or until the orange slices are tender but still hold their shape. Lift the orange slices out of the syrup and leave to cool on the prepared baking sheet.

5 Return the syrup to a low heat and simmer 8 to 10 minutes until it is thick enough to coat the back of a spoon, then leave to cool. When the oranges a cool, cut each slice in half into a half-moon shape. Arrange the orange slices, slightly overlapping, on top of the cake. Brush the warm syrup over the top of the oranges, then sprinkle the remaining tarragon over the top.

Orange-blossom Strawberries with Lime Shortbread

When I was younger, we used to grow strawberries, and our favorite dessert was freshly picked ripe strawberries folded into whipping cream, just a touch, sprinkled with sugar and chilled for an hour or so. We would then crush them with a fork before eating them. When I go home in the summer, I still love to eat them like this. Another family favorite is this stylish strawberry dessert, which I often call Strawberry Soup, although it isn't really a soup. I just call it that because the strawberries are served with lots of wonderful fresh fruit juice, scented with orange blossom. You could use the orange zest to make candied orange (see page 77) and sprinkle it over the top of the soup before serving.

SERVES 4
PREPARATION TIME 25 minutes, plus
  20 minutes macerating
COOKING TIME 20 minutes

3⅓ cups strawberries, hulled and
  quartered
4 teaspoons sherry vinegar
½ cup superfine sugar
juice of 2 oranges
4 teaspoons orange blossom extract

FOR THE LIME SHORTBREAD
finely grated zest of 1 lime
1½ sticks unsalted butter, soft
⅓ cup superfine sugar, plus extra
  for sprinkling
1½ cups plus 1½ tablespoons
  all-purpose flour

1 Heat the oven to 315°F. To make the lime shortbread, beat together the lime zest, butter and sugar in a large bowl, using an electric mixer, until light and fluffy, then fold in the flour to make a soft dough. Roll the dough out between two sheets of parchment paper until it is about ½ inch thick. Transfer it to a baking sheet and lift off the top sheet of paper. Mark a pattern on the top with a fork, if you like. Bake 12 to 18 minutes until just light golden and slightly firm to the touch.

2 Cut the shortbread straightaway into whatever shape you like and sprinkle with sugar. You must cut the shortbread as soon as it comes out of the oven, while still soft and pliable. Put the baking sheet on a wire rack and leave the shortbread to cool and become crisp.

3 While the shortbread is baking, put the strawberries into a bowl and add the sherry vinegar. Reserve 2 tablespoons of the sugar, then sprinkle the remainder over the strawberries. Toss them together, cover with plastic wrap and put in the refrigerator to macerate 15 to 20 minutes only.

4 Pour the orange juice into a bowl and add the orange blossom extract. Take the strawberries out of the refrigerator and turn them in the macerating liquid. Using a slotted spoon, divide the strawberries into four large *coupé* glasses, leaving the residual juice in the bowl. Add the orange juice to the strawberry juice and mix well, then spoon over the strawberries and serve with the lime shortbread.

Blood Orange and Star Anise Tart

SERVES 4 to 6
PREPARATION TIME 30 minutes, plus
   1 hour infusing and at least
   2 hours 50 minutes chilling
COOKING TIME 20 minutes

FOR THE SWEET ORANGE PASTRY DOUGH
¾ stick unsalted butter, soft, plus
   extra for greasing
finely grated zest of ½ blood orange
a pinch salt
½ cup confectioner's sugar
¼ cup very fnely ground blanched
   almonds
1 egg
1⅓ cups plus 1 tablespoon
   all-purpose flour, sifted

FOR THE ORANGE AND STAR ANISE FILLING
1½ leaves gelatin, about ¹⁄₁₆ ounce
   total weight
juice of 4 unwaxed blood oranges
2 star anise
3 eggs
½ cup less 1 tablespoon sugar
5 tablespoons unsalted butter, soft

FOR THE CANDIED ORANGE ZEST
finely pared zest of 3 unwaxed blood
   oranges
2 tablespoons sugar

1 To make the pastry dough, lightly grease a 7-inch loose-bottomed tart pan that is 1 inch deep. Beat together the butter, orange zest, salt, confectioner's sugar, ground almonds and egg in a large bowl, using an electric mixer, until light and fluffy. Fold in the flour to form a dough. (Try not to overwork the dough; it is ready as soon as it comes together.) Wrap it in plastic wrap and chill 20 minutes.

2 Roll out the dough between two sheets of parchment paper until it is ⅛ inch thick, then use it to line the bottom and the side of the prepared pan, pressing it into the side without overstretching the dough. Trim off any excess dough, prick the bottom with a fork and chill 30 minutes to prevent the dough shrinking during baking.

3 Heat the oven to 350°F. Line the dough with parchment paper and baking beans. Bake 6 minutes, then turn the oven down to 315°F. Remove the beans and parchment paper, then return the pan to the oven and bake the pastry 3 to 4 minutes longer until it is baked through and light golden brown. Leave to cool on a wire rack.

4 To make the filling, soak the gelatin leaves in a bowl of cold water about 5 minutes until they are soft, then squeeze out the water. Pour the orange juice into a saucepan and bring to a boil over high heat. Remove the pan from the heat and whisk in the soft gelatin, then add the star anise. Cover the pan with plastic wrap and leave the orange juice to infuse 1 hour in a warm place. You don't want the gelatin to set.

5 After 50 minutes, beat the eggs with the sugar, using an electric mixer, 3 to 4 minutes until the mixture is pale and thickened. Beat in the butter, a little at a time, then remove the star anise and whisk in the orange juice mixture. (Blitz in a blender if you prefer a smooth filling.) Pour into the baked pastry case and chill at least 2 hours until it is set.

6 Meanwhile, make the candied orange zest. Line a baking sheet with parchment paper. Put the orange zest in a small saucepan, cover with cold water and bring to a boil, then remove the pan from the heat and drain and refresh the zest in cold water. Drain again and repeat the entire process once more. Return the zest to the pan and add the sugar and 3 tablespoons water, then bring to a boil, stirring until the sugar dissolves. Boil 4 to 5 minutes until the zest becomes transparent, then remove the pan from the heat and leave the zest to cool in the syrup. Strain the zest, discarding the syrup, then spread it out on the prepared baking sheet. Remove the tart from the tart pan and decorate with the candied zest.

Lemon and Chili Cake with Chili Glaze

I'm not a pastry chef but when I have the time, I love to work with my head pastry chef, Anthony, in the restaurant. We have tried all sorts of desserts, but I wanted to do a cake with chili, lemon, flecks of fresh chili and a chili confit that I just knew would work. So, here it is... lemon is a classic flavoring for cake, but the chili is the icing on the cake, so to speak! Make sure you soak the cake while it's still warm so it absorbs the syrup. This makes a fabulous dessert, but you can also enjoy a slice with a cup of tea.

SERVES 6 to 8
PREPARATION TIME 25 minutes, plus 5 minutes infusing and 30 minutes cooling
COOKING TIME 40 minutes

¾ cup plus 2 tablespoons all-purpose flour or 1 cup cake flour
½ teaspoon baking powder
finely grated zest and juice of 2 small lemons
1 cup superfine sugar
4 eggs
¼ cup crème fraîche
3 red chilies, seeded and finely chopped

1 Heat the oven to 315°F. Line the bottom and sides of a nonstick 12 x 5 x 3½-inch bread pan with parchment paper. Sift together the flour and baking powder into a bowl.

2 Beat together half the lemon juice, just over half of the sugar and the eggs in a large bowl, using an electric mixer, about 10 minutes until the mixture is pale and double in volume. Beat in the crème fraîche, then fold in the flour mixture. Fold in 2½ of the chilies and all the lemon zest.

3 Pour the batter into the prepared bread pan, smooth the top and bake 15 minutes, then open the oven door. Carefully pull the shelf out slightly with the bread pan on it and mark the cake with a knife lengthwise down the middle. (This will help the cake open up and give it a light texture.) Slide the pan back into the oven and bake 20 minutes longer.

4 While the cake finishes baking, make the syrup. Put the remaining lemon juice, 2 tablespoons of the sugar and 2 tablespoons water in a saucepan and heat over high heat 2 minutes until the sugar dissolves and the liquid turns slightly syrupy. There should be 3 to 4 tablespoons of liquid. Remove the pan from the heat and leave to one side.

5 Check to see if the cake is baked by inserting a skewer into the deepest part and if it comes out clean, the cake is ready. If not, return the cake to the oven, bake 5 minutes longer and check again. Leave the cake to cool 5 minutes, then turn it out onto a wire rack placed over a baking sheet. Peel away the parchment paper and put the cake top-side up. Immediately spoon the lemon syrup evenly over the top of the cake, then leave it on the rack to cool completely.

6 Put the remaining sugar in a saucepan with 3½ tablespoons water over medium heat 5 minutes, or until it forms a thick, shiny syrup. Remove from the heat and add the remaining chili, then leave to infuse 5 minutes. When the cake is completely cool, brush the top with the chili glaze to give a nice, shiny coating.

EGALITÉ

Democratic recipes that elevate humble ingredients to starring roles

"*Egalité*" is a lovely word, and it would be great to drift away into all sorts of discussions and explanations—but that's not for now. In this chapter, I will be talking about ingredients that were originally perceived as peasant fodder, but are now being rediscovered and enjoying new recognition. I'm sure you know what I mean by that—ingredients like rabbit, mushrooms, potatoes and simple herbs.

Underpin that with beautifully complementary ingredients. I've tried to create recipes in which the relationship between two, or sometimes more, ingredients, when combined with one another, make a perfectly balanced pairing—they are just great for each other. So you see, in that brief description, what we have captured in *egalité*.

So let me give you an example of some of the ingredients I have used in these recipes. There's a beautiful Rabbit Terrine with Onion Marmalade (see page 86), a great Pomme Farcie with Braised Boston Butt (see page 117), Flounder with Celery Root and Pancetta Galette (see page 130) and Lamb Sweetbreads and Wild Mushroom Vol-au-Vents (see page 123). *Egalité* of high-quality ingredients!

Game, Chestnut and **Golden Raisin** Terrine

Game birds, such as pheasant and partridge, are a seasonal favorite of mine, and much underused. I've combined these two in this terrine and, to add to the autumnal theme, I've added chestnuts, with their lovely earthiness, as well as golden raisins for a touch of sweetness. You can buy cooked and peeled chestnuts in the supermarket, which are wonderfully easy to use. I find Muscatel golden raisins give the best flavor. Make sure you follow the timings, because you don't want a dry terrine, which can easily happen when bird game is overcooked.

SERVES 6 to 8
PREPARATION TIME 45 minutes, plus 3 to 4 hours marinating, cooling and 2 days chilling
COOKING TIME 1 hour

¼ cup golden raisins, such as Muscatel
3 tablespoons Madeira
2 pheasant breasts and legs, about 7 ounces total weight, skinned, boned and cut into large cubes
4 partridge breasts and legs, about 7 ounces total weight, skinned, boned and cut into large cubes
10 ounces pork belly fat, ground
5 tablespoons Manzanilla or other dry sherry
¾ teaspoon sea salt
½ teaspoon freshly ground black pepper
12 slices smoked bacon
2 eggs
7 tablespooons heavy cream
¾ teaspoon dried tarragon
1½ tablespoons roughly chopped cooked cooked chestnuts
chargrilled warm toast and mixed leaf salad, to serve

1 Put the golden raisins in a bowl with the Madeira and leave to soak while you prepare the pheasant and partridges. Put the pheasant and partridge leg meat into a food processor and pulse until coarsely ground. Put the ground mixture in a bowl with the diced pheasant and partridge and ground pork fat, and mix well. Add the soaked golden raisins and any Madeira left in the bowl, the sherry, salt and pepper and mix again. Cover and leave the mixture to marinate in the refrigerator 3 to 4 hours.

2 Heat the oven to 275°F. Use a double layer of plastic wrap to line the bottom and sides of a 10- x 4- x 3-inch terrine with a lid, ideally a cast-iron one. Line with the bacon, allowing both ends to overhang the sides. Leave the terrine to one side.

3 Whisk together the eggs, cream and tarragon until combined. Using a spatula, gradually mix them into the meat, then stir in the chestnuts. Spoon the mixture into the prepared terrine and press down with the back of the spoon until it is even. Fold the overhanging bacon over the top to cover, then fold over the plastic wrap and cover with the terrine's lid.

4 Put the terrine in a deep roasting pan and pour in enough just-boiled water to come two-thirds of the way up the sides of the terrine. Bake 1 hour, then check if it is cooked through by inserting a thermometer into the middle; it should read 154°F. If the terrine is not ready, carefully return it to the oven 15 minutes longer and check again. Alternatively, you can insert a knife into the terrine and it should come out hot and dry if the terrine is ready.

5 Remove the terrine from the roasting pan, take off the lid and top with a piece of parchment paper and a heavy weight, 2¼ to 2½ pounds. Leave the terrine to cool completely at room temperature. Once cool, cover and leave in the refrigerator couple of days before serving to let the flavors develop. Serve in thick slices with chargrilled toast and a mixed leaf salad.

Rabbit Terrine with Onion Marmalade

SERVES 12 to 14
PREPARATION TIME 35 minutes, plus
   at least 10 hours chilling
COOKING TIME 10 hours overnight
   cooking, plus 2 hours

16 small rabbit legs, about
   6½ pounds total weight
2 tablespoons olive oil, plus extra
   for brushing
4 thyme sprigs
12 pearl onions, peeled and cut
   in half
8 scallions
6 rabbit tenderloins, about
   10 ounces total weight
1 teaspoon roughly chopped flat-leaf
   parsley leaves
sea salt and freshly ground
   black pepper

FOR THE ONION MARMALADE
2 tablespoons olive oil
6⅔ cups halved and thinly sliced
   large white onions
¾ cup plus 2 tablespoons sugar
¾ cup plus 2 tablespoons apple
   cider vinegar
2 cups dry white wine
2 tablespoons white balsamic
   vinegar
1 thyme sprig

1 Heat the oven to 150°F. Put the rabbit legs on a baking sheet, season with salt and pepper, drizzle with the oill and scatter the thyme over, then cover with parchment paper. Cook overnight, or at least 10 hours. The next day, remove the baking sheet from the oven and leave to one side.

2 Turn the oven up to 315°F. Put the pearl onions and scallions on a baking sheet, brush with oil and roast 20 minutes. Remove the scallions and leave to one side, then roast the pearl onions 25 minutes longer. Remove from the oven and leave to one side, then turn the oven down to 150°F.

3 Put the rabbit tenderloins on a baking sheet, season with salt and bake 12 minutes so they remain soft, then leave to one side. Take the leg meat off the bone and put in a large bowl. Strain the cooking juices through a fine strainer into a saucepan. Bring to a boil, then turn the heat down to medium and simmer 10 minutes, or until the liquid reduces by two-thirds. Shred the leg meat using forks, then stir in the parsley and reduced liquid.

4 To assemble the terrine, use plastic wrap to line the bottom and sides of a 10- x 4- x 3-inch terrine, letting it hang over the sides. Cover the bottom with some of the rabbit leg mixture, then lay the pearl onions along the middle of the terrine at regular intervals. Cover with more of the rabbit leg mixture, then lay half of the tenderloins side by side along the middle. Put half the scallions on each side of the tenderloins and cover with more rabbit leg mixture. Repeat with the remaining tenderloins and scallions, then cover with the remaining rabbit leg mixture. Fold the plastic wrap over the terrine to cover completely, then put 2¼ to 2½ pounds of weights, such as a small bag of sugar wrapped in plastic wrap, on top. Leave in the refrigerator to chill at least 10 hours, or overnight.

5 To make the onion marmalade, put the oil in a saucepan over medium-low heat. Add the onions and cook slowly 15 minutes, or until soft, but not colored. Meanwhile, dissolve the sugar in the cider vinegar in a nonmetallic bowl. Add the vinegar solution to the pan with the wine, balsamic vinegar and thyme. Bring to a boil, then turn the heat down to medium and cook 15 minutes longer, stirring occasionally, then turn the heat down to medium and cook 10 minutes longer, or until the liquid becomes thick and syrupy. Remove the pan from the heat and leave the syrup to cool completely, then remove and discard the thyme and spoon the marmalade into a sterilized jar and seal. Serve the terrine with the onion marmalade. The marmalade can be stored in the refrigerator up to 2 months.

Lentil and Bacon Soup with Mushrooms and Thyme Cream

Where I'm from in the Haute-Saône region of France we use lentils a lot, particularly the slate-green-colored Puy lentils. The first record of the famous *lentilles vert du Puy* dates from 1643, and the Puy lentil was awarded Protected Designation of Origin status (PDO) in 2009. Known as the "caviar of the poor," the earthy flavor of these lentils blends beautifully with the pancetta, mushrooms and thyme.

SERVES 4
PREPARATION TIME 25 minutes, plus making the stock
COOKING TIME 30 minutes

1 tablespoon olive oil
3½ ounces thick pancetta or bacon, cut into small lardons
1 shallot, finely sliced
1 carrot, peeled and diced
1 bouquet garni, made with 1 thyme sprig and 1 parsley sprig, tied together with kitchen string
1 cup Puy lentils, picked over and rinsed
5⅓ cups Vegetable Stock (see page 17)
⅔ cup whipping cream
leaves from 2 thyme sprigs
3 tablespoons unsalted butter
1½ cups thickly sliced crimini or button mushrooms
sea salt and freshly ground black pepper
crusty bread, to serve

1 Heat a saucepan over medium heat. Add the oil and pancetta and fry 3 to 4 minutes, stirring occasionally, until the pancetta is golden brown. Add the shallot and carrot and cook 2 to 3 minutes longer until they are slightly soft, then add the lentils, bouquet garni and stock. Bring to a boil, then turn the heat down to low and simmer 8 minutes. Pour in slightly less than ½ cup of the cream, then return the liquid to a simmer and cook 7 to 8 minutes longer until the lentils are tender. Discard the bouquet garni.

2 Ladle the soup into a blender and blitz until smooth and creamy. Return the soup to the cleaned pan and add a little water or more stock to the pan if the soup is too thick. Season to taste with salt and pepper, cover the pan with a lid and keep the soup warm.

3 Whip the remaining cream until soft peaks form, then fold in two-thirds of the thyme and season with a touch of pepper.

4 Heat a skillet over high heat. Add the butter and when it is foaming, add the mushrooms and sauté 3 to 4 minutes until they are golden brown. Season with salt and pepper to taste, then add the remaining thyme. Divide the mushrooms into four shallow soup bowls, piling them in the middle and put a spoonful of the thyme cream on top. Finally ladle the soup around the mushrooms and cream and serve with crusty bread.

Snail, Fennel and Almond Casserole in Red Wine Sauce

You might recall the classic dish of snails with garlic butter, which, when made the correct way, is delicious. Well, this recipe is different, but no less flavorsome. It's a bit like a boeuf bourguignonne, but with snails, toasted almonds and fennel. You will have to buy some cooked snails, and just make sure you rinse them properly before use. This is delicious served with Rutabaga Boulangère (see page 20) or sautéed potatoes with pancetta.

SERVES 4
PREPARATION TIME 15 minutes, plus making the stock
COOKING TIME 35 minutes

1 pound 2 ounces canned snails, shells discarded
2 tablespoons unsalted butter
1 tablespoon olive oil
1 shallot, finely chopped
2 tablespoons dry sherry vinegar
5 tablespoons Burgundy red wine
2 cups Beef Stock (see page 16)
2 fennel bulbs, outer leaves discarded and fronds reserved, finely sliced using a mandolin, if possible
1 handful slivered almonds, toasted
sea salt and freshly ground black pepper
crusty bread, to serve

1 Rinse the snails in warm water, then tip them onto paper towels, pat them dry and leave to one side.

2 Melt the butter and half the oil in a nonstick skillet over low heat. Add the shallot and fry slowly 2 minutes, or until it is soft. Pour in the sherry vinegar, turn the heat up to high and deglaze the pan by stirring to remove any caramelized bits stuck to the bottom, then cook until the liquid almost evaporates. Add the red wine and cook 3 to 4 minutes longer until it reduces by half. Then add the stock and simmer 10 to 15 minutes until it reduces by two-thirds and the sauce becomes glossy and almost syrupy. Season with salt and pepper to taste. Cover the pan, leave the sauce to one side and keep warm.

3 Meanwhile, heat the oven to 400°F and bring a saucepan of salted water to a boil. Add the sliced fennel and blanch 2 to 3 minutes until slightly soft. Drain and refresh in ice water, then drain again and pat dry with paper towels.

4 Heat the remaining oil in a large, nonstick skillet over medium heat. Add the fennel and fry 2 to 3 minutes, stirring, until it is just golden brown. Add the snails and the reserved fennel fronds and fry 2 to 3 minutes longer until everything is just heated through—you don't want to overcook the snails. Add the toasted slivered almonds and toss to combine. Finally, season with salt and pepper to taste.

5 Divide the snails into four small ovenproof dishes or wide ramekins. Spoon the red wine sauce over the top of the snails until they are just coated. Put the dishes in a baking sheet and cook in the oven 4 to 5 minutes until heated through and just bubbling. Serve hot with plenty of crusty bread.

Pickled Mackerel with **Warm Potato** and **Radish Salad**

This colorful salad reminds me of the time I spent in Sweden, as it is fairly typical of something you would eat for breakfast there. I was staying in the Grand Hotel, in Lund, and remember so well the breakfast table laden with smoked, marinated and pickled fish. It was amazing! My version features warm potatoes and cilantro with a yogurt-based French dressing. You can use some of the pickling liquid instead of the French dressing, if you like.

SERVES 4
PREPARATION TIME 20 minutes, plus 30 minutes cooling and 6 hours marinating
COOKING TIME 25 minutes

2 large pinches coriander seeds
½ cup white balsamic vinegar
½ cup Chardonnay vinegar or white wine vinegar
4 tablespoons light soft brown sugar
4 whole mackerel, about 9 ounces each, filleted
1 tablespoon sea salt
1 small red onion, finely sliced
2 cilantro sprigs, plus 2 tablespoons chopped cilantro leaves
1 garlic clove
10 ounces small new potatoes, scrubbed
3 tablespoons French Dressing (see page 18)
2 tablespoons Mayonnaise (see page 18)
1 tablespoon plain Greek yogurt
finely grated zest and juice of 1 lime
8 large radishes, very thinly sliced
1 scallion, thinly sliced diagonally
sea salt and freshly ground black pepper

1 Heat a skillet over medium heat. Add the coriander seeds and lightly toast 1 minute, shaking the pan occasionally, until they color slightly and smell aromatic. Tip them onto a plate and lightly crush with the blade of a knife, then leave them to one side.

2 Pour both types of vinegar into a small saucepan. Add the sugar and put over medium heat to warm 2 to 3 minutes, or just long enough for the sugar to dissolve, stirring occasionally. Remove the pan from the heat, stir in the toasted coriander seeds and leave the liquid to cool.

3 Put the mackerel in a shallow, nonmetallic dish, skin-side down, and sprinkle with the sea salt. Pour the cool vinegar mixture over and top with three-quarters of the red onion. Cover with plastic wrap and leave the mackerel to marinate in the refrigerator about 6 hours, or until pickled, turning the fish over after 3 hours.

4 Just before the mackerel is ready, bring a saucepan of water, one-third full, to a simmer with a steamer insert on top. Put the remaining red onion, the cilantro sprigs and garlic in the water. Put the potatoes in the steamer, cover and steam 12 to 18 minutes until they are just tender. Turn the heat off and continue to steam the potatoes in the residual heat 5 minutes longer.

5 While the potatoes are cooking, whisk together the French dressing, mayonnaise and Greek yogurt in a bowl, then stir in the lime juice and zest. Season with salt and pepper to taste. When the potatoes are cool enough to handle, cut them into ¼-inch-thick slices and put them in a large serving bowl. Add the radishes and chopped cilantro, then drizzle the dressing over and toss gently without breaking up the potato slices. Scatter with the scallion. Lift the mackerel out of the pickling liquid and put on serving plates. Scatter some of the red onion over the top and serve with the potato salad.

Heirloom Beet "Tagliatelle" and Carpaccio

Heirloom beets come in fantastic colors—from ruby red to vibrant yellow—and heir earthy, nutty flavor goes really well with the freshness of the chervil. Try not to overcook the beets though, because they will break when you cut them into thin slices. They should be soft, but still with a slight crunch. You can scatter some small, crisp lardons or bacon over the top instead of the goat cheese, if you like, and serve with some crusty bread.

SERVES 4
PREPARATION TIME 25 minutes
COOKING TIME 1½ hours

4 heaped tablespoons sea salt, plus extra to season
4 beets, different colors if possible
¾ cup plus 2 tablespoons beet juice
1 tablespoon balsamic vinegar
2 tablespoons extra virgin olive oil
1 small bunch chives, cut into 2-inch pieces
1½ teaspoons chervil leaves
1 handful yellow frisée lettuce
1 handful corn salad
3½ ounces soft goats cheese log, such as Ste. Maure, rind removed, crumbled
freshly ground black pepper
crusty bread, to serve (optional)

1 Heat the oven to 315°F. Take a 20- x 12-inch piece of aluminum foil and sprinkle the sea salt over the middle in a thick layer. Put the beets on top of the salt, then fold the foil over and scrunch the edges to make a secure package. Put the package on a baking sheet and roast 1½ hours, or until the beets are just tender when pierced with the tip of a knife. Remove the package from the oven and leave the beets, still wrapped, until cool enough to handle. Open the package and discard the salt, then peel the beets and leave to one side until ready to use.

2 While the beets are cooking, make the dressing. Pour the beet juice into a small saucepan over medium heat and bring to a simmer, then turn the heat down to low and simmer about 10 minutes until the juice reduces to about 2 tablespoons. Whisk in the balsamic vinegar and season with salt and pepper to taste, then leave the dressing to cool.

3 Thinly slice 3 of the cooked beets, then put the slices on a serving plate and brush with the oil. Season with salt and pepper and scatter the chives and chervil over the top.

4 Using a mandolin or sharp knife, cut the remaining beet into very fine julienne strips to make "tagliatelle," then spoon half the beet dressing over the strips. Spoon neat piles of beet "tagliatelle" in the middle of the beet carpaccio. Toss the frisée and corn salad in a bowl, spoon the remaining dressing over and toss again until the leaves are coated. Scatter the leaves over the top of the beets, sprinkle with the goat cheese and serve with crusty bread, if you like.

Radish, Belgian Endive and Marinated Pear Salad

This is the perfect salad for fall, the best season for buying pears. In France, there are lots of different varieties of pear, so there is a wide selection to choose from. I'm a fan of the Pascatan, but I guess it's best to choose your own favorite. Using two colors of Belgian endive makes the salad particularly attractive, but you can just use yellow Belgian endive, if you'd rather or if that is all you can find. You can serve this salad as a meal on its own, or it goes very well with a charcuterie board, or even a chicken liver terrine.

SERVES 4
PREPARATION TIME 15 minutes, plus 2 hours marinating
COOKING TIME 10 minutes

2 tablespoons unsalted butter
2 large slightly underripe pears, peeled, cored and each cut into 8 wedges
1 tablespoon light soft brown sugar
4 tablespoons white balsamic vinegar
1 shallot, halved lengthwise and thinly sliced
2 teaspoons Dijon mustard
5 tablespoons light olive oil, plus 1 tablespoon for the croutons
2 slices stale sourdough bread, torn into bite-size pieces
1 tablespoon olive oil
12 small radishes, finely sliced
2 large yellow Belgian endives, outer leaves discarded and leaves separated, cut into 3 diagonally
2 large red Belgian endives, outer leaves discarded and leaves separated, quartered lengthwise
4 scallions, green part only, roughly chopped
½ cup walnuts, toasted and lightly crushed

1 Melt the butter in a nonstick skillet over medium heat. Add the pears and cook 3 to 4 minutes, turning them once, until they are just tender and light golden. Sprinkle with the sugar, then turn the pears to coat them in the sugary butter. Transfer the pears to a dish, spoon the balsamic vinegar and shallot over and stir together. Cover and leave to marinate at room temperature 2 hours.

2 Pour off the marinade from the pears and put 2 tablespoons in a small bowl, discarding the rest. Whisk the mustard into the marinade, then slowly add the light olive oil, whisking until it thickens and becomes glossy. Leave to one side.

3 Heat the broiler to high. Scatter the bread in the broiler pan, then drizzle with the olive oil and mix until combined. Broil 2 to 3 minutes, turning the pieces over halfway through, until they are golden and crisp. Tip the croutons and any crumbs into a bowl, carefully wipe the pan clean and put the pears in the pan. Broil them 1 to 2 minutes until just warmed through.

4 Gently toss the pear wedges with the radishes, endives and scallions. Scatter the croutons and walnuts over the top, drizzle with the dressing and serve while the pears are still warm.

Goat Cheese and Dandelion Salad

This is definitely a salad to try, because it's both interesting and very different. We used to eat a more traditional version at my aunt's house and she would send us into the garden to collect the dandelion leaves—called *pissenlit* in French! We would bring back loads and then prepare them with my uncle. His version of this salad included lardons, but my vegetarian alternative features a crumbly goat cheese and tangy orange to go with the bitterness of the dandelion leaves. It's a perfect summer dish to serve with a glass of Viognier.

SERVES 4
PREPARATION TIME 15 minutes, plus making the croutons
COOKING TIME 3 minutes

1 tablespoon blanched hazelnuts
4 handfuls dandelion leaves, washed thoroughly
5 ounces soft goat cheese log, such as Golden Cross or Ste. Maure, rind removed, crumbled
1 small bunch of chives, cut into 2-inch pieces
1 tablespoon chopped chervil leaves
2 small oranges
1 tablespoon small Croutons (see page 18)

FOR THE DRESSING
1 tablespoon clear honey
2 to 3 tablespoons Chardonnay vinegar or white wine vinegar
3 tablespoons extra virgin olive oil
sea salt and freshly ground black pepper

1 To toast the hazelnuts, put them in a small, dry skillet over medium heat. Toast 2 to 3 minutes, shaking the pan occasionally, until the nuts are light brown all over. Tip them out onto a plate and leave to cool, then lightly crush.

2 Put the dandelion leaves on four large plates. Scatter the goat cheese over the tops, then add the chives and chervil.

3 Peel the oranges, removing all the the bitter white pith. Cut it into segments, then cut each segment into 3 pieces, reserving the juice. Scatter the pieces over the salad, then finish with the toasted hazelnuts and croutons.

4 To make the dressing, whisk together the honey, reserved orange juice, vinegar and oil in a small bowl until almost opaque, or you can blitz it with a hand-held blender. Season with salt and pepper to taste, then drizzle the dressing over the salad and serve immediately.

Jerusalem Artichoke Velouté with **Truffle Oil** and **Chive Cream**

Jerusalem artichokes are an indulgent root vegetable that can be roasted, pureed or served, as here, in a velouté. When cooked this way, with a delicious chive cream, they become beautifully velvety and nutty and make a memorable cream soup for a special occasion.

SERVES 4
PREPARATION TIME 25 minutes,
  plus making the stock
COOKING TIME 30 minutes

2 tablespoons unsalted butter
1 shallot, finely diced
1 pound 5 ounces Jerusalem
  artichokes, peeled and chopped
4½ to 5 cups Chicken or Vegetable
  Stock (see pages 16–17)
14 ounces white asparagus, peeled
  and woody ends discarded
½ cup whipping cream
1 tablespoon finely snipped chives
6 drops truffle oil
1 baguette, sliced, to serve
sea salt and freshly ground
  black pepper

1 Melt the butter in a large saucepan over low heat. Add the shallot and artichokes and cook 5 minutes, stirring occasionally. Turn the heat up to high, add 4½ cups of stock and bring to a boil. Turn the heat down to low and simmer 10 to 12 minutes until the artichokes are just soft.

2 Meanwhile, cut off the asparagus tips and leave to one side. Roughly chop the stalks, add to the soup and cook 4 minutes, or until they are just tender. Whip half the cream, using an electric mixer, until soft peaks form.

3 Transfer the soup to a blender, season with salt and pepper and blend until smooth. You might have to do this in batches, depending on the size of your blender. Add the whipped cream and blend once more, then pass the soup through a fine strainer, using a ladle to help you, into the cleaned pan. Leave to one side.

4 Whip the remaining cream until soft peaks form, then fold in the chives and half the truffle oil and season with salt and pepper to taste. (You can use a hand-held blender to add the chive cream to the soup at this stage, or keep it separate and serve on top of the soup as below.)

5 Bring a saucepan of salted water to a boil. Add the reserved asparagus tips and cook 2 to 3 minutes until they are just tender when pierced with the tip of a knife. Drain and season with the remaining truffle oil and with salt and pepper to taste. Put into four soup bowls.

6 Gently reheat the soup, adding the remaining stock if it is too thick, until bubbles just start to form on the top. Do not let it boil. Ladle the soup over the asparagus and top with a spoonful of the truffle oil and chive cream. Serve with slices of baguette.

Rutabaga and Butternut Squash Soup with Caramelized Chestnuts

SERVES 4
PREPARATION TIME 20 minutes,
  plus making the stock
COOKING TIME 55 minutes

1 rutabaga, about 14 ounces total
  weight, peeled and diced
2 tablespoons olive oil
1 butternut squash, about
  1 pound 2 ounces total weight,
  peeled, seeded and diced
3 tablespoons unsalted butter
1 small onion, chopped
5 cups Vegetable Stock (see page
  17), plus extra for thinning,
  if necessary
¾ cup plus 2 tablespooons whipping
  cream
¾ cup plus 2 tablespoooons whole
  milk
½ cup cooked whole chestnuts
1 tablespoon sugar
2 tablespoons extra virgin olive oil
sea salt and freshly ground
  black pepper

I think rutabaga has been ignored for too long, but I feel it's making a bit of a comeback. It certainly makes a great warming winter soup, which goes brilliantly with the sliced caramelized chestnuts.

1 Heat the oven to 400°F. Put the rutabaga in a roasting pan, drizzle the olive oil over and season with a little salt and pepper. Roast 5 minutes, then add the squash, stir to coat in the oil and continue roasting 7 to 10 minutes longer until the vegetables are just beginning to color around the edges but are not cooked through. Remove from the pan from the oven and drain the rutabaga and squash on paper towels.

2 Meanwhile, heat a large saucepan over medium heat. Add half the butter and the onion and cook 3 to 4 minutes until it is just soft, but not colored. Add the roasted rutabaga and squash to the pan and toss together, then pour in the stock, cream and milk and bring to a simmer. Turn the heat down to low and simmer about 30 minutes, uncovered, until the vegetables are very soft. The soup must not boil or the cream will curdle.

3 While the soup is cooking, make the caramelized chestnuts. Melt the butter in a nonstick skillet over medium heat. When it is foaming, add the chestnuts and sugar and cook 3 to 4 minutes, turning the chestnuts over once, until they start to caramelize, but take care they don't burn. Tip the chestnuts onto parchment paper and leave to cool and become crisp, then then roughly slice them.

4 When the soup is ready, ladle it into a blender and blend until smooth. You might have to do this in batches, depending on the size of your blender. Pass the soup through a fine strainer into the cleaned pan; it should be very creamy and velvety. Season with salt and pepper to taste and warm the soup through. If you think it is a little thick, add some more stock. Serve drizzled with extra virgin olive oil and topped with the caramelized chestnuts.

Goat Cheese, Summer Vegetable and **Herb Quiche**

This quiche says summer to me—the warmth and sun of the Mediterranean—with its colorful mix of artichokes and red chard and aromatic lemon thyme. Not forgetting the crumbly goat cheese, which, when cooked slowly, adds an almost almondy flavor to the quiche. Do try it with the Reduced Balsamic Vinegar, because it gives the tart an added depth of flavor. Enjoy the quiche with a red chard salad and pickled shallots.

SERVES 4

PREPARATION TIME 20 minutes, plus making the dough and vinegar and 30 minutes chilling

COOKING TIME 1 hour

1 tablespooon unsalted butter, plus extra for greasing

9 ounces Savory Piecrust Dough (see page 22)

all-purpose flour, for dusting

¾ cup plus 2 tablespooons heavy cream

3½ ounces soft goat cheese log, such as Golden Cross or Ste. Maure, rind removed, crumbled

2 lemon thyme sprigs

2 tablespoons olive oil

1 onion, finely chopped

2½ ounces bottled artichokes, drained and thinly sliced

½ cup peeled and finely chopped carrot

handful red chard leaves

small handful watercress leaves

2 eggs, lightly beaten

¼ teaspoon freshly grated nutmeg

1 tablespoon Reduced Balsamic Vinegar (see page 19)

sea salt and freshly ground black pepper

1 Lightly grease an 8-inch loose-bottomed tart pan. Roll out the dough on a lightly floured countertop until it is 10 inches across and ⅛ inch thick, then use it to line the bottom and the side of the tart pan, gently pressing it into the edges without overstretching the dough. Trim any excess dough, prick the bottom with a fork and chill 30 minutes to prevent the dough shrinking during baking.

2 Meanwhile, make the filling. Pour the cream into a saucepan, add two-thirds of the goat cheese and the lemon thyme and warm over low heat 3 to 5 minutes, whisking, until smooth and silky. Remove the pan from the heat and leave the mxiture to cool while you make the rest of the filling.

3 Melt the butter with the oil in a nonstick skillet over medium heat. Add the onion and fry 5 minutes, stirring occasionally, or until soft, but not brown. Add the artichokes and carrot, mix well and cook 5 minutes longer, or until they are soft. Add the red chard and watercress and cook 2 minutes longer, or until they wilt. Tip the vegetables onto paper towels and press dry.

4 Add the eggs and nutmeg to the cool cream mixture, season with salt and pepper and whisk to combine.

5 Meanwhile, heat the oven to 325°F. Line the dough case with parchment paper and cover with baking beans. Put the tart pan on a cookie sheet and bake 12 minutes, then remove the paper and baking beans and turn the oven up to 350°F. Brush the bottom of the pastry case with the reduced balsamic vinegar. Spoon in the vegetable mixture, sprinkle with the remaining goat cheese and pour in the egg mixture. Bake 35 minutes, or until the filling is firm to the touch. Slice and serve either warm or at room temperature.

Pumpkin and Goat Cheese Lasagne

This "lasagne" is made with very thin layers of pumpkin, rather than pasta, as you would traditionally expect. For me, goat cheese is perfect with pumpkin, while the addition of pumpkin seeds and a drizzle of pumpkin oil make this a delicate, light and surprisingly lovely meal. I have also suggested a tasty little salad that you might like make to serve with the lasagne.

SERVES 4
PREPARATION TIME 40 minutes
COOKING TIME 50 minutes

4½-pound piece pumpkin, skin removed and seeded
¾ cup plus 2 tablespoons whole milk
2 cups whipping cream
1 rosemary sprig
a pinch freshly grated nutmeg
10 ounces soft goat cheese log, rind removed, crumbled
3 tablespoons unsalted butter
2 pinches toasted pumpkin seeds
1 tablespoon toasted pumpkin seed oil
3½ ounces firm sheep's milk cheese, such as Ossau Iraty, diced
sea salt and freshly ground black pepper

FOR THE GOATS CHEESE AND PUMPKIN SALAD

2½ ounces corn salad leaves
1 tablespoon toasted pumpkin seeds
2 ounces soft goat cheese log, rind removed, crumbled
1 teaspoon toasted pumpkin seed oil
2 tablespoons extra virgin olive oil
1 tablespoon Chardonnay vinegar or white wine vinegar

1 Cut a 5- x 3-inch rectangle, 2 inches thick, from the pumpkin, then cut it into twelve ¹⁄₁₆-inch-thick slices, using a mandolin or a very sharp knife. Chop the remaining pumpkin into bite-size cubes (about 6¼ cups).

2 Put the cubed pumpkin in a saucepan with the milk, half the cream, the rosemary sprig and the nutmeg and cook over very low heat 10 to 15 minutes until the pumpkin is just tender, but with a little resistance. Using a slotted spoon, lift out the pumpkin and leave it to one side. Reserve the milk mixture in the pan.

3 Meanwhile, bring a saucepan of salted water to a boil. Add the pumpkin slices, a few at a time, and cook 2 to 3 minutes until they are just tender and pliable, then use a slotted spoon to transfer them to a bowl of ice water and leave 1 minute. Lift them out and drain on paper towels, keeping the slices separate, then season with salt and pepper.

4 Return the saucepan containing the milk mixture to medium heat. Add the remaining cream and the goat cheese. Turn the heat down to low and cook, whisking continuously, until the cheese melts and the sauce thickens to a silky texture. Discard the rosemary sprig.

5 Meanwhile, heat the oven to 350°F and grease a 8½- x 7-inch baking dish with the butter. Overlap 4 slices of the pumpkin on the bottom of the dish. Scatter with half the pumpkin cubes, then add half the toasted pumpkin seeds and pumpkin oil and finish with one-third of the sauce. Repeat with another 4 slices of pumpkin, then the rest of the pumpkin cubes, seeds and oil. Spread another one-third of the sauce over the top, then finish with the remaining pumpkin slices. Add the remaining sauce and sprinkle with the sheep's milk cheese. Bake 20 minutes, or until golden and bubbling. Turn the oven up to maximum and continue cooking 5 to 8 minutes until golden brown. Leave to rest 2 to 3 minutes.

6 Meanwhile, prepare the salad, if you like. Toss the corn salad, pumpkin seeds and crumbled cheese together in a bowl. In a separate bowl, whisk together the oils and vinegar and season with salt and pepper. Drizzle the salad with the dressing, toss and serve with the lasagne.

Glazed Belgian Endive and Thyme Tart

Belgian endive is a very versatile vegetable and while it is perfect raw in a salad, it also tastes delicious baked in a tart. Here, it is combined with orange juice, a drop of honey and fresh thyme, which lift the Belgian endive to new heights. The orange zest and walnuts sprinkled over the top to finish the dish beautifully.

SERVES 4
PREPARATION TIME 25 minutes, plus 30 minutes chilling and 20 minutes cooling
COOKING TIME 1 hour

5 tablespoons unsalted butter, plus extra for greasing
9 ounces puff pastry dough, thawed if frozen
all-purpose flour, for dusting
6 heads Belgian endive, trimmed and halved lengthwise
finely grated zest and juice of 1 orange
2 tablespoons honey
¼ teaspoon thyme leaves
¼ cup walnuts, chopped
2 tablespoons chopped celery leaves
¼ apple, peeled, cored and diced
sea salt and freshly ground black pepper

1 Lightly grease an 8-inch loose-bottomed tart pan. Roll out the dough on a lightly floured countertop until it is 10 inches across and ⅛ inch thick. Use it to line the bottom and side of the tart pan, gently pressing it into the edges without overstretching the dough. Trim any excess dough, prick the botom with a fork and chill 30 minutes to prevent the dough shrinking during baking.

2 Meanwhile, make the filling. Melt slightly less than 2 tablespoons of the butter in a large sauté pan over medium heat. Add the Belgian endives, cut-side down, and cook 4 to 5 minutes until lightly colored. Take care not to let the butter burn. Pour enough water into the pan to fill by ½ inch, then add the remaining butter. Pour in the orange juice, season with salt and pepper and stir to combine. Cover the Belgian endives with a *cartouche* (see page 218), turn the heat down to very low and simmer 35 to 40 minutes until they are very tender and caramelized. Check occasionally to make sure the mixture is not burning and add more water, if necessary.

3 While the Belgian endives are cooking, heat the oven to 325°F. Line the pastry case with parchment paper and cover with baking beans. Bake 12 minutes, then remove the paper and baking beans and bake 3 to 5 minutes longer until the pastry is cooked and just golden. Remove the tart pan from the oven and leave the pastry case to to cool in its pan on a wire rack. Turn the oven up to 400°F.

4 Lift the Belgian endives out of the pan and place on a clean dish towel to dry, then leave to cool. Add the honey and thyme to the pan and warm through, gently stirring, until you have a light syrup. Remove the pan from the heat.

5 When the Belgian endives have cooled, lay them tightly together in the pastry case, then brush generously with the orange-honey syrup. Bake 10 to 12 minutes until the tart is warmed through. Remove it from the oven and the pan. Scatter the walnuts, orange zest, celery leaves and apple over the top and serve warm.

Sous-vide Lettuce with **Sheep's Milk Cheese**

With this dish, I'm trying to encourage you to cook more salad vegetables, because this is a much-neglected style of cooking. My home-style "vacuum-packed" Little Gem lettuces are topped with a slightly crumbly sheep's milk cheese, crunchy croutons and a drizzle of olive oil, and are just delicious. Enjoy this recipe as a vegetaian dish with sourdough bread or serve it as an accompaniment to roast pork. If you have a small vacuum-pack machine, follow the instructions in the method, using vacuum bags instead of plastic wrap. Alternatively, you can use small freezer bags with a seal, making sure the air is squeezed out before you close them. You can also cook the lettuce packages in a microwave for just 40 seconds on full power.

SERVES 4
PREPARATION TIME 15 minutes,
  plus making the croutons
COOKING TIME 20 minutes

4 baby Little Gem lettuces or hearts
  of lettuce, outer leaves removed
  and quartered lengthwise
½ cup olive oil
4 ounces sheep's milk cheese, such
  as Ossau Iraty, crumbled
1 tablespoon small Croutons (see
  page 18)
sea salt and freshly ground
  black pepper

1 Put four 8-inch square sheets of plastic wrap on the countertop. Top each sheet with a quartered Little Gem, putting the pieces in a pile in the middle. Drizzle 1 tablespoon of the oil over each pile, then season with a little salt and pepper. Tightly wrap the Little Gem in the plastic wrap to make 4 small packages, pressing out any air.

2 Bring a saucepan of water to a simmer, with a steamer insert on top. Put the lettuce packages in the steamer, cover and gently steam 12 to 14 minutes until the lettuce quarters are just tender.

3 Remove the packages from the steamer and unwrap over a small saucepan to catch any juices. Pat the lettuce quarters dry with paper towels, then put them in a broiler pan, arranging the contents of each package closely together so you have four separate portions. Scatter the cheese over the lettuce, then season with more salt and pepper and leave to one side.

4 Meanwhile, heat the broiler to high. Put the pan of reserved cooking juices over medium-high heat and cook until it reduces by half, then whisk in the remaining oil. Drizzle the sauce over the Little Gems, then put them under the broiler 2 to 3 minutes until the cheese is golden brown and a little puffed up. Sprinkle with the croutons and serve hot.

SOUS-VIDE COOKING

I am sure everyone is familiar with using *sous-vide*—a vacuum—as a way of storing food, as we see vacuum-packed food all over the place, from spices and coffee to cured meats and rice. It is a great way of packing food for transport. But, although it has been around for a while now and is used a lot in professional kitchens, you might not be so familiar with cooking *sous-vide*.

At The Vineyard

In The Vineyard kitchen, we sometimes use this method, and we have a professional vacuum-pack machine that seals the food ready to go in a special water bath. It's usually a great way of cooking, although I have to confess it has gone wrong once or twice and given us all a good laugh—although laughter is not quite the reaction if it happens in the middle of a busy service! If a bag is not sealed properly—or the plastic wrap isn't tied securely if you are trying it at home—and no one notices in time, it can cause a mini disaster, and you can find yourself with an empty bag or a chicken breast swimming in water. So just watch those knots and tie them tightly!

Why would you prepare food this way?

So, what are the advantages of cooking in this way? Well, to start with, you can prepare dishes one or two days ahead and keep them refrigerated, or portioned up and frozen ready to cook when you need them. Imagine how useful that would be when you have a party coming up and you can spread the preparations so you have less to do on the day.

Then there's the fact that, when prepared this way, the food develops some beautiful flavors as it cooks in its own juices, with all the flavors locked in. As nothing is lost, there's an intensity of flavor in the finished dish.

Then we come to temperature, which is critical in *sous-vide* cooking. When you cook *sous-vide*, you can cook at a low temperature, about 158°F. This is important because meat, in particular, can be adversely affected when cooked at very high temperatures, as the collagen fibers within the meat can become tough. This is less important with fish, but it can still happen. So, to keep the meat tender, it is recommended you cook at less than 158°F. That makes this style of cooking perfect for the cheaper cuts of meat and also for variety meat. Many people don't like to cook variety meat in case they overcook and ruin it, but with *sous-vide* cooking that's not a problem, because the cooking method is so gentle. You'll be sure to get perfectly tender results every time.

Sous-vide cooking at home

So, how can you try *sous-vide* cooking at home without a professional vacuum-packing machine? I will show you how to cook a chicken breast, and you can use the same procedure for other foods. Just glance through the recipe options in the book that I've listed on page 107 and you'll see how versatile the technique is.

Firstly, make sure you use plastic wrap and not wax or parchment paper. Plastic wrap is perfect for cooking, because as it withstands the necessary temperatures,.

- Put four layers of plastic wrap on a countertop. Put a boneless chicken breast half in the middle of the plastic wrap, then roll it up tightly, pressing out the air to each side as you roll. Make a knot in one end, then press the air out the other side before you knot that end. This gives you a partial *sous-vide*.
- Of course, you cannot keep the product as though it had been properly vacuum-packed because you have not created a full vacuum. Therefore, you need to treat the packages as you would any nonvacuumed product and store it properly in the refrigerator or freezer for the recommended time only. If you follow your common sense, you'll be fine.

- For most *sous-vide* dishes, there are two alternative cooking methods, boiling and steaming. To boil, place the package in a saucepan large enough to hold it comfortably, then just cover it with water. Put the pan over medium heat and bring the water up to 158°F. Keep it at that temperature for the time indicated in the recipe, which will depend on the size of the portion. A 6-ounce chicken breast will take about 20 minutes; if it is stuffed, it will take 5 to 10 minutes longer.
- Alternatively, you can steam the package. Bring a large saucepan of water to a simmer, with a steamer insert on top. Put the chicken package in the steamer, cover and cook 20 to 25 minutes.
- When the food is ready, just cut off one end of the plastic wrap, push the meat through and pat it dry on paper towels or a clean dish towel.
- Then, to regain the crisp skin, heat a nonstick skillet over medium heat and pan-fry the chicken, skin-side down, for a minute or so until crisp and brown. Finally, serve it with a delicious sauce, or *jus*.

Just as a reminder, if you only want to prepare the package in advance, make sure you keep it refrigerated and for a maximum of 2 days. Do not cook it in advance.

Some meats have a stronger texture, and I usually wrap them in plastic wrap in the same way, but then cook them as a confit, in other words in hot fat. This method is suitable for chicken leg meat, or the dark meat from poultry or game birds.

Now that you understand the technique, I hope you'll try some of my recipes, such as Sous-Vide Lettuce with Sheep's Milk Cheese (see page 105), Stuffed Chicken Breasts with Cabbage and Chestnuts (see page 111), Pork Tenderloin with Mushrooms, Figs and Chestnuts (see page 118), Salmon in Cabbage Leaves with Lemon Butter Sauce (see page 126), Steamed Cabbage with Pork and Hazelnut Stuffing (see page 177) and Pancetta-wrapped Monkfish with Carrot and Mandarin Puree (see page 186).

Enjoy a quail salad—or, perhaps, a poussin

Quail is the quickest and easiest option if you want to try cooking *sous-vide*, and this recipe also works well with poussins, which are available from some supermarkets. This is one example of when it is best to cook the legs as a confit, because the texture of the meat is different.

Simply wrap two quail legs and two quail breasts separately in plastic wrap, as described in the general instructions on page 106. Cook the legs very gently in goose or duck fat 40 minutes, or until the meat is super-tender and falls off the bone. When the legs are almost cooked, steam the breasts very gently about 4 minutes until they are tender and cooked through. You can test if the meat the meat is cooked by piercing the plastic wrap with a sharp knife, and the juices will run clear when it is cooked.

Once unwrapped, heat a nonstick skillet over high heat. Add the breasts, skin-side down, and brown 2 minutes, then turn them over and cook 2 minutes longer. Deglaze the pan with a splash of white wine vinegar and a little salt and pepper, stirring to remove any caramelized bits stuck to the bottom.

I make a delicious salad to serve with the quail by tossing together a handful arugula leaves, a handful pea shoots and a few Belgian endive leaves. Then I sprinkle some shredded tarragon leaves and a quartered boiled new potato over. That's just enough per person. Cut the quail legs and the breasts in half, then put them on top of a pile of fresh salad. As an extra bonus, you can finish the dish with a quail egg per portion, boiled for just 2½ minutes so the yolk is perfectly runny.

Stuffed Chicken Breasts with Cabbage and Chestnuts

SERVES 4
PREPARATION TIME 20 minutes, plus making the stock
COOKING TIME 35 minutes

1 stick unsalted butter
4 tablespoons olive oil
2⅓ cups thinly sliced button mushrooms
4 chicken breast halves, skin on
1 large Savoy cabbage, shredded
12 cooked whole chestnuts
4 tablespoons Chicken Stock (see page 16)
4 tablespoons whipping cream
1 tablespoon chopped tarragon leaves
sea salt and freshly ground black pepper

1 Melt 2 tablespooons of the butter with 1 tablespoon of the oil in a large, nonstick skillet over high heat. When the butter is foaming, add the mushrooms and sauté 4 to 5 minutes until they release all their juices and are just golden. Remove and tip them onto paper towels to dry. Wipe the skillet, then return it to medium heat. Melt another 2 tablespoons of the butter with 1 tablespoon of the oil. When the butter is foaming, add the chicken breast halves, skin-side down, and cook one side only 5 minutes, or until the skin is light golden brown. Remove them from the pan and put them, skin-side up, on a cutting board.

2 Cut the chicken breasts horizontally through the middle and three-quarters of the way through so you can open them out like a book. Spread half the mushrooms over the bottom half of each breast and season with salt and pepper, then fold the top half back over to make a chicken-mushroom sandwich. Tightly wrap each chicken breast in plastic wrap to make a sausage shape. Twist and secure each end with a knot, pushing out any air.

3 Bring a large saucepan of water to a simmer, with a steamer insert on top, and bring another pan of salted water to the boil. Put the chicken packages in the steamer, cover and cook 12 minutes, or until cooked through. Remove them and leave them to rest on a plate 6 minutes.

4 While the chicken is cooking, blanch the cabbage in the boiling, salted water 3 to 4 minutes until it is only just tender, then drain well and pat dry. While the chicken is resting, melt another 2 tablespoons of the butter with 1 tablespoon of the oil in the skillet over medium heat. When the butter is foaming, add the blanched cabbage. Cook 2 to 3 minutes, then add the remaining cooked mushrooms and the chestnuts and toss 2 to 3 minutes longer until heated through. Transfer the cabbage mixture to a warm bowl, cover and leave to one side.

5 Once the chicken has rested, remove the plastic wrap and pour any juices into a small pan over medium-high heat. Add the stock and boil 2 to 3 minutes until the liquid reduces by half. Whip the cream until soft peaks form, then add it to the pan and let it melt into the sauce, without stirring. As soon the sauce starts to simmer, remove the pan from the heat. Season with salt and pepper to taste, then stir in the tarragon.

6 Meanwhile, melt the remaining buter and oil in the skillet over medium-high heat. Add the chicken and fry, skin-side down, about 3 minutes until the skin is crisp and golden. Quarter the chicken rolls and serve alongside the braised cabbage with the sauce.

Chicken and Cucumber En Papillote with Toasted Almonds

SERVES 4
PREPARATION TIME 20 minutes
COOKING TIME 30 minutes

4 chicken breast halves, about
 6 ounces each, skin on
4 teaspoons unsalted butter
2 tablespoons sunflower oil
1 cucumber, peeled, halved
 lengthwise and seeded
2 tablespoons olive oil
1 teaspoon smoked sweet (mild)
 paprika
¾ cup whipping cream
1 tablespoon chopped flat-leaf
 parsley leaves
2 tablespoons slivered almonds,
 toasted
sea salt and freshly ground
 black pepper

1 Season the skin of the chicken with salt and pepper. Melt the butter with the sunflower oil in a large skillet over medium-high heat. When the butter is foaming, add the chicken, skin-side down, and cook about 5 minutes until the skin is golden and crisp. Remove the breasts from the pan and leave to one side.

2 To prepare the cucumber, cut each piece in half crosswise about the same length as the chicken breast halves, then cut into strips, about ⅛ inch thick. Wipe the skillet clean, then heat over medium-high heat. Add the olive oil and cucumber, season with salt and pepper and sauté 4 to 5 minutes, tossing continuously, until the cucumber is translucent but still retaining its crunch. Add the paprika and stir to coat the cucumber, then remove it from the pan and drain on paper towels.

3 Meanwhile, heat the oven to 350°F. Lay four large sheets of parchment paper, each about 12 inches square, on the countertop. Put one-quarter of the cucumber on one of the sheets, arranging it lengthwise in the middle. Put the chicken lengthwise on top, then fold in the sides and the bottom end of the paper so the top is still open. Pour 3 tablespoons of the cream into the top, then fold the paper over and tightly fold the top to seal and make a package. Repeat to make 4 packages in total.

4 Put the packages in a roasting pan and cook 8 to 10 minutes. Remove the pan from the oven and leave the packages to rest 2 minutes until they are cool enough to handle. Turn the oven off and leave the door ajar, which will keep the chicken breasts warm without overcooking them. Carefully open one end of each package and pour the cooking juices into a small sauté pan. Close the packages again and return the chicken to the oven. Bring the cooking juices to a boil, then turn the heat down to low and simmer, uncovered, about 5 minutes until the juices reduce by half.

5 Meanwhile, whip the remaining cream until soft peaks form. Remove the sauté pan from the heat and whisk the cream into the reduced chicken juices. Return the pan to the heat and bring to a simmer, then immediately remove it from the heat. Stir in the parsley and season with salt and pepper to taste. Slide the paper packages carefully onto plates and open the tops. Sprinkle with the toasted almonds before serving and serve with the sauce alongside.

Pan-roasted Duck Breast with Spiced Peaches

Wild duck goes very well with lots of different fruit and spices. I like to use peaches, which you should still be able to find in early fall when wild duck comes into season. If possible, you want meat from a female, which is generally more tender a male's. I also like to use whole spices rather than ground, but don't overdo the spices, or they will be overpowering.

SERVES 4
PREPARATION TIME 15 minutes, plus making the stock
COOKING TIME 40 minutes

½ cup sugar
1-inch piece cinnamon stick, broken
4 unripe peaches
4 duck breasts, preferably wild, thawed if frozen
2 pinches roasted, crushed Szechuan peppercorns (see page 69)
4 tablespoons sunflower oil
3 tablespoons unsalted butter
1 shallot, chopped
4 tablespoons sherry vinegar
½ cup Chicken Stock (see page 16)
sea salt and freshly ground black pepper

1 Put the sugar in a large sauté pan over medium heat and add the cinnamon stick and 3 cups water. Cook until the sugar dissolves, stirring occasionally, and the syrup comes to a simmer. Add the peaches and poach 10 minutes. Using a slotted spoon, lift the peaches out of the syrup and leave to cool slightly, then remove the skins. Transfer the poaching syrup and cinnamon to a bowl and leave to one side. Halve the peaches, remove the pits and cut each half into 4 long slices.

2 Meanwhile, heat the oven to 350°F. Season both sides of the duck, then sprinkle the Szechuan pepper over the skin. Heat an ovenproof skillet over medium heat. Add the oil and when it starts to shimmer, add the duck, skin-side down, and cook 4 to 5 minutes until golden brown. Turn the duck over and put the pan in the oven 4 to 5 minutes. Remove the pan from the oven and put the duck in a small baking sheet, then cover and leave to rest 5 minutes. Reserve the fat and turn the oven up to maximum.

3 Meanwhile, put the cleaned sauté pan over medium heat. Add half the butter and the peaches and cook 5 minutes, turning occasionally, until they are lightly colored. Remove them and leave to one side on a plate. Add the cinnamon and ½ cup of the reserved poaching syrup to the pan. Cook over medium heat 3 to 4 minutes until the syrup just starts to turn a caramel color, then return the peaches and toss to coat them in syrup, Remove the pan from the heat, cover with foil and leave to one side.

4 Discard all but 1 tablespoon of the fat in the duck pan and return it to medium heat. Add the shallot and cook 5 minutes until soft, then pour in the sherry vinegar and deglaze the pan by stirring to remove any caramelized bits stuck to the bottom. Add the stock and bring to a boil, then simmer, stirring, about 5 minutes until it reduces by half. Add the remaining butter and swirl the pan to combine and make a shiny sauce. Add the juices from the rested duck, cover and leave to one side.

5 Reheat the duck in the hot oven 2 minutes. If the peaches have cooled, warm them through. Cut the duck brasts in half lengthwise, Pour the peach juices into the sauce and bring it quickly to a boil. Serve the duck surrounded by the peaches, with the sauce spooned over the top.

Guinea Fowl with **Buckwheat Spaetzle**

Spaetzle means "little sparrow," and this type of pasta traditionally comes from Baden, in Germany, but it is also very popular near my home region of Alsace, in the east of France, where I first tried it. The dough for the spaetzle can be made with spinach puree or cheese and it is often served with meat, but at The Vineyard restaurant we serve it with guinea fowl.

SERVES 4
PREPARATION TIME 30 minutes
COOKING TIME 35 minutes

2½ cups buckwheat flour
6 extra-large eggs
¼ teaspoon roughly chopped
 tarragon leaves
½ garlic clove, finely chopped
2 tablespoons very finely grated
 Parmesan cheese
4 tablespoons olive oil
4 guinea fowl breast halves, skin on
3 tablespoons unsalted butter
½ teaspoon finely chopped
 rosemary leaves
sea salt and freshly ground
 black pepper

1 To make the spaetzle, put the flour, eggs, tarragon, garlic and Parmesan in a large mixing bowl and whisk with a strong whisk or wooden spoon 5 minutes, or until the mixture starts to become elastic. Finish the dough by hand, almost slapping the mixture on the side of the bowl about 3 minutes until it becomes an elastic, sticky dough. Meanwhile, bring a large saucepan of water to a boil and stir in 3 tablespoons of the oil. Fill a large bowl with ice water. Heat the oven to 350°F.

2 Put one-third of the dough in a large metal colander then, holding it about 2 inches above the pan of gently boiling water, press the dough through the holes of the colander into the water, using either your hand or a spatula; they look like little worms going through and will break off naturally, so you don't need to cut them. Cook the spaetzle 1 to 2 minutes until they float to the surface. Scoop them out with a slotted spoon and drop them straight into the ice water. When they are cold, lift out with a slotted spoon and dry on a clean dish towel. Repeat with the remaining dough until all of it is used. Leave the spaetzle to one side on the towel.

3 Heat a large, ovenproof skillet over medium heat. Season the skin of the guinea fowl with salt. Add the remaining oil and half the butter to the pan. When the butter is foaming, add the guinea fowl, skin-side down, and cook 2 to 3 minutes until it is golden brown. Turn the breasts over, transfer the pan to the oven and roast 8 to 10 minutes until the guinea fowl are cooked through. Cover them with foil and leave to rest in a warm place.

4 Return the skillet to medium heat and heat until the cooking juices and butter start to turn a hazelnut brown color. Add the spaetzle and cook 2 to 3 minutes, turning once, until they are golden and crisp on the outside but still soft inside. Carefully lift out them out with a slotted spoon and drain on paper towels.

5 Add slightly less than ½ cup of water to the pan and deglaze by stirring to remove any caramelized bits stuck to the bottom. Add the remaining butter and the rosemary and simmer 1 minute, then season with salt and pepper to taste. Thickly slice the guinea fowl, top with the spaetzle and spoon over the cooking juices to serve.

Pomme Farcie with **Braised Boston Butt**

I love all the less expensive, and often forgotten, cuts of pork, beef or lamb. Here, I'm using Boston butt, from the hog's shoulder, which isn't so rare these days, but is best when it's braised, rather than roasted. Ask your butcher to cut the pork into large cubes and to keep the fat on, because it will make the dish much more flavorsome and also keep it moist, which for me is essential. For the best texture, crush the cooked meat partially using a fork—you are not making a rillette so you don't want it too smooth.

SERVES 4
PREPARATION TIME 30 minutes, plus making the stock
COOKING TIME 2 hours 25 minutes

4 teaspoons unsalted butter
2 tablespoons olive oil
1 pound 5 ounces boneless, fatty Boston butt, cut into large cubes
2 small carrots, peeled and chopped
2 shallots, chopped
2 garlic cloves, unpeeled, lightly crushed
½ cup dry white wine
2 cups Chicken Stock (see page 16)
4 Idaho potatoes, about 7 ounces each, peeled
1 tablespoon chopped sage leaves
sea salt and freshly ground black pepper
green salad, to serve

1 Heat the oven to 275°F. Melt the butter with 1 tablespoon of the oil in a large Dutch oven over high heat. When the butter is foaming, add the pork, carrots, shallots and garlic and cook 5 minutes, or until everything is just beginning to brown. Add the white wine and simmer, deglazing the pan by stirring to remove any caramelized bits stuck to the bottom, until the liquid reduces by two-thirds. Pour in the stock and bring to a simmer. Reduce the heat to low, partially cover and cook 2 hours, stirring every 30 minutes, until the meat is very tender but not quite falling apart. The sauce should be thick enough to coat the back of the spoon.

2 While the pork cooks, make a horizontal cut along the length of each potato, about one-quarter of the way down, to make a lid. Set its lid next to each potato. Using a teaspoon, scoop out the insides of the potatoes, leaving a ¼-inch shell. (You can discard the flesh or save it for another recipe.) Season the insides with salt and pepper and divide the remaining oil between them. Put the lids back on and tightly wrap in plastic wrap. Bring a large saucepan of water on to a simmer, with a steamer insert on top. Put the potatoes in the steamer, cover and cook over very low heat 1 to 1¼ hours until they are just tender. Turn off the heat, then leave the potatoes in the steamer to cook in the residual heat 10 to 15 minutes.

3 When the meat is nearly ready, remove the plastic wrap from the potatoes, lift off the lids and turn the potatoes upside-down on a clean dish towel to absorb any condensation. Turn the potatoes over and put them in a roasting pan.

4 Remove the pork from the heat, spoon slighly less than ½ cup of the cooking juices into a bowl and leave to one side. Lightly crush the meat with a fork, stir in the sage and season with salt and pepper. Fill each potato with the mixture, taking care not to break them, cover with the potato lid, then spoon the reserved juices over the top. Put the potatoes in the oven 15 minutes, or until they are hot and bubbling. Serve with a green salad.

Pork Tenderloin with **Mushrooms, Figs** and **Chestnuts**

Not only is fall the mushroom season, but it is also the best time for figs and chestnuts. They all have an "earthy" quality, but with different textures. Remember to look out for packaged cooked and peeled chestnuts, which are really good and save a lot of time, too! I have given you the option of cooking the pork in different ways and I hope you'll try both methods to appreciate the differences in flavor, color and texture.

SERVES 4
PREPARATION TIME 20 minutes, plus making the stock
COOKING TIME 15 minutes

4 pieces pork tenderloin, about 5 ounces each, trimmed
5 tablespoons unsalted butter
2 tablespoons sunflower oil
7 ounces mixed wild or cultivated mushrooms
12 cooked whole chestnuts
4 tablespoons sherry vinegar
2 medium-firm figs, quartered
¾ cup plus 2 tablespoons Chicken Stock (see page 16)
1 tablespoon snipped chives
sea salt and freshly ground black pepper
boiled rice, to serve (optional)

1 Season the pork tenderloin with pepper, then tightly wrap each one in plastic wrap. Twist and secure each end with a knot, pushing out any air. Bring a large saucepan of water to a simmer, with a steamer insert on top. Put the pork packages in the steamer, turn the heat down to low, cover and cook 12 minutes, then remove and leave to rest 1 minute, or until cool enough to handle. Remove the pork from the plastic wrap and pat the meat dry with paper towels.

2 Melt 2 tablespoons of the butter and 1 tablespoon of the oil in a large skillet over medium heat. When the butter is foaming, add the pork and cook 3 to 4 minutes, turning occasionally, until it is brown all over. The pork should still be slightly pink in the middle, which is perfect. (Alternatively, brown the pork in an ovenproof skillet as above, then, instead of steaming, transfer it to an oven heated to 275°F and roast 7 to 9 minutes. Remove it from the oven and leave to rest 1 minute before continuing with the recipe.)

3 While the pork is cooking, melt 1½ tablespoons of the butter and the remaining oil in a skillet over medium-high heat. When the butter is foaming, add the mushrooms and fry 2 minutes until they release all their juices and are golden brown. Add the chestnuts and cook 2 minutes longer. Add the sherry vinegar and deglaze the pan by stirring to remove any caramelized bits stuck to the bottom. Add the figs, pour in the stock and cook 3 to 4 minutes until the stock reduces by one-quarter, then add the remaining butter. Cook 2 minutes longer, or until the sauce reduces and is thick enough to coat the back of a spoon. Season with salt and pepper to taste and stir in the chives.

4 Cut each pork tenderloin into diagonal slices and spoon the mushroom mixture over the top before serving with rice, if you like.

Morteau Sausage and **Warm Cranberry Bean Salad**

The town of Morteau gave its name to this well-known sausage and it comes from the same part of France as I do, which is Franche-Comté, to the east of the country next to the Jura mountains. Local cooks only use pork from the region, because the animals are fattened traditionally. In addition, to be permitted to use the label *saucisse de morteau*, the sausage must be smoked at least 48 hours over sawdust from conifer and juniper trees. In this recipe, the cranberry beans bring a nuttiness, which is complemented by the sweet flavor of the oven-dried tomato. Throw in some garlic and herbs and a drizzle of French dressing and this dish is sure to impress!

SERVES 4
PREPARATION TIME 15 minutes, plus overnight soaking and 30 minutes infusing
COOKING TIME 2½ hours

3 tablespoons olive oil
6 garlic cloves, 3 unpeeled, lightly crushed, plus 1 whole and 2 chopped
9 ounces cherry tomatoes, cut in half crosswise and gently squeezed
1 teaspoon confectioner's sugar
leaves from 1 thyme sprig
¾ cup dried cranberry beans, soaked overnight, drained and rinsed
1 large carrot, peeled
1 shallot
1 flat-leaf parsley sprig, plus 1 tablespoon chopped leaves
2 morteau sausages or other smoked sausage, about 10 ounces each, pricked with a knife
3 tablespoons French Dressing (see page 18)
sea salt and freshly ground black pepper

1 Heat the oven to 225°F. Put the oil and the whole unpeeled garlic cloves in a small roasting pan in the oven 30 minutes to infuse. Remove and leave the garlic to one side. Add the tomatoes to the pan, cut-side up, then sprinkle with the confectioner's sugar and season with salt and pepper. Scatter the thyme over the top and roast 2½ hours until the tomatoes are dried and wrinkly.

2 After the tomatoes have been cooking 1 hour, put the soaked cranberry beans in a saucepan and cover with plenty of cold water. Bring to a boil, then skim off any foam that rises to the surface. Add the carrot, shallot, parsley sprig and the peeled whole garlic clove. Turn the heat down to a simmer, cover the pan and simmer 30 minutes. Add the sausages to the pan, re-cover it and simmer 30 minutes longer, or until the beans are tender and the sausages cooked through.

3 Use a slotted spoon to transfer the sausages to a bowl, then cover with plastic wrap. Strain the beans, reserving the cooking liquid in a separate pan. Tip the beans into a bowl. Discard the garlic clove and parsley sprig, then cut the carrot into small dice and add to the beans. Return the cooking liquid to the heat, bring to a a boil and boil about 5 minutes until it reduces by half. Whisk in one-third of the French dressing.

4 Add the oven-dried tomatoes to the beans along with the remaining chopped garlic, chopped parsley and another one-third of the dressing and mix gently. Discard the skin from the sausage and cut the meat into thick slices. Serve the sausage on top of the beans and drizzle with the remaining dressing to serve.

Lamb Sweetbreads and Wild Mushroom Vol-au-Vents

For a while now I've wanted to cook lamb sweetbreads in a puff pastry case, and here it is. This is a very flavorsome dish, but it's best to ask a butcher to prepare the sweetbreads for you, which can be a bit fiddly. Serve two vol-au-vents per person for a generous portion with vegetables of your choice. Mine would be pan-fried zucchini or steamed spinach or red chard.

SERVES 4
PREPARATION TIME 15 minutes
COOKING TIME 25 minutes

1 pound 2 ounces all-butter puff
  pastry dough, thawed if frozen
2 tablespoons all-purpose flour, plus
  extra for dusting
1 egg, beaten
10 ounces prepared lamb
  sweetbreads
2½ tablespoons unsalted butter
2 tablespoons olive oil
1 tablespoon very fine dry
  bread crumbs
10 ounces mixed wild or button
  mushrooms
4½ tablespoons whipping cream
1 tablespoon snipped chives
sea salt and freshly ground
  black pepper
vegetables of your choice, such
  as pan-fried zucchini or steamed
  spinach or chard, to serve

1 Heat the oven to 375°F and line a cookie sheet with parchment paper. Roll out the dough on a lightly floured countertop until ¼ inch thick, then cut out eight 3½-inch circles. Put 4 of the dough circles on the prepared cookie sheet. Using a 3-inch round cutter, cut out a circle in middle of the remaining dough cirles, leaving an outer ring. (Use the dough from the cut out circles for another recipe.) Brush the top of the circles on the cookie sheet with beaten egg, making sure the egg does not go over the edge, then lay a dough ring neatly on top of each one. Carefully brush the top of the rings with egg, then bake 20 minutes, turning the baking sheet halfway through, until the vol-au-vents are risen and golden.

2 While the pastry is baking, bring a saucepan of salted water to a boil. Add the sweetbreads and blanch them 1½ minutes, then drain, refresh in a bowl of ice water, pat dry and remove the skin. Cut the sweetbreads into large cubes. Toss in the flour to coat and tap off any excess.

3 Melt half the butter with the oil in a large skillet over medium heat. When the butter is foaming, add the sweetbreads and fry 4 to 5 minutes until golden brown and crisp. Add the bread crumbs and toss to combine, then cook 1 minute longer until the crumbs are crunchy. Drain the sweetbreads and bread crumbs on paper towels.

4 When the vol-au-vent cases are baked, turn the oven down to 200°F. Lift off the middle top layer to of each vol-au-vent to make a hollow. Keep them warm in the oven, with the door ajar, while you finish the filling.

5 Melt the remaining butter with the remaining oil in the cleaned skillet over medium heat. When the butter is foaming, add the mushrooms and fry 1 to 2 minutes until they are soft. Add the cream and bring to a boil. After 2 to 3 minutes, when it starts to coat the mushrooms, add the cooked sweetbread mixture and the chives. Toss to combine all the ingredients and season with salt and pepper to taste. Spoon the mixture into the baked vol-au-vent cases and serve with your favorite vegetables.

Braised Ox Cheeks with Crushed Potatoes

Here is a cut of meat you might not be familiar with. Until a few years ago, ox cheeks were a forgotten cut of meat, but they're becoming popular again and no wonder—they are so delicious. They can be a little tricky to prepare, because as you need to trim them carefully, removing all the sinew before cooking, but if you have a butcher, ask him or her to do this for you. Crushed new potatoes are perfect with this dish, and if you have a choice of variety I recommend Vitelotte, Jersey Royal, Charlotte, or even Ratte—just don't forget a good glug of olive oil and the herbs.

SERVES 4
PREPARATION TIME 25 minutes, plus making the stock
COOKING TIME 5 hours

2 cloves
4 tablespoons olive oil
2 garlic cloves
2 carrots, peeled and cut into ⅝-inch chunks
2 shallots, cut into ¾-inch-thick rings
2¾ pounds large ox cheeks, sinew and fat trimmed
6 tablespoons sherry vinegar
1¼ cups red wine
1¼ cups Chicken Stock (see page 16)
¾ cup plus 2 tablespoons Beef Stock (see page 16)
¼ star anise
8 large new potatoes, such as Charlotte, scrubbed
1 tablespoon snipped chives
sea salt and freshly ground black pepper

1 To blanch the cloves, bring a small saucepan of water to a boil. Add the cloves, then lower the heat and simmer 1 minute. Drain and refresh them in cold water and leave to one side.

2 Heat a large Dutch oven over medium-high heat. Add 1 tablespoon of the oil and the garlic, carrots and shallots and cook about 5 minutes until soft. Remove them with a slotted spoon and leave to one side.

3 Add the beef to the pot and cook 15 to 20 minutes, turning the meat occasionally, until it is brown all over. Add the sherry vinegar and deglaze the pan by stirring to remove any caramelized bits stuck to the bottom. When the vinegar evaporates, add the red wine and cook 5 minutes longer, or until it reduces by half. Add both stocks, the star anise and the cloves, then return the cooked vegetables to the pan and bring the stock to a low simmer. Turn the heat down to low, partially cover the pot with a lid and simmer 4½ hours, stirring every 30 minutes, until the beef is very tender.

4 While the beef is cooking, prepare the potatoes. Put the potatoes in a saucepan, cover with water and bring to a boil. Turn the heat down to low and simmer 30 minutes, or until they are very tender when pierced with the tip of a knife. Remove the pan from the heat and leave the potatoes to cool in the water.

5 Fifteen minutes before the beef should finish cooking, drain the potatoes, peel them carefully and return them to the pan. Drizzle with the remaining oil and season with salt and pepper, then cover the pan. Put the pan over very low heat and leave 5 to 10 minutes until the potatoes are just heated through. Remove the lid and lightly crush the potatoes with the back of a fork until they are just broken up, but not mashed. Add the chives and stir through. Serve the ox cheeks, carrots and sauce on top of the crushed potatoes.

Salmon in Cabbage Leaves with Lemon Butter Sauce

SERVES 4
PREPARATION TIME 25 minutes
COOKING TIME 45 minutes

4 large Savoy cabbage leaves,
  for wrapping
4 salmon fillets, about 4 ounces
  each
2 tablespoons unsalted butter
12 pearl onions, peeled
1 teaspoon sugar
2 ounces thick pancetta, cut into
  ¼-inch lardons
1 tablespoon olive oil
3½ cups fresh podded peas
sea salt and freshly ground
  black pepper

FOR THE LEMON BUTTER SAUCE
4 tablespoons whipping cream
7 tablespoons unsalted butter,
  cut into small pieces
finely grated zest and juice
  of 1 lemon

1 Bring a large saucepan of salted water to a boil. Add the cabbage leaves, then turn the heat down to medium and cook 5 minutes, or until tender. Using a large slotted spoon, lift out the leaves and transfer them to a bowl of ice water and leave 1 minute; remove and pat dry. Cut along each side of the central stem, about three-quarters of the way up a leaf from the stem end. Discard the stem, leaving the leaf still attached at the top; repeat with the remaining leaves. Season the leaves with a little salt and pepper, then put the leaves, stem-end facing up, on the countertop. Lay a salmon fillet horizontally on the bottom half of a leaf, fold in the sides and wrap up to make a package; repeat to make 4 packages. Wrap each package tightly in plastic wrap. Twist and secure each end with a knot, pushing out any air. Leave in the refrigerator until ready to cook.

2 Melt the butter in a skillet over medium heat. When it is foaming, add the pearl onions and cook 4 to 5 minutes, stirring occasionally, without browning. Season with salt and pepper, add enough water to cover and simmer 15 minutes, uncovered, or until the onions are soft and the liquid reduces by half. Add the sugar and cook, stirring, 3 to 4 minutes longer until the onions become glazed and transparent, then leave to one side.

3 Meanwhile, bring a small pan of water to a boil. Add the pancetta and blanch 1 to 2 minutes until just cooked. Drain, then refresh in cold water, tip onto paper towels and pat dry. Heat the oil in a skillet over medium heat. Add the pancetta and sauté 7 to 8 minutes until crisp and golden brown. Leave to one side.

4 Bring a large saucepan of water to a simmer, with a steamer insert on top. Put the salmon packages in the steamer, cover and steam 9 minutes, or until they are cooked but still slightly pink in the middle, then leave to rest in a warm place 2 minutes.

5 Meanwhile, make the lemon butter. Pour the cream into the cleaned small pan and bring to a boil. Remove the pan from the heat and add 1 tablespoon cold water, then whisk in the butter, a little at a time. If becomes too thick, add a little lemon juice to thin it. Continue until all the butter is incorporated. Season with salt and pepper to taste, then add the lemon zest, cover with plastic wrap and leave to one side.

6 Add the peas to the pan with the onions and simmer 3 to 4 minutes, stirring occasionally, until tender. Add the pancetta and season with salt and pepper to taste. Remove and discard the plastic wrap from the salmon and serve with the pea mixture and the lemon butter sauce spooned over the top or served separately.

Poached Pollock with **Lemongrass** and **Coconut Milk**

In this recipe, I have poached the pollock in coconut milk with lemongrass to add an Asian accent, but not too much as I'm still influenced mainly by the cooking of my home country, France. This is a favorite of my wife, Claire—say no more, the girl knows! You can mash any leftover sauce into your mashed potatoes to go with this dish, if you like.

SERVES 4
PREPARATION TIME 10 minutes
COOKING TIME 20 minutes

2½ cups whipping cream
1¾ cups coconut milk
2 tablespoons unsalted butter
1 tablespoon olive oil
4 pollock fillets, skin on, about
   5 ounces each
4 garlic cloves, unpeeled, lightly
   crushed
1 lemongrass stalk, bruised
sea salt and freshly ground
   black pepper
Creamed Mashed Potatoes
   (see page 20), to serve

1 Put the cream and coconut milk in a wide, shallow sauté pan over medium heat and bring to a simmer.

2 Meanwhile, melt the butter with the oil oil in a large, nonstick skillet over medium heat until the butter turns golden. Season the skin of the pollock with salt and pepper. Put in the skillet, skin-side down, with the garlic and cook 3 to 4 minutes until the skin is crisp and golden brown.

3 Turn the pollock over and pour in the simmering cream and coconut milk—the liquid needs to be just below the height of the fish so the skin doesn't soften. Add the garlic cloves and lemongrass to the liquid and simmer 8 minutes, or until the fish is cooked through. To check the fish is ready, press lightly on the skin and you will see the flesh at the side of the fillet just start to flake away.

4 Lift the fish out of the pan, cover and keep it warm. Return the sauté pan to the heat and simmer 5 to 8 minutes until the liquid reduces by at least half and is thick enough to coat the back of a spoon. Add any juices from the resting fish and season with salt and pepper to taste, then pass the sauce through a fine strainer, using a ladle to help you. Spoon the sauce over the fish and serve with mashed potatoes.

Pan-fried Cod with White Bean Puree and Garlic Chips

This dish is similar to one I make at The Vineyard restaurant and it is always popular. Make sure the cod is super-fresh and line-caught, if possible, but you can use hake or pollock instead. The white bean puree is smooth in contrast to the crisp garlic chips and delicate, tender loins of cod.

SERVES 4
PREPARATION TIME 20 minutes, plus
  overnight soaking
COOKING TIME 40 minutes

8 garlic cloves, unpeeled
4 cod loins, skin on, about 5 ounces
  each, patted dry
3 tablespoons unsalted butter
2 tablespoons olive oil

FOR THE WHITE BEAN PUREE
¾ cup dried butter beans, soaked
  overnight, drained and rinsed
1 carrot, peeled
1 shallot
1 garlic clove
2 tablespoons extra virgin olive oil
1 tablespoon chopped flat-leaf
  parsley leaves
finely grated zest and juice of 1 lime

FOR THE GARLIC CHIPS
sunflower oil, for deep-frying
¾ cup plus 2 tablespooons
  whole milk
4 large garlic cloves, thinly sliced
3 tablespoons all-purpose flour
sea salt and freshly ground
  black pepper

1 To make the white bean puree, put the butter beans in a saucepan, cover with cold water and bring to a boil, skimming off any foam that rises to the surface. Add the carrot, shallot and garlic, turn the heat down to a simmer, partially cover and simmer 40 minutes, or until the beans are tender.

2 While the beans are cooking, make the garlic chips. Heat enough sunflower oil to deep-fry the garlic to 315°F, or until a cube of bread browns in 45 seconds. While the oil is heating, bring the milk to a slow boil in a small saucepan. Add the sliced garlic and blanch 2 to 3 minutes until slighly soft but not breaking up. Remove and pat dry with paper towels, discarding the milk. Lightly dust the garlic in the flour, then drop a few slices at a time into the hot oil and deep-fry 2–3 minutes until golden brown and crisp. Drain on paper towels. Season with salt and leave to one side.

3 Blanch the 8 garlic cloves in a small saucepan of boiling water 4 to 8 minutes until soft, then drain, refresh in cold water and pat dry with paper towels.

4 Season the skin of the cod with salt and pepper. Melt the butter and olive oil in a large, nonstick skillet with a lid over high heat. When the butter is foaming, add the cod, skin-side down, and cook 3 to 5 minutes until the skin is crisp and golden brown. Turn the heat down to medium-low, add the blanched garlic cloves, partially cover with a lid and cook about 4 minutes. Uncover the pan, carefully turn the fish over and cook 3 to 4 minutes longer until just cooked through.

5 Meanwhile, strain the beans, reserving 3 to 4 tablespoons of the cooking liquor, then discard the carrot, shallot and garlic. Transfer the beans to a blender with 3 tablespoons of the reserved cooking liquid and blend to a smooth puree. Add the extra virgin olive oil and blend once more. Add the remaining cooking liquid if the puree is too thick. Season with salt and pepper to taste, then stir in the parsley, half the lime zest and all the lime juice. Serve the cod on a bed of the bean puree with the buttery garlic sauce spooned over the top. Sprinkle with the garlic chips and the remaining lime zest before serving.

Flounder with Celery Root and Pancetta Galette

This is my alternative to the classic *sole meunière*, using flounder. The flounder must be in prime condition, and I would recommend your fish merchant skin it for you, because it is fiddly. Celery root is a beautiful vegetable, which I personally love when it's roasted or, like here, grated with potatoes and mixed with pancetta to make a crisp and golden galette. If you don't have a pan large enough to cook both flounder at once, cook one, then keep it warm in a 300°F oven while to cook the second. Add extra butter and olive oil to the skillet, if necessary.

SERVES 4
PREPARATION TIME 15 minutes
COOKING TIME 30 minutes

2 ounces thick pancetta, cut into lardons
1 cups peeled and grated Idaho or other baking potatoes
2 cups peeled and grated celery root
1 tablespoon chopped flat-leaf parsley leaves
1 stick unsalted butter
3 tablespoons olive oil
3 tablespoons all-purpose flour
2 flounder, skinned and left on the bone
finely grated zest and juice of 1 lime
sea salt and freshly ground black pepper

1 Heat the oven to 315°F. To make the galette, bring a small saucepan of water to a boil. Add the pancetta and blanch 1 to 2 minutes until just cooked. Drain and refresh the pancetta in cold water, then tip it onto paper towels and pat dry. Mix the potatoes, celery root and pancetta in a bowl with half the parsley and season with pepper.

2 Melt 1½ tablespoons of the butter with 1 tablespoon of the oil in a large nonstick, ovenproof skillet over medium heat. When the butter is foaming, add the potato mixture and lightly press it down with a spatula into an even layer. Fry it 5 minutes, or until golden brown, then put the pan in the oven 3 minutes. Remove the pan from the oven and put a large plate on top to cover the pan, then carefully turn the pan and plate upside-down to flip the galette onto the plate. Slide it back into the pan, uncooked side up.

3 Return the pan to medium heat. Add another 1½ tablespoons of the butter and cook the galette 3 minutes, then return the pan to the oven 3 minutes longer. Slide the galette onto paper towels to drain a few seconds, then wrap in kitchen foil to keep warm while you cook the fish.

4 Turn the oven up to 350°F. Put the flour on a plate and season with salt and pepper. Dust the fish in the seasoned flour, patting to remove any excess. Melt 1½ tablespoons of the butter with 1 tablespoon of the oil in the cleaned skillet over high heat. When the butter is foaming, add the fish and cook 6 minutes, then turn it over, add another 1½ tablespoons of the butter and, when it melts, spoon it over the fish. Put the pan in the oven 6 minutes, or until the fish is cooked through and flakes easily.

5 Remove the fish from the oven, cover and leave to rest on a warm plate. Return the skillet to the stovetop, add the remaining butter and oil and stir in the remaining parsley and the lime zest and juice. Heat through briefly. Spoon the sauce over the fish and serve with portions of the galette.

Casserole of **Fall Vegetables** with **Pears** and **Ceps**

At home, I often make casseroles and it is very much the way my mother likes to cook. It is not by accident I have chosen pears and ceps; not only do I love them but they bring so much to this casserole with their superb flavor and texture.

SERVES 4
PREPARATION TIME 30 minutes, plus making the stock
COOKING TIME 1 hour 10 minutes

5 tablespoons unsalted butter
1 tablespoon sunflower oil
1½ cups peeled carrots cut into ¾-inch chunks
1½ cups peeled rutabaga cut into ¾-inch chunks
2 firm pears, peeled, cored and cut into 8 wedges
2 large shallots, cut into thick rings
1½ ounces dried ceps or porcini, soaked in ⅔ cup warm water
2 thyme sprigs
1½ cups peeled celery root cut into ¾-inch chunks
12 garlic cloves, unpeeled
1½ cups peeled butternut squash cut into ¾-inch chunks
4 small new potatoes, such as Charlotte or Ratte, scrubbed and each cut into 3 pieces
½ cup Chicken Stock or Vegetable Stock (see pages 16–17)
1 tablespoon chopped flat-leaf parsley leaves
sea salt and freshly ground black pepper

1 Melt 1½ tablespoons of the butter with the sunflower oil in a large Dutch oven over medium-high heat. When the butter is foaming, add the carrots and immediately turn the heat down to medium. Partially cover the pot and cook 12 to 15 minutes, stirring occasionally, until the carrots just start to soften around the edges but not color. Add the rutabaga, cover the pot again with the lid and cook 10 to 12 minutes longer, stirring occasionally.

2 Meanwhile, melt 1½ tablespoons of the butter in a large skillet over medium heat. When the butter is foaming, add the pears and shallots and cook 8 to 10 minutes until just they are tender and starting to caramelize.

3 Using a small slotted spoon, remove the ceps from their soaking water, taking care not to stir the bowl, then put them on paper towels and pat them dry. Strain the soaking water though a fine strainer. Add the ceps to the pan with the pears and shallots, then stir in the thyme sprigs and sauté over medium-low heat 3 to 4 minutes longer until the ceps become soft. Season well with salt and pepper, then remove the pan from the heat and leave to one side.

4 Add another 1½ tablespoons of the butter to the Dutch oven with the celery root and garlic, partially cover and cook 8 to 10 minutes, stirring occasionally, until they are slightly soft. Add the butternut squash and potatoes and cook 8 to 10 minutes, stirring occasionally. Turn the heat up to high, remove the lid and add the remaining butter, the stock and reserved cep water, making sure there is not any sediment from the ceps in the water. Cook 5 to 8 minutes until the liquid reduces enough to just coat the vegetables; do this quickly so the vegetables don't overcook. Remove the pot from the heat, add the pear mixture and parsley, stir gently to combine and heat through, then serve hot.

Jerusalem Artichoke and Red Chard Omelet with Pickled Shallots

Red chard is a salad leaf that's not used so much in the home kitchen, but is popular with chefs. It's almost like spinach, but less buttery and cooks very quickly so you want to add the leaves at the very last minute, just before the eggs. Also, to intensify the flavor of the dish, I have added pickled shallots, which bring a touch of acidity and crunch. But the main feature is the Vacherin Mont d'Or, which is a soft, rich, creamy cow's milk cheese from the Jura region, in Franche-Comté. It is made by traditional methods and is only available during the September to April season. My region, I love it and what memories it brings...

SERVES 4
PREPARATION TIME 10 minutes, plus 10 minutes cooling
COOKING TIME 20 minutes

4 teaspoons unsalted butter
7 ounces Jerusalem artichokes, peeled, quartered lengthwise and thinly sliced
1 large red onion, sliced
3¼ ounces red chard leaves
8 eggs, lightly beaten
2 ounces soft, creamy cheese, such as Vacherin Mont d'Or
olive oil, for dressing
sea salt and freshly ground black pepper

FOR THE PICKLED SHALLOTS
¾ cup plus 2 tablespoons Chardonnay vinegar or white wine vinegar
4 teaspoons sugar
1 large banana shallot, thinly sliced into rings

1 To make the pickled shallots, put the vinegar and sugar in a small saucepan over medium heat, stirring to dissolve the sugar, and bring to a boil. Put the shallots in a heatproof bowl and when the liquid is boiling, pour it over the shallots. Leave them to cool about 10 minutes, which is long enough to pickle the shallots perfectly.

2 Meanwhile, heat the oven to 315°F. Melt the butter in a large, nonstick, ovenproof skillet over medium heat. When it is foaming, add the Jerusalem artichokes and onion and cook 4 to 5 minutes until they are just soft and slightly caramelized. Add half of the red chard leaves and toss twice to mix.

3 Season the eggs with salt and pepper, then pour them over the vegetables in the pan. Turn the heat up to high and spoon the cheese in small dollops all over the top. When the edges of the omelet start to bubble and thicken slightly, run the edge of a rubber spatula quickly around the pan to loosen, then put the pan in the oven 4 to 5 minutes until the omelet is just cooked. Check the omelet is cooked by gently pressing the top to see if it springs back lightly. If it doesn't, return the omelet to the oven 2 minutes longer and check again.

4 Dress the remaining red chard with a little olive oil and a touch of salt and pepper. Drain the shallots. Serve the omelette topped with the shallots and finished with the dressed red chard on top.

Spiced Fall Fruit and **Pan-fried Brioche**

I've chosen my favorite fruit for this recipe—including yellow peaches, which I love—but be adventurous, because this is a great way of using up any surplus pitted fruits or apples or pears you might have. You can also use a vanilla bean instead of star anise, or even black pepper instead of the cinnamon, but use them with care to avoid overpowering the fruit. I like to use Drambuie but you can use Scotch instead, if you like.

SERVES 4
PREPARATION TIME 15 minutes
COOKING TIME 10 minutes

4 plums, halved and pitted
4 greengages, halved and stones removed
1 yellow peach, quartered and pitted
1 nectarine, quartered and pitted
2 figs, quartered
⅓ cup light soft brown sugar
2 small cinnamon sticks
2 star anise
4½ tablespoons Drambuie
juice of ½ lime
2 extra-large eggs
4 slices brioche loaf, each about ⅝ inch thick
3 tablespoons unsalted butter
Real Vanilla Ice Cream (see page 23), to serve

1 Heat a large, nonstick skillet over medium-high heat. Add the fruit in a single layer, cut-side down, and cook 1 minute. Sprinkle one-third of the sugar over the top and add the cinnamon and star anise, then continue to cook 3 to 4 minutes longer until the fruit start to release their juices and become slightly soft; they should still keep their shape.

2 Pour the Drambuie into the pan and immediately set it alight (it should burn for a few seconds), then turn the heat down to low so some of the Drambuie remains in the pan and cook 1 to 2 minutes longer, taking care not to let the fruit become too soft. Stir in the lime juice and remove the pan from the heat. Cover the pan to keep the fruit warm while you cook the brioche.

3 Beat the eggs with the remaining sugar in a large, shallow bowl until thick and creamy. Dip each side of the brioche briefly into the egg mixture until it is just coated, then leave to one side.

4 Melt the butter a second large, nonstick skillet over medium-high heat. When it is foaming, add the brioche and cook for a few minutes on each side until just golden brown and slightly crisp. Serve with the fruit and their juices spooned over the top and with vanilla ice cream.

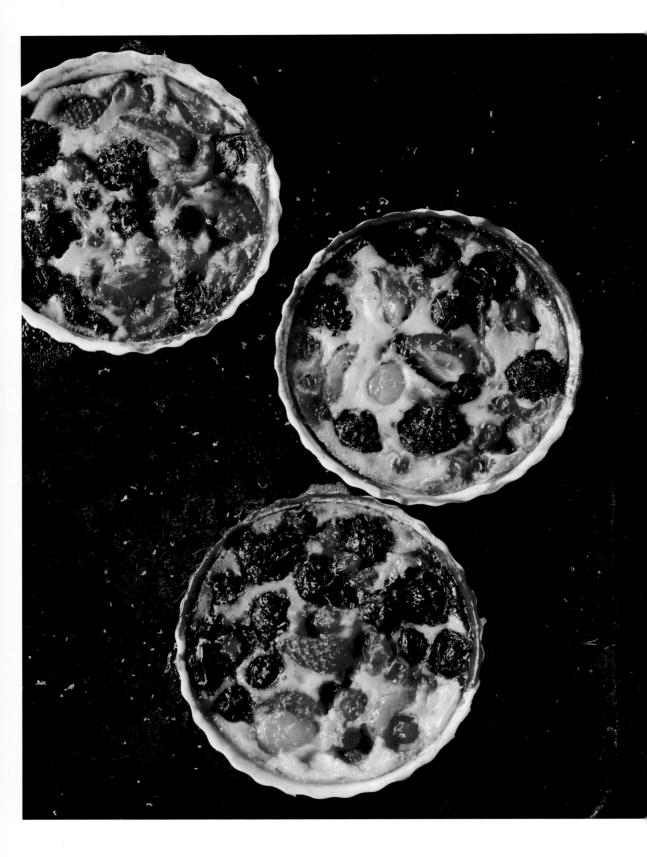

Red Fruit Clafoutis and **Flavored Greek Yogurt**

Imagine all the colors and flavors of these lovely summer berries in a rosemary-infused clafoutis. And the individual clafoutis are really just as good made with thyme or lavender flowers, but make sure the flowers are edible and untreated. Another great flavor combination is crushed black pepper and grated lime zest—enjoy experimenting!

SERVES 4
PREPARATION TIME 15 minutes, plus
  1 hour macerating
COOKING TIME 12 minutes

⅓ cup blueberries
⅓ cup blackberries
½ cup red currants
⅓ cup cherries, pitted
⅓ cup strawberries, hulled
  and quartered
scant ½ cup sugar
½ teaspoon very finely chopped
  young rosemary leaves (from
  the tips)
4 tablespoons plain Greek yogurt
3 tablespoons unsalted butter, half
  soft and half melted
½ cup all-purpose flour, sifted
a pinch salt
1 egg
2 egg yolks
¾ cup plus 2 tablespoons whole milk

1 Wash the fruit, drain it well and put it into a bowl. Add 2 tablespoons of the sugar and the rosemary and turn to coat. Cover and leave the fruit to macerate at room temperature 1 hour to release some of the juices from the fruit.

2 Heat the oven to 350°F. Strain the fruit and add half of the juices to the yogurt, reserving the other half. Mix the juices into the yogurt, then cover with plastic wrap and chill until ready to serve.

3 Grease four large ramekins with the soft butter and sprinkle with 2 tablespoons of the sugar, carefully turning the ramekins to make sure the sugar coats the insides, then tip out any excess.

4 Sift the flour and salt into a mixing bowl. In a separate bowl, whisk together the egg, egg yolks and remaining sugar, then slowly add to the flour, mixing until incorporated and smooth. Gradually add the milk and the reserved fruit juices, stirring until the mixture has the consistency of a crepe batter, then add the melted butter and mix well until combined.

5 Divide the berries into the prepared ramekins and pour the batter over to just below the top. Bake 10 to 12 minutes until the clafoutis are set and golden brown. Serve with a dollop of the flavored Greek yogurt on top, if you like, or you can serve it separately.

Honey Parfait with Poached Rhubarb

There are so many types of honey to choose from, so experiment to find the ones you like the best. I find the subtle flavors of flower honeys delicious, and here they perfectly complement the flavor of delicate pink rhubarb.

SERVES 4
PREPARATION TIME 20 minutes, plus at least 8 hours freezing
COOKING TIME 10 minutes

5 egg yolks
1 cup less 1½ tablespoons honey, such as lavender, thyme, chestnut or acacia
1 vanilla bean, split in half lengthwise and seeds scraped out
⅔ cup whipping cream
4 rhubarb sticks, chopped into large pieces
a few edible lavender flowers, to serve

1 Line a 12- x 5- x 3½-inch bread pan or terrine with plastic wrap, leaving a generous overhang. Put the egg yolks in a mixing bowl and add the vanilla seeds, reserving the bean for another recipe. Melt 2½ tablespoons of the honey in a small saucepan over low heat, then scrape it into the egg yolks and beat about 10 minutes, using an electric mixer, until the mixture is cool and forms a light ribbon when the beaters are lifted out of the bowl.

2 Whip the cream, then fold it into the cold egg and honey mixture. Pour the mixture into the prepared bread pan, cover with the overhanging plastic wrap and put in the freezer at least 8 hours until firm.

3 To poach the rhubarb, pour 2 cups water and the remaining honey into a saucepan and bring to a boil. Turn the heat down to low and simmer 3 to 4 minutes until a very light syrup forms. Add the rhubarb and poach slowly about 5 minutes until it is just soft. Using a slotted spoon, scoop out the rhubarb and put it on a plate to cool. At the same time, leave the syrup to cool. When both are cool, return the rhubarb to the syrup, then sprinkle with the lavender flowers and serve with a slice of the honey parfait.

Deconstructed Poached Rhubarb with **Pistachio Crumble**

This is a very different type of crumble from the one your grandmother might have made—the rhubarb is gently poached in a lemongrass-infused syrup and then elegantly layered in a glass with a lemon- and lime-flavored cream and topped with a crisp pistachio crumble. It makes a deliciously elegant and modern twist on an old favorite.

SERVES 4
PREPARATION TIME 20 minutes,
  plus at least 3 hours chilling
COOKING TIME 50 minutes

3½ cups peeled rhubarb cut into
  1-inch-long pieces, with the
  trimmings reserved
½ cup sugar
1 lemongrass stalk, split and
  bruised

FOR THE LEMON AND LIME CREAM
¾ cup heavy cream
2 tablespoons sugar
2 tablespoons lemon juice
finely grated zest of ½ lemon
finely grated zest of ½ lime

FOR THE PISTACHIO CRUMBLE
¾ cup plus 1 tablespoon
  confectioner's sugar
¾ cup plus 1 tablespoon
  all-purpose flour
a pinch salt
¾ cup very finely ground
  blanched almonds
⅓ cup shelled pistachios,
  roughly chopped
7 tablespoons unsalted butter, soft

1 To make the lemon and lime cream, put the cream and sugar in a small saucepan over high heat and bring to a boil. Put the lemon juice and both zests in a small measuring jug and as soon as the cream comes to a boil, pour it into the jug and mix quickly to combine. Pour the hot cream mixture into four small, heatproof sundae glasses. Leave to cool completely, then put in the refrigerator and leave to thicken at least 3 hours before serving.

2 Put the rhubarb, rhubarb peelings, sugar and lemongrass in a sauté pan and just cover with water. Heat over low heat until simmering, then simmer 15 to 20 minutes until the rhubarb is just tender but keeps its shape. Strain the rhubarb through a fine strainer into the cleaned pan, then return the syrup to the heat and cook until it reduces by half and is thick and syrupy. Meanwhile, discard the rhubarb peelings and the lemongrass and put the rhubarb in a shallow nonmetallic dish. Pour the reduced syrup over the top of the rhubarb and leave to cool while you make the crumble.

3 Heat the oven to 315°F. Put all the crumble ingredients in a large mixing bowl and rub gently with your fingertips to make a coarse crumb mixture. Tip the crumb mixture into a baking sheet in an even layer and bake 20 to 25 minutes until it is golden brown. Turn the crumble mixture, bringing the edges into the middle and then spreading it out into an even layer again, every 6 to 8 minutes to make sure it bakes evenly. Remove the baking sheet from the oven and leave the crumble to cool completely until it is crunchy.

4 Take the cream-filled glasses out of the refrigerator and top with the rhubarb. Drizzle with the syrup and finish with the crumble, gently sprinkling it over the top. Serve immediately while the crumble topping is still crunchy.

Confit Tomato Marmalade and Goat Milk Yogurt with Langues de Chat

Langues de chat are thin, crisp cookies that we normally serve at The Vineyard restaurant with afternoon tea or coffee. As I'm a lover of goat milk I wanted to see if I could make a version of the cookie with goat butter and goat crème fraîche, and here it is. These are delicious dipped into the sweet and slightly acidic confit tomato marmalade and goat milk yogurt dessert. Goat milk products are available online if you can't source them locally.

SERVES 4
PREPARATION TIME 30 minutes,
  plus cooling
COOKING TIME 40 minutes

4 ounces vine cherry tomatoes,
  halved
¼ cup superfine sugar
2 basil leaves
1 teaspoon balsamic vinegar
1 pound plain goat milk yogurt
finely grated zest of 1 lime

FOR THE LANGUES DE CHAT
7 tablespoons goat butter, soft,
  plus extra for greasing
½ cup superfine sugar
3 egg whites
1 cup white bread flour, sifted,
  plus extra for dusting
½ vanilla bean, split in half
  lengthwise and seeds scraped out
6 tablespoons goat milk
  crème fraîche

1 To make the confit tomato marmalade, put the tomatoes, sugar, 1 basil leaf and the vinegar in a sauté pan with ¾ cup plus 2 tablespoons water and bring to a boil. Turn the heat down to low and simmer 20 to 30 minutes until the tomatoes thicken to the consistency of marmalade or a thick jam. Remove the pan from the heat and spoon the mixture into a bowl, cover and leave to cool. When it is cool, strain it through a fine strainer into a bowl to collect the juices (leave the tomatoe mixture to one side).

2 Roughly chop the remaining basil leaf and add to the goat milk yogurt with the strained juices, then mix until just combined. Cover and leave in the refrigerator until ready to serve.

3 Heat the oven to 400°F. To make the *langues de chat*, beat together the butter and sugar, using an electric mixer, 5 minutes, or until light and well blended. Whisk in the egg whites, one at a time, because the mixture will split if you add them all at once, until incorporated. Gradually fold in the flour, then beat in the vanilla seeds and crème fraîche until the batter is soft, pale and creamy. Spoon the batter into a disposable pastry bag.

4 Grease and flour a large cookie sheet. Trim the end off the pastry bag to a ½-inch opening, then carefully pipe the cookies, 3 inches long, onto the cookie sheet, leaving a 4-inch gap between each one, because they spread during baking. Bake 5 to 6 minutes, turning the cookie sheet halfway through, until the cookies are dark golden brown around the edges and pale in the middle. Remove the cookie sheet from the oven, transfer the cookies to a wire rack and leave to cool and become crisp.

5 To serve, spoon the confit tomatoes into the bottom of small sundae glasses, top with the yogurt and a sprinkling of lime zest and serve with the cookies.

Strawberry Jelly Puree with Elderflower Yogurt and Sesame Nougatine

I recommend you wait for the strawberry season before making this dish —the quality of the fruit will make a massive difference to the taste of the jelly. I also use a lovely elderflower cordial, which is not as sweet as some cordials. To finish the dessert, I use black and white sesame seeds made into a lovely transparent, glasslike nougatine, which is very crunchy, but absolutely delicious! If you cannot find liquid glucose, use light corn syrup.

SERVES 4
PREPARATION TIME 35 minutes, plus at least 30 minutes chilling and cooling
COOKING TIME 25 minutes

FOR THE STRAWBERRY JELLY PUREE
2 gelatin leaves, about 1/16 ounce total weight
3 1/3 cups strawberries, hulled
1 tablespoon sugar
2 tablespoons white balsamic vinegar

FOR THE ELDERFLOWER YOGURT
1 1/4 cups plain Greek yogurt
2/3 cup cream cheese
3 tablespoons elderflower cordial
1 tablespoon confectioner's sugar, sifted

FOR THE SESAME NOUGATINE
1/3 cup black sesame seeds
1/3 cup white sesame seeds
2 tablespoons liquid glucose
1/2 cup less 1 tablespoon superfine sugar
5 tablespoons unsalted butter

1 To make the strawberry jelly puree, put the gelatin in a medium bowl with enough cold water to cover, then leave to soften 5 minutes. Drain and return the gelatin to the bowl. Heat a large, nonstick skillet over high heat. Add 2 cups of the strawberries and the sugar and cook 2 minutes, tossing to coat the strawberries in the sugar. Remove the pan from the heat, cover and leave to one side 3 minutes.

2 Transfer the strawberries and any juices in the pan to a blender and blend to a puree, then pass through a fine strainer, using a ladle to help you, directly onto the soaked gelatin and whisk briskly until it dissolves. Put the bowl directly in a larger bowl of ice water to cool rapidly. When the mixture starts to set, divide it equally into four tumblers. Put them in the refrigerator to set at least another 30 minutes. Meanwhile, finely dice slightly less than 1 cup of the remaining strawberries, then put them into a bowl with the vinegar and leave to macerate 20 minutes.

3 Put all the elderflower yogurt ingredients in a separate bowl and mix well to combine, then cover and leave in the refrigerator until needed.

4 When the strawberry mixture has set, spoon the yogurt into the four glasses. Using a slotted spoon, add the macerated strawberries on top, then leave in the refrigerator to set while you make the nougatine.

5 Heat the oven to 350°F and line a baking sheet with parchment paper. Put all the nougatine ingredients in a nonstick skillet. Add 1 tablespoon water and stir to combine, then heat over medium heat 3 minutes, or until the butter melts and the sugar dissolves. Turn the heat up and cook 4 to 5 minutes until the mixture just starts to turn golden brown. Pour it onto the prepared baking sheet and spread out using a wet spatula. Bake 12 minutes, or until golden brown; it shouldn't be as dark as caramel. Remove the baking sheet from the oven and leave the nougatine to cool on the tray until crisp. Break the nougatine into large pieces. Remove the glasses from the refrigerator and balance a piece of nougatine in the top of each dessert, then put the rest in a bowl to share.

Balsamic and Lime Raspberries with Goat Milk Ice Cream

This was a bit of a discovery for me. I've been thinking about making a goat milk ice cream for some time and I was really pleased with the results, both because it is easy to make and the lift from the lime zest is perfect. Buy raspberries in season for the best flavor and you need a very good, aged balsamic vinegar for the marinade—one that is slightly syrupy, but not too acidic—and the age will be specified on the label if it is a really good product. The Langues de Chat (see page 139) go really well with this, too. The finished dessert is summer itself!

SERVES 4
PREPARATION TIME 20 minutes, plus
   at least 3½ hours freezing
COOKING TIME 5 minutes

Langues de Chat (see page 139),
   to serve
1 tablespoon fennel seeds
1 tablespoon confectioner's sugar

FOR THE GOAT MILK ICE CREAM
1¼ cups goat milk
¾ cup plus 2 tablespoons
   goat cream
¾ cup plus 2 tablespoons plain goat
   milk yogurt
1 cup confectioner's sugar
finely grated zest of ½ lime

**FOR THE BALSAMIC AND LIME
   RASPBERRIES**
1⅔ cups raspberries
3 tablespoons balsamic vinegar
finely grated zest of ½ lime, plus
   extra for sprinkling
2 drops lime juice

1 Line a medium-deep freezerproof tray with parchment paper. Put all the ice cream ingredients in a bowl and whisk together until smooth. Pour the mixture into the prepared tray and freeze for at least 3 hours, or until hard. Remove from the freezer and break into small chunks, then put them into a food processor and blend briefly to a smooth, firm puree; you don't want the mixture to thaw too much. Spoon the mxiture into a small freezerproof container, smooth the top, cover and return to the freezer at least 25 to 30 minutes until hard again.

2 Meanwhile, put the raspberries in a large bowl with 2 tablespoons of the balsamic vinegar, the lime zest and juice. Gently stir until combined, cover with plastic wrap and put in the refrigerator.

3 Heat the oven to 400°F and line a baking sheet with parchment paper. Put the fennel seeds on the prepared baking sheet and dust with the confectioner's sugar until lightly coated. Put in the oven 4 to 5 minutes until light golden and caramelized. Return the baking sheet to the oven a couple of minutes at a time if the seeds are not ready. Remove the baking sheet and leave the seeds to cool, breaking up any that might have stuck together.

4 Remove the raspberries from the refrigerator and, using a slotted spoon, spoon into serving bowls. Put a small scoop of ice cream on top of each bowl of raspberries. Drizzle any of the liquid from the raspberries and the remaining balsamic vinegar over the top and finish with a scattering of caramelized fennel seeds and a little extra lime zest. Serve with *langues de chat*.

Pain de Gênes with **Rosemary** and **Tonka Bean Crème Anglaise**

I have loved *pain de gênes* since I was a boy. It was an afternoon cake at home and often served when we had visitors, and is similar to a genoise sponge but with toasted slivered almonds on top. For an exotic twist, I'm serving it with a chili, rosemary and tonka bean crème anglaise and sprinkling it with hazelnuts. Tonka beans, by the way, are wrinkled black seeds with an aroma reminiscent of vanilla and almond. You can buy them online if they are not available in your supermarket.

SERVES 4 to 6
PREPARATION TIME 40 minutes, plus 30 minutes infusing and cooling
COOKING TIME 50 minutes

FOR THE PAIN DE GÊNES
4 tablespoons unsalted butter, softened, plus extra for greasing
⅓ cup plus 1 tablespoon white bread flour, sifted, plus extra for dusting
7 ounces soft marzipan, ideally containing half almonds and half sugar
3 eggs
1 tablespoon baking powder, sifted
2 tablespoons blanched hazelnuts, toasted and chopped

FOR THE ROSEMARY AND TONKA BEAN CRÈME ANGLAISE
½ cup whole milk
½ cup whipping cream
leaves from 1 small rosemary sprig
1 small red chili, seeded and finely chopped
1 tonka bean or 1 vanilla bean, split in half lengthwise and seeds scraped out
3 extra-large egg yolks
¼ cup sugar

1 Heat the oven to 300°F. Grease and flour a deep 8-inch loose-bottomed cake pan.

2 To make the *pain de gênes*, put the marzipan and butter in a food mixer fitted with a paddle, or use a bowl and an electric hand mixer, and beat 5 minutes, or until soft and light. Add the eggs, one at a time, making sure each is properly incorporated before adding the next one. When all the eggs have been added, continue to beat at least 20 minutes until the mixture is white and fluffy. Add the flour and baking powder and fold in very gently with a large metal spoon. Pour the batter into the prepared cake pan and sprinkle the hazelnuts over the top. Bake 35 to 40 minutes until the cake is risen and golden brown on top. To check the cake is ready, insert a skewer through the deepest part, and if it comes out clean the cake it is baked. If not, bake 5 minutes longer and check again. Remove the pan from the oven, put on a wire rack for the cake to cool slightly, then turn the cake out of the pan and leave to cool completely on the rack.

3 While the cake is baking, make the rosemary and tonka bean crème anglaise. Put the milk and cream in a saucepan over medium heat and bring to a simmer, then remove the pan from the heat. Add the rosemary leaves, half the chili and the tonka bean and stir to combine, then cover and leave to infuse 30 minutes.

4 Put the egg yolks and sugar in a bowl and whisk until the sugar dissolves. Return the pan of infused cream and milk to medium-high heat and bring to a simmer, then pass through a strainer onto the egg mixture, whisking continuously. Discard the solids in the strainer. Return the mixture to the pan and simmer over medium heat 5 to 8 minutes, stirring continuously with a wooden spoon (otherwise you'll get scrambled eggs!) until it starts to thicken. You will be able to tell when the crème anglaise is ready if you run two fingers down the back of the spoon and the two lines don't immediately join. Stir in the remaining chili. Serve the *pain de gênes* cut into wedges with a generous spoonful of the crème anglaise.

Paris–Brest with Chicory and Coffee Cream

This is a twist on the beautiful, classic Paris–Brest choux pastry dessert, which I've given a whole new dimension by filling it with a delicious mixture of chicory and coffee cream. You will find granulated chicory and coffee online or in specialist coffee stores.

SERVES 4
PREPARATION TIME 45 minutes, plus cooling and 35 minutes resting
COOKING TIME 40 minutes

FOR THE CHOUX PASTRY
1½ sticks unsalted butter
¾ teaspoon salt
¾ tablespoon superfine sugar
2 cups all-purpose flour
8 medium eggs
a few drops vanilla extract
1 teaspoon granulated chicory and coffee mixture

FOR THE CHICORY AND COFFEE CREAM
1⅓ cups whole milk
2 teaspoons chicory and coffee granules
3 eggs
½ cup superfine sugar
¼ cup cornstarch
1¼ sticks unsalted butter, soft

1 To start the chicory and coffee cream, put the milk in a small saucepan over medium heat and bring almost to a boil. Stir in the chicory and coffee until it dissolves. Remove from the pan the heat, cover and leave to cool.

2 To make the choux pastry dough, put the butter, salt, sugar and 2 cups water in a large saucepan and bring to a boil. Remove the pan from the heat and whisk in the flour. Return the pan to the heat and gently stir the mixture with a wooden spoon until it starts to come away from the side of the pan and falls off the spoon easily. Remove the pan again from the heat and whisk in the eggs, one at a time, until they are all incorporated. Stir in the vanilla, then cover with plastic wrap and leave to rest 35 minutes.

3 Meanwhile, heat the oven to 350°F. Using a 3¼-inch round biscuit cutter or upturned cup as a template, draw eight circles on a large sheet of parchment paper. Turn the paper over and put it on a cookie sheet.

4 Spoon the choux pastry dough into a disposable pastry bag, snip off the end to a ¾-inch opening, then carefully pipe eight circles using the circles drawn on the parchment paper as templates. Sprinkle the granulated chicory and coffee on top and bake, with the door ajar by 2 inches, 30 minutes, or until the pastry is medium golden brown. (Leaving the door open allows the pastry to dry as it bakes and makes it very light.)

5 While the pastry is baking, complete the chicory and coffee cream. Beat together the eggs, sugar and cornstarch, using an electric mixer, 5 minutes, or until light and fluffy. Strain the chicory-coffee milk onto the egg mixture and whisk to combine, then return it to the pan. Put over medium-low heat and stir continuously 10 minutes, or until the mixture starts to thicken. Remove the pan from the heat and continue to stir until the mixture cools and is smooth, thick and slightly trembling. Beat the softened butter in a separate mixing bowl until very soft, then add the chicory-coffee cream, a little at a time, until incorporated. Continue to whisk 10 minutes, or until you have a very light buttercream.

6 To assemble, halve the choux rings horizontally and spoon the chicory-coffee cream into a pastry bag the same size you used to pipe the pastry. Pipe the cream over the bottoms, then gently put on the pastry tops.

Cider-soaked Babas with Cinnamon Chantilly Cream

In my version of the classic rum baba I'm using an infusion of hard cider and cinnamon to give a welcome, refreshing, tangy flavor. They are served with a cinnamon Chantilly cream, or you can use ice cream—I know which one I would go for, though!

SERVES 4
PREPARATION TIME 25 minutes, plus 50 minutes proving and 10 minutes cooling
COOKING TIME 12 minutes

FOR THE BABAS
1½ cups plus 1½ tablespoons white bread flour
a pinch salt
1 tablespoon sugar
2 eggs
4 tablespoons unsalted butter, very soft, plus extra for greasing
¼ ounce compressed yeast, or ½ envelope (1 teaspoon) active dry yeast mixed with 1 tablespoon warm water

FOR THE CIDER AND CINNAMON INFUSION
1½ quarts dry hard cider
½ cup sugar
1 cinnamon stick

FOR THE CINNAMON CHANTILLY CREAM
¾ cup plus 2 tablespoons heavy cream
4 teaspoons sugar
a pinch ground cinnamon or ½ teaspoon vanilla extract

1 To make the babas, put all the ingredients in a food mixer bowl and, using the dough hook, mix slowly until it forms a soft dough, then remove the bowl from the machine. (Alternatively, put all the ingredients in a mixing bowl and mix using a wooden spoon 2 minutes until it forms a soft dough. Tip out onto a lightly floured countertop and knead about 6 minutes until smooth.) Cover the bowl with a clean dish towel and leave at room temperature 30 minutes, or until it rises by half. When the dough has risen, press it down with one hand to punch out the air.

2 Lightly grease a 12-hole muffin pan and put on a baking sheet. Divide the dough into 12 pieces, each about the size of a golf ball. Take a ball of dough in your hand, form a fist and squeeze the dough out through the bottom of your fist into a muffin hole. Repeat with all the dough. (It is important the muffin holes are only half filled to let the dough rise.) Cover the pan with a clean dish towel and leave the babas to rise in a warm place 20 minutes, or until double in size.

3 Meanwhile, make the cider and cinnamon infusion. Put the cider and sugar in a large saucepan and bring to a boil. Stir to dissolve the sugar, then remove the pan from the heat. Add the cinnamon stick, cover and leave to infuse 30 minutes.

4 To make the cinnamon Chantilly cream, whip the cream with the sugar and ground cinnamon, using an electric mixer, until soft peaks form. Cover and put in the refrigerator until ready to serve.

5 Meanwhile, heat the oven to 375°F. Bake the babas about 12 minutes, turning the pan around once, until they are golden and baked through. Remove the muffin pan from the oven and leave the babas to cool in the pan 5 minutes, then turn them out onto a wire rack to cool completely.

6 Remove the cinnamon stick and check that the cider and cinnamon infusion is still warm. If not, reheat it briefly. Carefully dip the babas, two at a time, into the cider infusion, pushing them under until wet and heavy. Serve the babas with the cinnamon Chantilly cream.

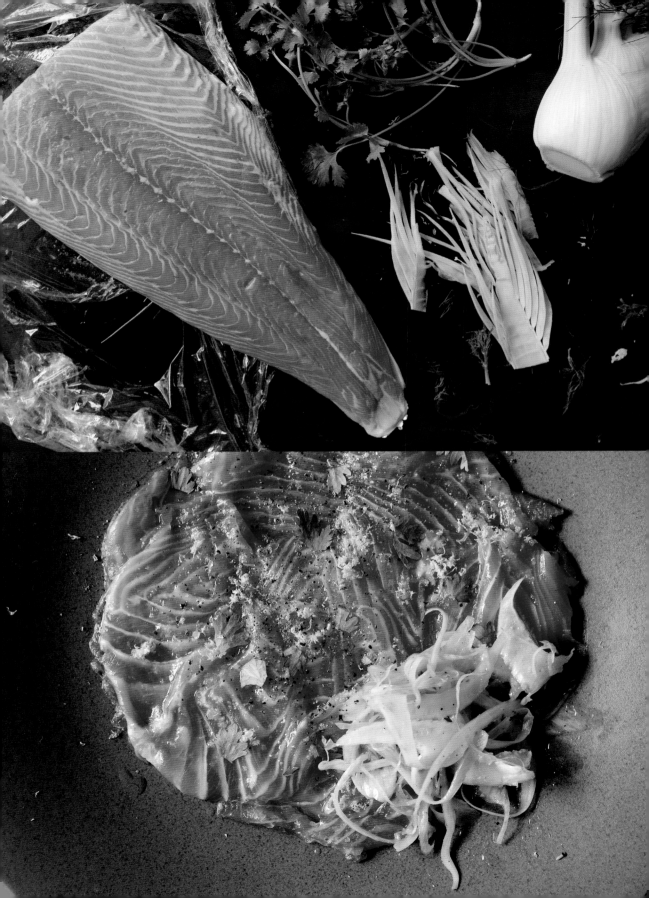

FRATERNITÉ

Dishes that bring innovation and style to classic combinations of ingredients

In these recipes, you'll find a sense of originality, as I have taken ingredients that are classically put together, but combined them in innovative ways— in a kind of union, a friendship that can be achieved by modern association. There is more imagination in the construction of these dishes, so some might be more challenging to cook, but also more fun. I am sure your guests and family will enjoy these creative recipes.

There are some lovely ideas to discover in this chapter, from Smoked Duck and Lentils with Lavender (see page 154) to Chocolate, Chili and Lemongrass Tart (see page 208). You'll find ingredients you might not have thought of putting together, but which will lift the dish and delight you when you taste them, so I am very much hoping you will try the recipes and give me some favorable feedback.

Chicken, Leek and Wild Mushroom Packages

I wanted to try a twist on a *pithivier*, a puff pastry torte, and I decided phyllo pastry would make it lighter and also unusual. I have created a wonderful way of using the dough, which I am sure you will enjoy making and eating.

SERVES 4
PREPARATION TIME 20 minutes, plus making the stock and 30 minutes marinating
COOKING TIME 1 hour

2¼ sticks plus 1 tablespoon unsalted butter
2 boneless, skinless, corn-fed chicken breast halves, about 6 ounces each, cut into ¾-inch cubes
grated zest and juice of 1 lemon, plus 1 whole lemon
2 tablespoons plain Greek yogurt
2 teaspoons finely chopped tarragon leaves
1 small young leek, green part cut in half lengthwise and then into slices, white part reserved for another dish
7 ounces mixed wild or shiitake mushrooms
1 tablespoon sunflower oil
18 ounces fresh phyllo pastry dough, cut into sixteen 6¼- x 8½-inch rectangles
1 egg, beaten
2 tablespoons sherry vinegar
¾ cup plus 2 tablespoons Chicken Stock (see page 16)
¾ cup plus 2 tablespoons whipping cream
sea salt and freshly ground black pepper

1 To make the clarified butter, put 2¼ sticks of the butter in a saucepan over very low heat and leave 30 minutes, or until the butter melts and the solids fall to the bottom of the pan. Remove the pan from the heat.

2 Mix the chicken, lemon zest and juice, yogurt and half the tarragon in a nonmetallic bowl. Cover and marinate in the refrigerator 30 minutes.

3 Meanwhile, bring a saucepan of water to a boil. Add the leek, return the water to a boil and blanch 1 minute. Lift out using a slotted spoon and refresh in ice water, then lift out and pat dry. Add the mushrooms to a boiling water, blanch 1 minute, then lift out, refresh and pat dry.

4 Melt the remaining butter with the oil in a large, nonstick skillet over high heat. When the butter is foaming, add the mushrooms and sauté 2 minutes. Add the leek and chicken and sauté 2 minutes until starting to color. Remove from the pan and leave to cool at room temperature.

5 Heat the oven to 350°F. Cover the pile of phyllo dough with a clean, damp dish towel and work quickly with one piece at a time. Lay a sheet of dough on the countertop, brush lightly with clarified butter, then grate a little lemon zest from the whole lemon over the top. Lay a second sheet over the top and brush with butter as before, then season with a little salt. Put another sheet on top, brush with butter again and grate over a little lemon zest. Finish with a fourth sheet, then butter and a little pepper. Beat together the egg and 1 tablespoon water to make an egg wash. Brush the edges of the dough with the egg wash, then spoon one-quarter of the chicken onto the bottom half of the dough. Gently fold the dough over the filling, press the edges together and tuck them under to seal and form a package. Put on a cookie sheet and put in the refrigerator while you make 3 more packages. Brush the outsides with the clarified butter, then bake 20 to 25 minutes until golden brown and crisp.

6 Meanwhile, return the skillet to medium heat. Add the sherry vinegar and deglaze the pan by stirring to remove any caramelized bits stuck to the bottom. Add the stock and cream, turn the heat down to low and simmer 10 to 12 minutes until there is slightly less than 1 cup of sauce, thick enough to coat the back of a spoon. Add the remaining tarragon and season to taste. Spoon the sauce over the phyllo packages to serve.

Smoked Duck and **Lentils** with **Lavender**

If you have time, hot-smoke your duck at home using a wok (see page 170), otherwise substitute a cold-smoked, air-dried duck, sliced and served as a salad with the hot lentils. Either way, corn-fed and free-range birds give the best flavor, and the combination of honey, lavender and orange works well.

SERVES 4
PREPARATION TIME 20 minutes
COOKING TIME 35 minutes

FOR THE CANDIED ORANGE ZEST
1 large orange, washed and
   scrubbed
2 tablespoons sugar

FOR THE SMOKED DUCK
½ cup basmati rice
3 tablespoons green tea
1 teaspoon sugar
2 small lavender sprigs
1 tablespoon canola oil
2 duck breasts, about 7 ounces
   each
1 tablespoon honey
a few chervil leaves

FOR THE LENTILS
1 cup Puy lentils, picked over
   and rinsed
1 onion, finely chopped
2 cloves
1 bouquet garni, made with 1 thyme
   sprig and 1 parsley sprig, tied
   together with kitchen string
3 tablespoons unsalted butter
sea salt and freshly ground
   black pepper

1 To make the candied orange zest, use a sharp knife or vegetable peeler to pare the zest from the orange into fine strips, cutting away the pith. Put the zest in a small saucepan, cover with cold water and bring to a boil. Remove the pan from the heat and drain the zest, then refresh it under cold water and drain again. Repeat this blanching process.

2 Return the zest to the pan over low heat and add the sugar and 3 tablespoons water, stirring until the sugar dissolves. Raise the heat and bring to a boil, then turn the heat down to low and simmer 4 to 5 minutes until the zest becomes transparent. Remove the pan from the heat and leave the orange strips to cool in the syrup.

3 Put a large piece of aluminum foil, shiny-side down, in the bottom of a wok or steamer. Add the rice, tea, sugar and 1 lavender sprig, and drizzle with the canola oil. Cover with a wire rack or steamer insert and lid, then put over medium heat 5 minutes, or until the mixture starts to smoke. Quickly put the duck breasts inside, cover with foil to help seal the duck, then put the lid on, turn the heat to low and smoke 5 minutes.

4 Meanwhile, put the lentils in a small saucepan and cover with cold water. Bring to a boil, then skim off any foam that rises to the surface. Add the onion, cloves and bouquet garni, turn the heat down to low and simmer 5 to 7 minutes until they are just tender. Season with salt and pepper to taste, then strain and discard the flavorings.

5 When the duck is almost ready, heat a nonstick skillet over medium heat. Turn off the heat under the smoker, lift out the duck and put the lid back on the smoker. Put the duck, skin-side down, in the skillet and cook 4 to 5 minutes. Flip the duck over, brush the skin with the honey and sprinkle a little of the remaining lavender over, then cook 5 minutes longer. Lift out, cover with foil and leave to rest, quickly discarding the foil with the smoking ingredients.

6 Heat a nonstick skillet until hot. Add the butter and lentils and stir-fry a few minutes until hot. Cut the duck into chunks and serve on top of the lentils, sprinkled with the orange zest strips with a little of the syrup, the chervil leaves and a pinch more lavender.

Salmon Marinated in **Fennel** and **Coriander**

I have always loved marinated salmon and sea trout. It makes for a refreshing and delicate dish, which is unusual for your guests, as very few people make this at home. It is very much up to you which herbs and fruit you use, because there are many ways to make this recipe, but cilantro works well, as do chives and chervil. Chervil can be difficult to find, but as it is one of the most flavorsome herbs around, you might like to grow your own. You can also use other citrus fruit instead of the grapefruit. Orange, lemon, blood orange or kumquat all work well, but lime is my favorite. But as long as you get the essential sugar-salt combination, you will have a great spring or summer first course.

SERVES 4
PREPARATION TIME 20 minutes, plus 24 hours curing

1 salmon fillet, 1 pound 5 ounces weight, skin on
2 tablespoons sea salt, plus extra for seasoning
2 tablespoons sugar
1 teaspoon ground cumin
1 teaspoon ground coriander
2 small fennel bulbs, outer sections removed
finely grated zest of 1 and juice of ½ grapefruit
2 tablespoons roughly chopped cilantro leaves
1 tablespoon olive oil
freshly ground black pepper

1 Put the salmon, skin-side down, on a large piece of plastic wrap. Mix together the salt, sugar, cumin and ground coriander, then sprinkle the mixture over the flesh side of the salmon and finish with a little pepper. Using a mandolin, grate one of the fennel bulbs over the top of the mixture and press it down so it totally covers the fish. Wrap all the ingredients in the plastic wrap and put, flesh-side down, in a small baking sheet. Cover with another small baking sheet and put a can of beans or similar weight on top, then put both baking sheets and the weight into the refrigerator and leave to cure 24 hours in total, following the instructions in Step 2 during that time.

2 After the first 8 to 10 hours, remove the weight and turn the fish over, flesh-side up. Continue turning it flesh-side down and then flesh-side up, every following 4 to 5 hours. You can go to bed, just remember it turn it over before you go to bed, then again when you get up!

3 The following day, remove the salmon from the refrigerator and carefully rinse it under cold running water to remove the excess cure, then pat it dry on a clean dish towel. Slice as thinly as you can and put on a plate, spreading the slices attractively. Season with a little pepper and just a tiny touch of sea salt and sprinkle with some of the grapefruit zest and juice and half the cilantro leaves.

4 Finely slice the second fennel bulb on a mandolin or by hand, then toss it in a small bowl with the oil, grapefruit zest and the remaining grapefruit juice and cilantro leaves. Season with a little pepper to taste, then serve with the salmon.

Scallop Soufflé with **Mushroom** and Tarragon Cream

This is one of my favorite recipes to serve to friends. Although the soufflés include egg and cream, don't think for a minute they will be heavy—on the contrary, they are fantastically light. Add the freshness of the tarragon and the earthy mushroom cream and you'll want to make these more than once.

SERVES 4
PREPARATION TIME 30 minutes, plus
  making the stock
COOKING TIME 12 minutes

3½ ounces scallops, rinsed
1 extra-large egg
¾ cup plus 2 tablespoons
  whipping cream
1½ tablespoons unsalted butter
1¾ cups roughly chopped button
  mushrooms
1 tablespoon roughly chopped
  tarragon leaves, plus 4 tiny
  tarragon sprigs
4 tablespoons Vegetable Stock (see
  page 17)
sea salt and freshly ground
  white pepper

1 Remove the roes from the scallops, trim off any tough flesh and remove any veins. Put the scallop, egg and 4 tablespoons of the cream into a blender. Season with salt and white pepper and blend to a very fine, smooth, shiny puree. Pass the scallop mixture through a fine strainer into a bowl. Whip 4 tablespoons of the remaining cream to soft peaks, then into the puree. Spoon the mixture into a disposable pastry bag and chill.

2 Line a plate that fits inside a large steamer basket with parchment paper, then put four 2-inch chef's rings, 2 inches deep, on top, making sure they do not touch each other. Cut out four bands of parchment paper 3 inches long and 2 inches deep and use to line the chef's rings. The paper needs to sit snugly inside the rings with the ends overlapping.

3 Remove the scallop mix from the refrigerator and trim the pastry bag to a ½-inch opening. Pipe the filling into each ring until two-thirds full and about ½ inch below the rim, making sure you hold onto the ring to stop it slipping. Cover the plate loosely with plastic wrap so no condensation can get in, yet the soufflés have space to rise. Bring a large saucepan of water to a simmer, with a steamer insert on top. Put the plate of soufflés in the steamer, cover, then turn the heat down as low as possible and steam 12 minutes, or until risen. Turn the heat off, remove the lid and leave the soufflés to rest 2 minutes.

4 While the soufflés are cooking, make the mushroom cream. Heat a large skillet over high heat. Add the butter and mushrooms and sauté 3 to 4 minutes until they just turn golden brown. Add the chopped tarragon and toss to combine. Add the stock and the remaining cream and bring to a simmer, then season with salt and pepper to taste. Pour into a blender and blend to a fine, light, foamy puree.

5 Divide the mushroom cream into four warm bowls. Remove the plate from the steamer and carefully take off the plastic wrap then, using a small metal spatula, transfer a soufflé to the middle of a bowl of mushroom cream. Slide out the spatula, holding the edge of the ring so it doesn't move around. Lift the ring off and gently peel away the paper lining. Repeat with the remaining soufflés, then top each one with a tiny tarragon sprig to serve.

Langoustine or Shrimp Ceviche

What is ceviche? It is originally a Spanish word, and is a great specialty of Peru, as well as Ecuador and Chile. It is basically raw fish or shellfish marinated in plenty of citrus juice, fresh herbs, onions, shallot and other flavorings. When you use shellfish, make sure they are fresh or freshly frozen—trust your fish merchant, because he or she will have the expertise you need. You'll see that I use garlic here, just enough to bring a little accent to the dish. Enjoy your ceviche served with mango, perhaps, or an avocado, sweet potato and red onion salad with flat-leaf parsley. I use Chardonnay vinegar in many recipes, such as this one, in preference to ordinary white wine vinegar, because it imparts a better flavor, so it is worth buying a bottle.

SERVES 4
PREPARATION TIME 20 minutes, plus 3 hours marinating

20 medium to large raw, shelled langoustines or tiger shrimp, heads removed and deveined
grated zest and juice of 1 lime
1 red chili, seeded and finely chopped
2 garlic cloves, crushed
2 tablespoons Chardonnay vinegar
a pinch sea salt
1 teaspoon chopped tarragon leaves
1 hard, green eating apple, such as Granny Smith
Mayonnaise (see page 18), flavored with chili, tarragon or garlic, to serve

1 Reserve 4 whole langoustines, then cut the rest into ½-inch chunks and put in a nonmetallic bowl. Add the whole langoustines, then add the lime zest and juice, chili, garlic, vinegar and a pinch of salt and gently fold everything together. Cover and leave to marinate in the refrigerator 2 to 3 hours.

2 Just before you are ready to serve, core the apples, then cut them into thin slices, form top to bottom, discarding the ends that are all skin. Stack the slices and cut through them to form thin matchsticks.

3 When ready to serve, remove the bowl from the refrigerator and take out the whole langoustines, then add the tarragon and all but 1 tablespoon of the apple and fold together. Spoon the mixture into four glasses, then hang the whole langoustines on the edge of the glasses. Scatter the remaining apple over the top and serve immediately with mayonnaise flavored with your chosen spice or herb.

Crab Tian with Artichoke and Pepper Confit

Spring is the time for this recipe, when you can get some delicious crab, freshly cooked for you. Or, why not try cooking the crab yourself? If you like, you can also use a little of the brown meat and mix it with the white, which will give the dish more strength and flavor. The red bell peppers need to be roasted, which is very easy, but if you're short of time, just use some from a jar of roasted Spanish piquillo peppers. These ingredients make a brilliant combination with a light mayonnaise with a touch of tarragon for freshness.

SERVES 4
PREPARATION TIME 15 minutes, plus making the mayonnaise and dressing
COOKING TIME 12 minutes, plus 8 minutes cooling

2 small to medium red bell peppers
14 ounces fresh white crab meat
¼ cup whipping cream, lightly whipped
4 tablespoons Mayonnaise (see page 18)
2 teaspoons chopped tarragon leaves
1 teaspoon grainy mustard
grated zest and juice of 1 small lime
10 ounces whole chargrilled artichokes preserved in oil, drained
handful baby arugula leaves
a few drops Tabasco sauce
a few drops Worcestershire sauce
2 tablespoons French Dressing (see page 18)
sea salt and freshly ground black pepper

1 Heat the broiler to high. Put the peppers on a tray under the broiler and broil about 8 minutes, turning them regularly, until they are charred on all sides. Transfer them to a bowl, cover with plastic wrap and leave to cool. When the peppers are nearly cool, remove and discard the skin and seeds, then cut them into quarters.

2 Put the white crabmeat in a bowl with the cream, mayonnaise, tarragon, mustard, lime zest and juice and mix to combine, then season with salt and pepper to taste.

3 Put a piece of the red pepper into the base of individual soup plates. Take a spoonful of the crab mixture and put on top of each piece of red pepper, then top that with a piece of artichoke, then another piece of red pepper, another spoonful of crab, and finally another artichoke. Divide the arugula leaves among the plates. Whisk the Tabasco and Worcestershire sauces into the French dressing, then drizzle over the tops to serve.

Pan-fried Chili Squid with Garlic Mayonnaise

Squid is another of my favorite foods. In Spain, it is served everywhere, mainly as tapas, but also cooked and flavored in many different ways. At The Vineyard we sometimes prepare squid *sous-vide*—sealed in a bag and slowly cooked in a water bath—but I particularly like it this way, too, with the squid coated in spiced bread crumbs and fried until golden brown, then served with the perfect garlic mayonnaise. You can buy panko bread crumbs in Japanese food stores or online if you can't find them in your supermarket. In fact, the name just means "bread crumbs," but they are processed to form flakes rather than fine crumbs, so they tend to give a crispier coating.

SERVES 4
PREPARATION TIME 25 minutes
COOKING TIME 6 minutes

4 squid, about 6 ounces each
2 cups panko bread crumbs
1 teaspoon dried chili flakes
3 eggs, beaten
2 red chilies, seeded and
    finely chopped
¾ cup plus 1 tablespoon
    all-purpose flour
5 tablespoons unsalted butter
2 tablespoons sunflower oil
4 tablespoons very finely chopped
    flat-leaf parsley leaves

FOR THE GARLIC MAYONNAISE
2 egg yolks
1 tablespoon white wine vinegar
1 tablespoon Dijon mustard
⅔ cup sunflower oil
2 garlic cloves, crushed to a paste
grated zest of 1 lime
sea salt and freshly ground black
    pepper

1 Start by preparing the squid. Wash them thoroughly, then pat dry, remove the tentacles and leave to one side, then remove and discard the beaks. Cut the bodies in half lengthwise, then rinse and pat dry again. Cut each body in half lengthwise once more so you have 16 pieces, plus the tentacles. Pat everything dry with paper towels and leave to one side.

2 To make the garlic mayonnaise, put the egg yolks, vinegar and mustard in a bowl and whisk together. Whisking continuously, drizzle in the oil, a little at a time. until the mayonnaise is thick and creamy. Add the crushed garlic and lime zest and season with salt and pepper to taste. Cover and put in the refrigerator until ready to serve.

3 Put the bread crumbs into a food processor with the chili flakes and blitz to a fine powder. Pour the chili powder onto a plate. Break the eggs into a shallow bowl and whisk with the chopped fresh chili. Put the flour on another plate. Pass the squid through the flour, then drop into the chili-flavored egg and finally into the chili-flavored bread crumbs, tossing to coat on all sides.

4 Heat half the butter with the oil in a deep skillet over medium-high heat. When the butter is foaming, add half the squid and pan-fry 2 to 3 minutes, turning once, until golden brown and crunchy. Drain on paper towels, then repeat with the remaining butter and squid.

5 Pile the squid on a large plate, scatter the parsley over the top and put it in the middle of the table with the garlic mayonnaise and let everyone help themselves.

Red Onion Tartes Tatin with Goat Cheese

This is a twist on the classic tarte tatin, not made with fruit, but with onions—deliciously sweet red onions, to be precise—using more or less the same principle and technique. To go with my onion tarts, I have chosen goat cheese, which for me is the perfect partner, and I have also created these as individual tarts, which means they are ideal for serving for a first course or lunch, and make a fantastic dish to serve outdoors, sitting on your patio. My choice of accompaniment is fresh salad leaves, or a pea shoot or herb salad, either of which go well.

SERVES 4
PREPARATION TIME 25 minutes, plus
   30 minutes chilling
COOKING TIME 1 hour

13 ounces bought puff pastry dough,
   thawed if frozen
all-purpose flour, for dusting
1 cup superfine sugar
½ teaspoon lemon juice
4 thyme sprigs
6 red onions, peeled, root trimmed
   to the level of the base and cut
   into quarters
1 egg, lightly beaten
3½ ounces soft goat cheese log,
   such at Ste. Maure, rind removed
1 teaspoon black onion seeds
4 handfuls pea shoots
1 tablespoon extra virgin olive oil
sea salt and freshly ground
   black pepper

1 Roll out the dough on a lightly floured countertop and cut it into 4 circles, each about 8 inches in diameter. Put the circles on a cookie sheet, cover with plastic wrap and chill 25 to 30 minutes to prevent the dough shrinking during baking.

2 Meanwhile, heat the oven to 315°F. Melt the sugar, lemon juice and 5 tablespoons water in a nonstick skillet over low heat. Increase the heat to medium and cook 10 to 12 minutes until it turns into a rich golden brown caramel. Divide into four 6-inch nonstick cake pans or baking dishes. Put a thyme sprig in the middle of each pan, then put the red onion quarters, rounded-side down, into the caramel; there should be 6 quarters in each pan. Bake 20 minutes, then remove from the oven and turn the oven up to 375°F.

3 Take the cookie sheet out of the refrigerator and quickly and carefully put the dough on top of the onions, pushing the edges down into the side of the pans or dishes. Brush the tops with the egg wash. This needs to be done very quickly, or the dough will start to melt if you take too long. Sprinkle a little sea salt over the tops, then put the pans in the oven and bake 20 to 25 minutes until the pastry is golden brown and crisp.

4 Remove the tarts from the oven and leave them to cool for a few minutes. Put an upside-down plate the same size or slightly larger than the tart on top of the first tart and, holding both the plate and pan, flip it over to unmold the tart onto the plate. Crumble the goat cheese over the top of the tart and sprinkle with the black onion seeds. Repeat with the remaining tarts.

5 Toss the pea shoots with the extra virgin olive oil in a small bowl, then season with salt and pepper. Serve the tarts as the cheese just starts to melt, with the pea shoot salad served separately.

Celery Root and Apple Rémoulade with **Crystallized Celery Root Leaves**

What better to have as part of a fresh tray of crudités than a celery root rémoulade—well, perhaps, a rémoulade with freshly cut, crunchy green apple to bring some essential acidity to cut through the richness of the mayonnaise. You'll see what I mean when you try it, because the apple really raises the dish to another level. I have also used the leaves of the celery root, which you might be able to get if you buy your celery root from a farmers' market, but not usually from a supermarket. If you can't get them, just use ordinary celery leaves. They are more tender and a touch less bitter, but will work fine, because they will be sprinkled with superfine sugar before being dried in the oven and becoming crystallized. It is a fun idea that's worth doing if you happen to have some time to hand, and it really finishes the dish beautifully.

SERVES 4

PREPARATION TIME 25 minutes, plus
  making the mayonnaise and
  20 minutes marinating

COOKING TIME 6 to 8 hours

leaves from 1 head celery root
  or celery
1 egg white, lightly whisked
4 tablespoons superfine sugar
1 small celery root, about
  1 pound 2 ounces total
  weight, peeled
1 lemon, halved
grated zest of 1 lime
5 tablespoons Mayonnaise (see
  page 18)
2 tablespoons Dijon mustard
1 tablespoon whipping cream,
  lightly whipped
1 crisp green eating apple, such
  as Granny Smith, cored
sea salt and freshly ground
  black pepper

1 Heat the oven to 150°F, with the fan switched off if that is a feature of your oven. Line a baking sheet with parchment paper.

2 Pick all the leaves from the celery root. Leave to one side 24 to 28 very fine, pale, flat leaves from the middle, then roughly chop the remaining green, slightly firmer leaves. Put the fine leaves in a single layer on the prepared baking sheet, then brush with a little egg white on one side. Sprinkle the sugar lightly over the top of the egg white and put the baking sheet in the oven 6 to 8 hours until the leaves are fully crystallized and dry. Remove them from the oven and leave to one side.

3 Quarter the celery root lengthwise, then rub all over with the cut lemon to stop it from turning brown. Grate the celery root into long strips (you can use a mandolin if you have one, just take care) and put them in a bowl with another squeeze of lemon juice. Add the chopped celery root leaves and lime zest, then add the mayonnaise, mustard and cream and fold together. Cover and leave to marinate in the refrigerator 20 minutes.

4 Just before the rémoulade finishes marinating, cut the apple into thin slices from top to bottom, discarding the end slices that are all skin, then stack the slices and cut through through them to form thin matchsticks.

5 When ready to serve, fold the apple through the celery root mixture. Pile the rémoulade on a plate and carefully put 4 or 5 crystallized leaves on top. Serve immediately while the leaves are crisp.

Leek and Potato Terrine

This recipe needs a bit of care, but I think you will love the result. Just follow the instructions and you'll soon get the technique right. The recipe contains wild mushrooms and I normally use a summer truffle, but they might be difficult to find and are very expensive, so look out for the *trompette*, or horn-of-plenty mushroom, as it's also called, which you can buy dehydrated.

SERVES 6 to 8
PREPARATION TIME 30 minutes, plus making the stock and dressing and 24 hours chilling
COOKING TIME 30 minutes

a little oil, for greasing
4 cups Vegetable Stock (see page 17)
8 baby leeks
3 pounds 5 ounces Idaho potatoes, peeled and cut into 12 pieces
½ ounce dried horn of plenty mushrooms, crumbled
2 leaves gelatin, about ⅛ ounce total weight, soaked in cold water
2 to 5 drops truffle oil
½ to ¾ cup French Dressing (see page 18)
2 tablespoons chopped flat-leaf parsley leaves
sea salt and freshly ground black pepper

1 Lightly oil a terrine mold or 12- x 5- x 3½-inch bread pan, then line with three large sheets of plastic wrap, allowing a long overhang on all sides. Wrap two 2-pound bags of sugar in two layers of plastic wrap, then leave the pan and sugar to one side

2 Bring the stock to a boil in a wide skillet over high heat. Add the leeks, then turn the heat down to low and simmer 4 to 5 minutes until they are just tender. Lift the leeks out of the stock using a slotted spoon, and drain on paper towels. Cut in half lengthwise and leave to dry.

3 Add the potatoes to the stock a few at a time, then return the stock to a boil and simmer 10 to 12 minutes until the potatoes are almost tender; the tip of a knife should just go through with the barest resistance. Lift the potatoes onto paper towels to dry. Simmer the stock until it reduces by half.

4 Put 3 or 4 pieces of potato directly into the bottom of the terrine, making sure the bottom is completely covered. Cover the potatoes with half of the prepared leeks, cut-side down, then sprinkle half of the dried mushrooms over. Repeat with a layer of potatoes, the rest of the leeks, the mushrooms, then a final layer of potatoes.

5 By now the stock should have reduced to about 2 cups. Squeeze out the soaked gelatin and add to the hot stock, whisking until it melts. Season with salt and pepper, then strain through a fine strainer over the terrine so the liquid just covers the potatoes; you don't want it to come up too high up. As you pour, press down lightly on the potatoes so there are not any air pockets. Fold the plastic wrap over the top to cover completely, then put the prepared bags of sugar along the length of the terrine. Leave to cool, then chill in the refrigerator 24 hours until totally set.

6 Turn out the terrine in its plastic-wrap wrapping onto a small tray. Carefully cut into thick slices with a sharp, non-serrated knife, and only then remove and discard the plastic wrap. Add the truffle oil to the French dressing (remember, you only want a few drops of truffle oil, because it is very strong), then stir in the parsley and drizzle over the terrine to serve.

Warm White Asparagus Salad with **Grapefruit Zest Vinaigrette**

In France, we could almost change our national day to White Asparagus Day. Well, almost, but not quite! But when white asparagus comes into season, you will find it on all the tables at home, in restaurants, bistros, brasseries and *auberges*—it will be on every menu for that short season. I love it. It's just superb. Here, I am serving it with white grapefruit and a boiled egg and grapefruit dressing that complements the white asparagus perfectly. If you like, you can also serve it with crusty bread and my Belgian Endive and Radish Salad (see page 19) alongside.

SERVES 4
PREPARATION TIME 25 minutes, plus making the mayonnaise
COOKING TIME 20 minutes

1 egg
2¼ pounds white asparagus, peeled and woody ends discarded
1 white grapefruit
1 tablespoon Dijon mustard
4 teaspoons Mayonnaise (see page 18)
6 tablespoons sunflower oil
1 teaspoon chopped chervil leaves
sea salt and freshly ground black pepper

1 Bring a saucepan of water to a boil over medium heat. Add the egg and return the water to a boil, then turn the heat down to low and simmer 10 minutes. Drain and cool the egg under running cold water, then crack and peel it. Finely chop the egg yolk and white and leave to one side.

2 Divide the asparagus into 4 equal bunches and tie each bunch with kitchen string to secure. Bring a large pan of salted water to a boil over medium heat. Add the bunched asparagus and simmer 5 to 8 minutes, depending on the size of your asparagus, until it is tender but with just a little resistance when pierced with the tip of a knife.

3 Grate the zest from the grapefruit, reserve a pinch and put the rest in a small bowl. Peel the grapefruit, then take out 4 segments and cut each segment in half and leave to one side. Juice the rest of the grapefruit, pressing it through a fine strainer into the bowl with the zest. Add the mustard and mayonnaise and whisk together until well blended, then whisk in the sunflower oil in a steady stream. Stir in the chopped egg and chervil and season with salt and pepper to taste.

4 Remove the asparagus from the pan and drain quickly on paper towels or a clean dish towel. Remove the string and put the asparagus onto serving plates. Spoon the dressing over the top and finish with the reserved grapefruit segments and a sprinkling of the reserved zest.

SMOKING FOOD

I am a big fan of smoked foods, particularly meat, as I just love those smoky flavors. Although smoking was developed as a way of preserving food, I think it is more about the wonderful flavors it creates. Originally—going back to ancient times—people used to hang their kill to dry in their caves. Since there was no way out for the smoke from the fire, they noticed that both the flavor and the preserving qualities were improved by the smoke … and so it began!

Since then, smoking foods, usually over wood smoke, has become popular in many regions of the world and has developed commercially. In particular, smokehouses were built on farms to preserve meat—well away from the farm buildings to avoid fire spreading if an accident happened—and on the coasts, to be handy for the fishermen landing their catch.

The first commercial smoker here in the UK was set up in Scotland in 1939. Much later, when I worked in Scotland, there was a small smokehouse just down the road from us, which I used to drive past every day. Those memories will stay with me for ever, as I can still vividly recall the delightful smell of the burning wood.

Where I come from in Franche-Comté, smoking foods has always been a specialty and the technique is still very much alive today. On market day, I often used to go shopping with my mom or my sister, Dolores. They were both very good cooks—although that goes without saying in my family, as we are all enthusiastic gourmands. Anyway, you will see throughout this book, I like to use products from my home area, and one of those is Morteau, a delicious smoked sausage. We often bought this from the market, along with smoked pork shoulder (Boston butt), bacon or neck. To serve with it, Mom used to make sauerkraut with turnip instead of cabbage. That day was one day we all looked forward to.

At The Vineyard

We serve some smoked dishes in my restaurant. My friend, John, has supplied our smoked salmon, haddock and mackerel for the past twenty years and, trust me, he is very good at smoking! I also love to use other smoked ingredients, like smoked paprika and, of course, Morteau sausage. But we also do some smoking ourselves; my particular favorites are smoked beets, which have a wonderful earthy flavor, to serve as a side dish or as part of a salad, and smoked duck, a meat that seems perfect to prepare in this way.

Foods for smoking

All kinds of poultry and meat can be smoked, creating a range of products from spiced pastrami to smoked bacon. Smoked fish ranges from cod or haddock to salmon, herring or mackerel. Tofu and cheeses absorb fabulous flavors in the smoker, as do nuts, vegetables like peppers and beets and fruit like prunes, which are often smoked while drying. Teas, such as lapsang souchong, and even some Scotch whiskies are smoked. It is important to remember, though, there are various methods of smoking and not all act as a preservative.

Hot and cold smoking

Whatever their size, smokers create heat and smoke by burning wood chips or sawdust, or they might have gas burners. Here in the UK, where I am cooking, oak or alder are the woods of choice in most smokehouses, as well as beech and fruit-tree woods, such as apple. In the USA, corncobs are popular, while in New Zealand, they like to burn the wood from the manuka tree. Some smokers also have steam coils to create humidity and maintain the correct temperature, which is obviously crucial or the results will be dry and flavorless.

Hot smoking uses both smoke and heat in a wood-fired oven, a smoke-roaster or even a barbecue. The temperature reaches 125° to 176°F so, at the higher temperatures, the food is cooked as well as absorbing the smoky flavors.

Cold smoking does not cook the food, because the temperature of 62° to 68°F only imparts the wood-smoke flavor, so many cold-smoked foods are cured in brine first. For our smoked recipes, I'm using a method based on a Chinese technique known as tea smoking, because a combination of rice, tea and sugar is used to create the smoke. We'll then cook our smoke-flavored foods afterward. (I decided that the Icelandic tradition of smoking fish over dried sheep's dung was perhaps not one to try at home!)

How it's done

I hope you will try this method. You can buy smokers in packaged sets and there is a vast range of different wood chips available online for you to try. I recommend, however, you use my tea-smoking option first, because you can simply adapt your steamer or wok.

Just one reminder. Do be careful of the heat and smoke, especially when disposing of the smoking ingredients—they'll stay hot for a while even after you take them off the heat. Please do not burn yourself.

- You need a steamer with a lid, or a wok with a lid and a metal rack, and some aluminum foil.
- Your smoking mixture is ½ cup basmati rice, 2 tablespoons green tea and 2 teaspoons sugar.
- Prepare the food as if cooking it conventionally, so trimmed, pitted, left whole or sliced or whatever is necessary.
- Put a large piece of aluminum foil, shiny-side down, in the bottom of a steamer or wok. Put the rice, tea and sugar on the foil, cover with a steamer insert or a wire rack, then put on the lid. Put over medium heat about 5 minutes until the mixture starts smoking.

- Quickly lift the lid and put the food onto the rack. Put the lid back on, turn the heat down to low and smoke for the time recommended in the recipe; that's usually about 5 minutes for chicken or duck pieces.
- Lift out the food and put it on a plate to rest.
- Wrap the smoking ingredients in the foil and discard them carefully. Again, take care not to burn yourself.

Leave the food to cool, or continue cooking it, following the recipe instructions, then savor those stunning flavors. Try smoking a cod fillet following the method below, or try Smoked Duck and Lentils with Lavender (see page 154) or Smoked Chicken, Zucchini, Garlic and Rosemary Casserole (see page 174).

Fennel-smoked Cod with Warm Bean Salad

When you smoke fish with herbs, such as fennel, the subtle scent permeates the fish to complement the lovely smoky flavor. Try this simple cod recipe.

Add a pinch of dried fennel to the smoking mixture (left) in the foil-lined wok, then put 2 very fresh pieces of cod, in the smoker, skin-side down, and season with salt and pepper, cover the wok and smoke 5 minutes. Remove the cod from the smoker and brush the skin with a little olive oil. Heat a skillet over medium heat, then pan-fry the cod, skin-side down, about 5 minutes until the skin is crisp and golden brown. Flip it on the other side and cook 2 minutes longer to finish it off. Cool and discard the smoking ingredients.

The perfect accompiment is a warm white bean salad. Gently warm 1½ cups cooked white beans in a pan with 1 or 2 diced oven-dried tomatoes and a chopped garlic clove. Take the pan off the heat and stir in 2 teaspoons chopped parsley leaves, drizzle with extra virgin olive oil and top with your smoked cod fillet to serve. You should be in paradise! Can I join you for dinner?

Smoked Chicken, Zucchini, Garlic and **Rosemary** Casserole

A steamer works perfectly as a smoker, so, if you have one, do give this recipe a try. You put the smoking mix in the bottom and the chicken in the top, but be sure to keep the heat low—you don't want your kitchen smoke alarm to go off, so take it easy and don't get too excited! The green tea will bring a subtle flavor to the chicken, which will, in turn, infuse the zucchini. It's almost as if you'd grilled the zucchini, with the wonderful, smoky scent.

SERVES 4
PREPARATION TIME 10 minutes, plus making the stock
COOKING TIME 50 minutes

½ cup basmati rice
2 tablespoons green tea
2 teaspoons sugar
4 chicken legs, thighs and drumsticks separated
1 tablespoon unsalted butter
2 tablespoons sunflower oil
2 tablespoons olive oil
1½ cups zucchini cut in half lengthwise and then cut into 1-inch pieces
12 garlic cloves, unpeeled
4 tablespoons sherry vinegar
2 cups Chicken Stock (see page 16)
1 rosemary sprig
1 teaspoon chopped rosemary leaves
sea salt and freshly ground black pepper

1 Put a large piece of aluminum foil, shiny-side down, in the bottom of a steamer, then put the rice, tea and sugar on the foil. Cover with a steamer insert and lid and put over medium heat about 5 minutes until the mixture starts smoking. Quickly lift the lid and put all the chicken inside. Put the lid back on, turn the heat down to low and smoke 5 minutes. Lift out the chicken and put on a plate to rest, wrapping the smoking ingredients in the foil and discarding them as quickly as you can.

2 Season the chicken with salt and pepper. Melt the butter with the sunflower oil in a Dutch oven over medium-high heat. When the butter is foaming, add the chicken, skin-side down, and cook 6 to 8 minutes, turning the pieces occasionally, until they are golden brown all over. Transfer them to a bowl, cover with plastic wrap and leave to rest.

3 Discard the oil from the pot and lightly wipe the excess away with paper towels, taking care not to disturb the sediment. Return the pot to medium-low heat, add the olive oil, zucchini and garlic and cook gently 4 to 5 minutes until colored but only just tender.

4 Move the zucchini to the side of the pot, then and put the chicken pieces in the middle to reheat. Turn the heat up to medium and when you can actually hear the food starting to cook, add the sherry vinegar straightaway; it should evaporate immediately. Quickly pour the stock over the top and throw in the rosemary sprig. When the stock comes to a simmer, gently wriggle the pot around a little so nothing is stuck to the bottom, then put the lid on top without closing it completely—you just want a little gap so condensation doesn't create too much liquid, but not so large that all the liquid evaporates. Cook 15 minutes.

5 Remove the lid and discard the rosemary. Turn the heat to high and cook 5 minutes longer, stirring to remove any caramelized bits stuck to the bottom, or until the sauce is shiny and just thick enough to coat the back of the spoon. Add the chopped rosemary and season with salt and pepper to taste, then serve hot. Guests can squeeze the garlic out of the skins into the dish.

Poached Chicken with **Lemon Zest** and **Black Olives**

Here I have modernized a classic *poulet au pot,* bringing in Mediterranean flavors with olives and lemon. You would normally serve the bouillon first as a soup, then the garnish—the vegetables— with the chicken as the main course. But here I have taken some of the liquid and reduced it to a sauce, then added olives, thyme and lemon zest, which makes it very refreshing. Try both and see which one you prefer; that would make a really interesting comparison. Let me know what you decide.

SERVES 4
PREPARATION TIME 30 minutes
COOKING TIME 1½ hours

1 chicken, about 3 pounds 5 ounces
4 carrots, peeled
4 small turnips, peeled
4 small new potatoes, such
  as Charlotte, scrubbed
4 baby leeks
1 thyme sprig
⅔ cup whipping cream
1 large handful of pitted ripe olives
grated zest and juice of 1 lemon
1 tablespoon thyme leaves
1 tablespoon extra virgin olive oil

1 Tie the chicken legs together at the top of the cavity with a piece of kitchen string. Put the chicken in a large Dutch oven, cover with cold water and bring to a boil. When the water starts to simmer, skim off any foam that rises to the surface; this helps to keep the soup nice and clear.

2 Add the carrots and cook over very low heat 15 minutes, just keeping the water simmering. Add the turnips and cook 15 minutes, then the potatoes and cook 15 minutes. Finally add the leeks and thyme sprig and cook 15 minutes longer, by which time the chicken will have simmered 1 hour in total and should be cooked through, so the juices run clear when the thickest part is pierced with the tip of a sharp knife, and the vegetables all perfectly tender.

3 Remove the pot from the heat and ladle 1¼ cups of the cooking liquid straight into a sauté pan. Put over low heat, add ½ cup of the cream, bring to a simmer and simmer 10 to 12 minutes until the liquid reduces by half.

4 Whip the remaining cream in a small bowl, Add it to the sauce, return to a simmer and then remove the pan from the heat. The sauce should just be thick enough to coat the back of a spoon. Add the olives, lemon zest and a squeeze of lemon juice, then taste before adding any more lemon juice; it should just be slightly lemony, but not acidic. Add the thyme leaves and stir through.

5 Lift the chicken and potatoes out of the broth (you can use the broth and remaining vegetables to make a soup). Discard the string, cut the chicken into 4 portions and put straight onto a serving plate. Crush the potatoes with a little extra virgin olive oil and serve alongside, then spoon the sauce over the top.

Steamed Cabbage with **Pork** and **Hazelnut Stuffing** and **Creamy Mustard Sauce**

SERVES 4

PREPARATION TIME 25 minutes, plus making the stock

COOKING TIME 1 hour 20 minutes

1 large Savoy cabbage, 3 outer leaves discarded and root trimmed so it sits flat
1 tablespoon sunflower oil
1 pound 2 ounces boneless Boston butt, cut into small dice
1 small onion, chopped
2 small carrots, peeled and diced
6 garlic cloves, finely chopped
2 ounces thinly sliced pancetta, cut into julienne strips
⅔ cup Chicken Stock (see page 16)
3 ounces ground pork
2 ounces pig liver, finely chopped
1 egg
2 tablespoons fresh bread crumbs
2 tablespoons blanched hazelnuts, toasted and chopped
2 tablespoons chopped flat-leaf parsley
sea salt and freshly ground black pepper

FOR THE CREAMY MUSTARD SAUCE
2 tablespoons unsalted butter
2 tablespoons sunflower oil
1 shallot, finely chopped
5 tablespoons dry white wine
7 tablespooons Chicken Stock (see page 16)
5 tablespoons light cream
1 teaspoon wholegrain mustard
1 tarragon sprig

Sadly, cabbage is often overcooked, resulting in a virtually flavorlesss vegetable. I aim to rectify that sad situation with this throughly modern steamed cabbage recipe. I have used Boston butt, moister and tastier than lean cuts like tenderloin, which can be dry.

1 Cut off the top one-third of the cabbage, like a lid, and leave to one side. Gently pull out the leaves so you can get to the middle, without breaking them off. Use an ice cream scoop to scoop out most of the inner leaves, leaving an outer casing about ¾ inch thick. (Use the inner leaves for another dish or serve them sautéed with a little butter.)

2 Heat a large skillet over high heat. Add the oil and diced pork and sauté 4 to 5 minutes until it is golden brown, then transfer to a bowl. Add the onion, carrots, garlic and pancetta to the pan and sauté 4 to 5 minutes until the onion is just soft. Add the stock and deglaze the pan by stirring to remove any caramelized bits stuck to the bottom. Cook 5 to 8 minutes until it reduces by two-thirds and is syrupy. Mix with the pork.

3 In a separate bowl, put the ground pork, liver, egg, bread crumbs, hazelnuts and parsley, season with salt and pepper and mix well. Mix this into the now slightly cool pork and vegetable mixture.

4 Put two sheets of plastic wrap, about 20 inches long, on top of each other, then put another two sheets across the middle, giving you a cross shape. Put the hollowed-out cabbage in the middle, then gently open it out and fill it with the pork mixture. Set the lid back on top and then tightly wrap in the plastic wrap. Secure each end with a knot, pushing out any air.

5 Bring a large saucepan of water to a simmer, with a steamer insert on top. Put the cabbage in the steamer, cover and cook 50 minutes, or until the liquid runs clear when you pierce the pork through the plastic wrap with a knife. Turn off the heat and leave to rest in the pan 10 minutes.

6 Meanwhile, to make the sauce, melt the butter with the oil a nonstick skillet over medium heat. When it is foaming, add the shallot and cook 3 to 4 minutes, stirring occasionally, until golden brown. Add the wine, turn the heat up to high and cook until it reduces by half. Add the stock and continue cooking until it reduces by half again, then turn the heat down to low, bring to a simmer and slowly stir in the cream and mustard. Add the tarragon and season with salt and pepper to taste.

7 Lift out the cabbage, discard the plastic wrap and cut the cabbage into quarters. Serve with the creamy mustard sauce.

Casserole of Lamb and Pomegranate Molasses

I think this is my favorite casserole in this book. I like to use lamb shoulder, because it has excellent flavor, it's moist and there is just the perfect amount of fat needed for it to be tasty—ask a butcher to trim down the fat if there is too much. I'm pairing it with pomegranate molasses, which is a reduction of pomegranate juice that's taken right down to a thick, syrupy liquid. It's slightly tangy with a delicate sweet-and-sour accent. Just imagine the aromas in your kitchen when this casserole has been cooking for a couple of hours. Your guests will be wondering and asking questions. Make them wait a little longer, however, until they taste the casserole, when all will be revealed. Then you can tell them that the secret ingredient fraternizing with the lamb is pomegranate molasses, which lifts this humble, inexpensive cut to new heights.

SERVES 4
PREPARATION TIME 10 minutes
COOKING TIME 2½ hours

1 tablespoon unsalted butter
2 tablespoons sunflower oil
1 onion, roughly chopped
2 garlic cloves, roughly chopped
2¼ pounds boneless shoulder
   or neck of lamb, cut into
   large cubes
2 cups Lamb Stock or Chicken Stock
   (see page 16)
1 rosemary sprig
1 handful good-quality pitted
   ripe olives
2 tablespoons pomegranate
   molasses
grated zest of 1 lemon
sea salt and freshly ground
   black pepper
Creamed Mashed Potatoes (see
   page 20), to serve

1 Melt the butter with the oil in a Dutch oven over medium heat. When the butter is foaming, add the onion and garlic, reduce the heat to low and cook 5 to 8 minutes until the onion is slightly soft and translucent, but not colored.

2 Turn the heat up to high. Add the lamb and sauté 12 to 15 minutes until brown on all sides. Add the stock and rosemary and bring to a simmer, then cover with the lid without closing it completely—you just want a little gap so the condensation does not produce too much liquid—and simmer over very low heat 1¾ hours, making sure the liquid is just shimmering but not bubbling.

3 Check that the lamb is very tender and the liquid has reduced by about half, but no more. If not, continue cooking 15 minutes longer and check again. Add the olives and pomegranate molasses and cook 10 minutes longer, or until the sauce is shiny. Add the lemon zest and season with salt and pepper to taste. Serve with deliciously creamy mashed potato.

Slow-roasted Shoulder of Lamb with Garlic, Basil and Ginger

You might ask why I have included another recipe for lamb shoulder in this book. Firstly, because it's delicious, which should go without saying. And because, along with the neck and the belly, it is the tastiest cut—flavorsome, moist and succulent. These are the cuts we use in the restaurant. You can keep the shoulder on the bone if you want, because this is slowly roasted the bone will come out very easily at the end. Here, I have used basil, garlic and also ginger, the latter being slightly more unusual with lamb, but it adds an exotic touch that goes really well. Also, the Chardonnay vinegar brings a welcome sweet acidity. Just make sure you brown the lamb well first, then reduce the heat and follow the timings basting directions closely to slowly roast the lamb to perfection.

SERVES 4 to 6
PREPARATION TIME 10 minutes
COOKING TIME 3 hours 40 minutes

2¾ pounds shoulder of lamb, either bone-in or boned and tied if boned, at room temperature
1 tablespoon sea salt
3 tablespoons olive oil
4 large basil leaves
8 garlic cloves
2-inch piece gingerroot, peeled and chopped
2 banana shallots
¾ cup plus 2 tablespoons Chardonnay vinegar
3⅓ cups Lamb Stock (see page 16)
2 tomatoes, quartered
a few small rosemary sprigs
freshly ground black pepper
fried eggplant and zucchini slices, to serve

1 Heat the oven to 425°F. Season the lamb with the salt and plenty of black pepper, massaging the seasoning into the lamb really well. Put it in a deep, flameproof roasting pan, drizzle with the oil and roast 25 to 30 minutes, turning the roast once or twice, until brown all over.

2 Add 2 of the basil leaves, the garlic, ginger and shallots to the pan and return it to the oven 5 minutes. Remove the pan from the oven again and put over low heat. Add the vinegar, which should evaporate more or less immediately, and deglaze the pan by stirring to remove any caramelized bits stuck to the bottom. Add the stock and tomatoes and stir to combine everything, then cover with aluminum foil, leaving one edge open to let the steam escape.

3 Turn the oven down to 275°F. Return the lamb to the oven and roast 30 minutes. Remove the foil, baste the lamb and cover again. Repeat after 30 minutes, then remove the foil and cook 2 hours longer, basting every 30 minutes. The lamb should be very tender, almost falling apart.

4 Remove the pan from the oven, then pour the juices through a strainer into a sauté pan. Put over medium-high heat and cook 5 to 8 minutes, stirring continuously, until the sauce is thick enough to coat the back of a spoon. Chop the remaining basil leaves and add to the sauce, then season with salt and pepper to taste.

5 Carve the lamb, spoon the sauce over and top with the rosemary sprigs. Serve with fried eggplant and zucchini slices.

Slow-roasted Beef Ribeye Roast with **Carrot** and **Horseradish Puree**

This is a wonderful way of eating beef, and roasting it in a really low oven is an excellent way to get that melting texture. I like to serve this with a carrot puree, but with a really gorgeous twist—a little freshly grated horseradish. Make sure that you use a good blender so the puree is very smooth. Just drizzle a beef or red wine sauce on it and it's perfection.

SERVES 4
PREPARATION TIME 20 minutes, plus making the stock
COOKING TIME 2½ hours

1¾ pounds beef ribeye roast, trimmed and tied, bone reserved
1 tablespoon sunflower oil
1 carrot, peeled and chopped
1 onion, chopped
2 garlic cloves, chopped
2 thyme sprigs
¾ cup plus 2 tablespoons dry red wine
1¾ cups Beef Stock (see page 16)
sea salt and freshly ground black pepper

FOR THE CARROT PUREE
5 tablespoons unsalted butter
1 shallot, chopped
2¼ pounds carrots, peeled and roughly chopped
¾ cup plus 2 tablespoons whole milk
¾ cup plus 2 tablespoons heavy cream
2 tablespoons finely grated horseradish

1 Heat the oven to 200°F. Season the beef with salt and pepper. Heat a large skillet over medium-high heat. Add the oil and beef and roast 10 to 12 minutes, turning until it is a golden brown on all sides and taking care not to burn it on any side. Put the carrot, onion, garlic, thyme and reserved beef bone in a flameproof roasting pan and put the sealed beef on top. Cover loosely with aluminum foil, then roast 1½ to 2 hours. Check with a meat thermometer that the temperature in the middle of the beef is 131° to 140°F, which will give you medium-rare to medium. If you don't have a thermometer, insert the tip of a sharp knife into the meat, then carefully touch it on the inside of your wrist; it should be medium hot.

2 To prepare the carrot puree, melt half the butter in a saucepan over medium-low heat. Add the shallot and carrots and cook 10 to 12 minutes until they are just tender and the edges are soft, but not coloring. Add the milk, cream and horseradish and bring to a slow simmer, then cover with plastic wrap tightly so no air escapes, turn the heat down as low as it will go and cook 1½ hours. The carrots will be overcooked and create a delicious confit. Check occasionally and add 2 tablespoons water, if necessary.

3 Use a slotted spoon to put the carrots into a blender, then blitz to a fine puree, adding half the cooking liquid as you go to make a light, shiny puree. Add the remaining butter and blitz again to incorporate, then season with salt and pepper to taste.

4 Transfer the beef to a large plate, cover with aluminum foil and leave to rest in a warm place. Put the roasting pan over medium heat and stir until the juices start to bubble. Add the red wine and deglaze the pan by stirring to remove any caramelized bits stuck to the bottom. Simmer until there is barely any liquid left. Add the stock and bring to a boil, stirring up any sediment, then turn the heat down to low and simmer 8 to 10 minutes until it reduces by half and is shiny and thicker.

5 Remove the string from the beef, then cut it into slices. Spoon the sauce over the beef and serve with the carrot puree, putting any spare sauce into a bowl to serve at the table.

Fennel-roasted Porgy with Fennel Salsa

I have used porgy and fennel more than once in my demonstrations, although in very different ways, because these two ingredients work so well together. It always surprises me so few people cook with them. People tell me they find fennel's aniseed flavor too strong, or they don't know how to prepare fennel or don't normally use this particular fish. That's a shame, because porgy is very much underrated—it is tasty, sustainable and very affordable, and one is often enough for two people. So, try this delicious, refreshing recipe. It will show you just how light and pleasant this combination can be.

SERVES 4
PREPARATION TIME 20 minutes
COOKING TIME 20 minutes

4 fennel bulbs, as long as possible
2 tablespoons unsalted butter
1 tablespoon olive oil
2 porgy, about 1¾ pounds each,
  gills removed, scaled and gutted
1 small red onion, finely chopped
1 tablespoon chopped cilantro leaves
½ tablespoon chopped dill leaves
grated zest and juice of 1 lemon
1 tablespoon honey
3 tablespoons extra virgin olive oil
1 tablespoon white balsamic vinegar
sea salt and freshly ground
  black pepper

1 Heat the oven to 400°F and line a baking dish with aluminum foil. Cut the top one-third off the fennel bulbs and put them in the prepared dish. Peel off the first 2 layers of the remaining fennel bulbs and chop the layers roughly, then add them to the dish.

2 Melt the butter with the olive oil in a large, nonstick skillet over medium-high heat. When the butter is foaming, add the fish and fry 3 to 4 minutes on each side until the skin is light golden brown and slightly crisp. (A little tip—if you're not too sure how nonstick your pan is, cut a sheet of parchment paper to fit the bottom of the pan and put it into the hot pan before you add the butter and oil, then cook the fish. The paper will prevent the fish sticking, but it will not be hot enough to catch fire.) Season the fish with salt and pepper, then put it on top of the fennel in the baking dish. Spoon the cooking juices from the skillet over the top of the fish, then roast 12 minutes.

3 Meanwhile, to make the fennel salsa, thinly slice the remaining fennel hearts, using a mandolin if you have one. Put the slices in a large bowl, add the remaining ingredients and season with salt and pepper to taste, then toss together to combine.

4 By now, the fish should be ready—insert a knife into the flesh and it should slice through without any resistance. Remove the dish from the oven and leave to rest in a warm place 2 minutes. Serve the fish from the baking dish, with the salsa, allowing people to help themselves. The top fillet will lift off the bone very easily. Next, lift off and discard the whole bone from the tail end upward, revealing the succulent fillet on the other side.

Curry-spiced Cod and Mango Packages with Coconut and Chervil Sauce

I love cod, and I am always improvising new ways to cook it. My wife, Claire, always sneaks into the kitchen when I cook cod at home—it's the wonderful smells wafting through the house that attracts her. Cooking it *en papillote* is one of my favourite methods; it's fun, fresh, fast and delicious. Here, I give the recipe a modern twist with Asian ingredients. Even if you like strong spices, stick to a mild curry powder, or the cod will be overpowered and the balance of the dish will be lost. Ginger, red onion and Chardonnay vinegar set the right tone for the mango—flavorsome, but not too sweet. Then all that's left to do is to make a light, creamy sauce with coconut milk and herbs.

SERVES 4
PREPARATION TIME 15 minutes
COOKING TIME 30 minutes

4 cod loins, about 5 ounces each, skin on
1 teaspoon light soft brown sugar
2 tablespoons Chardonnay vinegar
1 small red onion, thinly sliced
1 firm mango, peeled, seeded and roughly chopped
1-inch piece gingerroot, peeled and grated
1 small red chili, halved, seeded and cut into julienne strips
1 teaspoon mild curry powder
1 tablespoon unsalted butter
1 tablespoon olive oil
¼ cup Fish Stock (see page 17)
¼ cup coconut milk
¾ cup plus 2 tablespoons whipping cream, lightly whipped
1 tablespoon chopped chervil leaves
1 teaspoon lemon juice
sea salt and freshly ground black pepper

1 Heat the oven to 400°F and cut out four 18- x 10-inch rectangles of parchment paper. The fish should have been pin boned but, if not, remove all small bones with a pair of fish tweezers.

2 Heat a small skillet until medium-hot. Add the sugar and Chardonnay vinegar and cook 1 to 2 minutes until the sugar dissolves. Add the onion and sauté 3 to 4 minutes, then reduce the heat to low, add the mango and ginger and cook about 8 minutes until the mango is soft, but still holding its shape. Add the chili and stir gently to combine, then remove from the heat and leave to cool.

3 Season the cod on both sides with curry powder, salt and pepper. Melt the butter with the oil in a nonstick skillet over medium-high heat. When the butter is foaming, add the cod, skin-side down, and sauté 3 to 4 minutes until the skin is golden brown and crisp.

4 Put the parchment paper rectangles on the countertop, then spoon the mango equally onto half of each sheet. Put the cod on top, skin-side up. Fold the paper over the filling and then fold along the edges to seal the liquid in securely. Put the packages in a baking sheet and bake 12 minutes. Remove from the oven and leave to rest 2 minutes.

5 While the fish cooks, make the sauce. Heat a sauté pan over medium heat. Add the stock and coconut milk and bring to a boil, then turn the heat down to low and simmer 4 to 5 minutes until they reduce by half.

6 Carefully open one side of each package and pour the juices into the sauce, then put the packages on serving plates. Whisk the cream into the sauce and return it to a boil, then remove from the heat and season with salt and pepper. Add the chervil and finish with the lemon juice. Serve the packages *en papillote* at the table with the sauce served separately, or open the packages, slide out the filling and spoon the sauce on top.

Pancetta-wrapped Monkfish with Carrot and Mandarin Puree

I can't stress often enough you will really taste the difference if you buy your fish fresh from a fish merchant. It is that simple with fish. Remember, too, how delicate the flesh is, so don't overcook fish; monkfish is a meaty fish and, therefore, dries out quickly. The pancetta needs to be very thinly sliced and, if possible, a touch longer than normal so you can overlap the slices when wrapping the fish.

SERVES 4
PREPARATION TIME 20 minutes
COOKING TIME 1 hour 20 minutes

4 monkfish fillets, about 5 ounces
   each, trimmed
20 thin slices pancetta
1½ cups peeled and thickly
   sliced carrots
1 cup plus 2 tablespoons freshly
   squeezed mandarin juice
1 lemongrass stalk, bruised
grated zest of 1 lime
2 tablespoons olive oil
2 tablespoons unsalted butter
a few cilantro leaves
sea salt and freshly ground
   black pepper

1 Season the monkfish with pepper, then wrap each fillet in the sliced pancetta until they are totally covered. Lay two sheets of plastic wrap on top of each other, then put a monkfish fillet at one edge. Tightly wrap in the plastic wrap to make a thick sausage shape. Twist and secure each end with a knot, pushing out any air. Repeat with each piece of monkfish. Put in the refrigerator while you prepare the carrots.

2 Bring a large saucepan of water to a simmer, with a steamer insert on top. Put the carrots in the steamer, cover and cook at least 1 hour until super soft.

3 While the carrots are steaming, put the mandarin juice in a small saucepan over medium heat. Add the lemongrass and half the lime zest and bring to a slow boil. Turn the heat down to low and simmer about 15 minutes until the liquid reduces by two-thirds and is syrupy. Remove the pan from the heat and keep the juice warm.

4 Remove the carrots from the steamer and pat dry with a clean dish towel. Put them in a blender, then strain in the reduced mandarin juice, discarding the lemongrass, and blend to a smooth, soft puree. Season with salt and pepper to taste, then leave to one side to keep warm.

5 Now put the monkfish in the steamer, cover and cook over very low heat 8 to 10 minutes. Remove from the steamer, then cut away and discard the plastic wrap. Put the monkfish onto a clean dish towel to absorb any of the liquid released while cooking.

6 Heat half the oil in a sauté pan over medium heat. Add the monkfish and cook 3 to 4 minutes until the pancetta is crisp and golden brown on all sides. Remove the fish from the pan and leave to rest on paper towels.

7 Gently reheat the puree until hot, then whisk in the butter and season with salt and pepper to taste. Cut each piece of monkfish in half on the diagonal—if it's cooked properly, you will see a tiny rainbow on the flesh of the fish. Sprinkle the monkfish with the cilantro, the remaining lime zest and oil, then serve warm with the puree.

Lemongrass-skewered Shrimp with **Sauce Vièrge**

I guess by now you have noticed that I really like Asian ingredients, perhaps because of my time in Singapore and traveling through Malaysia and the Far East. Using lemongrass as the skewer means it imparts its superb fragrance to the shrimp, so choose fresh green stalks. The sauce vièrge finishes the dish beautifully, so make sure you cook plenty as everyone will be asking for more!

SERVES 4
PREPARATION TIME 15 minutes
COOKING TIME 25 minutes

48 jumbo, raw shelled shrimp
12 lemongrass stalks
1-inch piece gingerroot, peeled
  and grated
5 tablespoons unsalted butter
½ cup olive oil
sea salt and freshly ground
  black pepper
Thai-style Pilaf Rice (see page 21),
  to serve

FOR THE SAUCE VIÈRGE
½ cup extra virgin olive oil
1 tomato, peeled, seeded and diced
1 teaspoon lightly crushed coriander
  seeds
grated zest and juice of 1 lemon
2 tablespoons chopped cilantro
  leaves

1 Heat the oven to 275°F and line a baking sheet with aluminum foil. Make a small hole through the middle of each shrimp with a sharp knife, then thread 4 shrimp onto each lemongrass stalk as a skewer. Sprinkle with the ginger, then season with salt and pepper.

2 Melt 1 tablespoon of the butter with 2 tablespoons of the oil in a large, nonstick skillet over medium-high heat. When the butter is foaming, add 3 skewers and fry 2 to 3 minutes on each side until the shrimp are just cooked through and lightly colored. You will be able to see the shrimp change color to pink as they cook. Transfer them to the prepared baking sheet and put it in the oven, but leave the oven door open—you just want to keep them warm, not for them to cook any more. Repeat with the remaining skewers, butter and olive oil.

3 While the last batch is cooking, make the *sauce vièrge*. Put the extra virgin olive oil, the tomato, coriander seeds, lemon zest and juice in a small saucepan over low heat and season with salt and pepper. Warm through very gently 2 minutes, stirring occasionally—you don't want the oil to actually get hot. Remove the pan from the heat, add the cilantro leaves, then stir to combine.

4 Simply serve the skewers with the sauce drizzled over the top, with an Asian-style steamed rice of your choice. I like to serve the skewers with Thai-style Pilaf Rice.

Crushed Pea and Mint Tortellini with Pea Shoot Salad

Not only is the pea a universally popular vegetable, it's also my wife and my son's favourite—although, botanically speaking, a pea is actually a fruit! Sometimes I serve this fresh-tasting pea coulis and tortellini on flameproof serving dishes and pop them under a hot broiler 1 to 2 minutes just until the cheese starts to melt. The salad is optional, but I like the combination.

SERVES 4
PREPARATION TIME 40 minutes, plus 60 minutes resting
COOKING TIME 15 minutes

FOR THE PASTA
2⅓ cups plus 1 tablespoon pasta flour
1 egg
1 egg yolk
1 tablespoon olive oil

FOR THE TORTELLINI
4 tablespoons unsalted butter
2 cups fresh podded peas (or use thawed peas if there are not any really fresh ones around)
1 tablespoon chopped mint leaves
semolina flour, for dusting
3½ ounces soft goat cheese log, such as Ste. Maure, rind removed
sea salt and freshly ground black pepper

FOR THE PEA SHOOT SALAD
large handful pea shoots
1 tablespoon olive oil
1 tablespoon pumpkin seeds

1 Blitz the pasta ingredients in a food processor until small granules form, then tip out onto a countertop and gather together quickly to form a firm dough. Wrap in plastic wrap and chill 30 to 60 minutes.

2 To make the filling, pour 3½ tablespoons water into a saucepan over medium heat. Add the butter, season with salt and pepper and bring to a boil. Add the peas and cook 4 to 8 minutes for fresh, 2 to 3 minutes for frozen, or until just tender. Taste one and it should be sweet but with the merest hint of a crunch. Using a slotted spoon, lift the peas out of the water and put 1⅓ cups in a bowl. Crush them lightly with a fork and season with salt and pepper to taste, then fold in the mint. The mixture should be really moist. Cover with plastic wrap and leave to one side.

3 To make a pea coulis, put the remaining peas in a food processor and blitz until very smooth, then add a little of the cooking liquid and blitz until it is thick enough to coat the back of a spoon. Pass the mixture through a fine strainer into pasta bowls, cover and leave to one side.

4 Lightly dust the countertop and a baking sheet with semolina flour. Roll out the pasta dough until ½ inch thick, then cut into 2 rectangles big enough to fit through your pasta machine. Roll through the machine, decreasing the thickness gauge each time, until it reaches the thinnest setting possible, dusting with semolina flour to prevent it sticking. Cut out twenty 3-inch circles of dough. Put a teaspoon of crushed peas onto each circle, just below the middle. Brush the edge of the pasta lightly with water, then fold the top half over the filling and press the edges to seal. Pick up the pasta crescent and twist the edges together, forming a lip on the outside edge, then put the tortellini on the prepared baking tray.

5 To make the salad, toss the pea shoots, oil and pumpkin seeds in a small bowl, then season with salt and pepper to taste.

6 Bring a large pan of salted water to a boil. Add the tortellini and cook 4 to 5 minutes until the pasta floats to the top of the pan. Drain the tortellini, then spoon on top of the coulis on serving plates. Crumble the cheese over the top, and finish with a little of the salad to serve.

Spring Vegetables with **Watercress** Dressing

I am not a vegetarian, but I do eat a lot of vegetarian dishes, especially in the spring and summer, when I really like like the colors, taste and freshness of them. The only downside is I am often left wanting more, so I like to make generous portions. That's what you'll find with these spring vegetables complemented with a modern watercress dressing and some perfectly poached quail eggs.

SERVES 4
PREPARATION TIME 20 minutes,
  plus making the dressing
COOKING TIME 50 minutes

2 bunches watercress, main
  stems discarded
1 cup French Dressing (see
  page 18)
4 ounces Chantenay or other young
  carrots, scrubbed
3 ounces baby leeks, trimmed
3 ounces baby turnips, trimmed
3 ounces baby zucchini
3 ounces baby corn cobs
2 small bunches thin, young
  asparagus, trimmed and cut in half
1½ cups thin, young green beans
  cut in half
3 ounces baby new potatoes,
  scrubbed
1 bunch scallions, white part only,
  green part kept for another dish
6 ounces baby chargrilled artichokes
  in olive oil, drained
16 quail eggs
2 teaspoons white wine vinegar
sea salt and freshly ground
  black pepper

1 Put 2 small handfuls of watercress leaves to one side. Bring a small saucepan of salted water to a boil. Add the remaining watercress and blanch 30 seconds. Drain and refresh the leaves in ice water, then drain again quickly so there's still water on the leaves. Put them into a spice grinder or small blender and blitz to a fine puree. Pass the puree through a fine strainer, pressing down into the strainer to release as much juice as possible; there should be about 6 tablespoons juice. Whisk the juice into the French dressing, season with salt and pepper and leave to one side.

2 Bring a large saucepan of salted water to a boil. Add the carrots and blanch 2 to 5 minutes until they are just tender. Use a slotted spoon to lift them out of the pan, then drain and refresh in ice water, drain again and tip carefully into a bowl. One at a time, blanch all the other vegetables, except the artichokes, in the same way in the same water, then transfer them to a bowl. Keep the saucepan of water for reheating when you are ready to serve.

3 Bring another small saucepan of salted water to a boil. Add the vinegar and then crack the eggs into the water and return it to just above a simmer—you want the water to be bubbling so the eggs don't stick to the bottom of the pan. Simmer 2 minutes, then lift out the eggs and cool them in a bowl of ice water. Drain them on paper towels, then season with salt and pepper.

4 Return the saucepan of vegetable water to a boil. Add all the vegetables, including the artichokes, and cook 2 minutes, or until they are hot. Lift them out of the pan using a slotted spoon and put on paper towels to drain. Add the quail eggs to the pan of water and heat through 15 to 20 seconds until hot, then drain and pat dry.

5 Drizzle the vegetables with the watercress dressing, and top with the quail eggs, then serve with a scattering of watercress leaves.

Zucchini Stuffed with **Camargue Rice** and **Melted Cheese**

My mom often used to make stuffed vegetables to use up leftover food, as when I was growing up, life was hard and food could not be wasted. But actually, we really liked it and sometimes the mix was fantastic—potatoes, tomatoes, eggplants, all with different fillings, lined up on a tray. I remember as though it were yesterday how delicious they were served with a freshly made tomato coulis tossed with fresh herbs. You can try different cheeses, such as a sharp farmhouse Comté or Gruyère, which are readily available, or try a Tomme de Savoie, which you should find at a good delicatessen.

SERVES 4
PREPARATION TIME 20 minutes, plus making the stock and coulis
COOKING TIME 50 minutes

4 large zucchini, trimmed
4 tablespoons olive oil
1 large onion, finely chopped
1 small bouquet garni, made with 1 thyme sprig and 1 parsley sprig, tied together with kitchen string
¾ cup Camargue rice or mixed white and wild rice
1¼ cups Vegetable Stock (see page 17)
7 tablespooons unsalted butter, chopped
1 recipe quantity Tomato Coulis (see page 21)
2 ounces semisoft sheep's milk cheese, such as Ossau Iraty, rind removed, grated
sea salt and freshly ground black pepper

1 Heat the oven to 300°F. Bring a saucepan of water on to simmer, with a steamer insert on top large enough to hold all the zucchini. Carefully cut a strip of the smallest amount lengthwise down each one, so they will sit flat on the countertop, then cut lengthwise again, taking off the top one-third to use later as a lid. Use a teaspoon to scoop out the inside of each zucchini, taking care not to make a hole in the bottoms or break the sides, then leave the zucchini to one side. If the scooped-out flesh don't have too many seeds, chop it to use in the rice stuffing.

2 Put the lids back on the zucchini and tightly wrap each one in plastic wrap. Twist and secure each end with a knot, pushing out any air, to keep the lid in place. Steam 12 to 15 minutes. Turn off the heat, remove the steamer lid and leave the zucchini to rest while you make the rice.

3 Heat an ovenproof skillet over medium heat. Add the oil, onion, chopped zucchini, if using, and the bouquet garni and fry 5 minutes until just soft. Turn the heat down to low and gently fold in the the rice, then fry 3 to 4 minutes. Add the stock, bring to a simmer and season with salt and pepper. Dot the butter over the top of the rice, then cover with a lid or a *cartouche* (see page 218) and put in the oven 25 minutes. Check to see if the rice is tender and the liquid has all been absorbed. If the rice is not quite tender, re-cover and return the pan to the oven 5 minutes, then check once more.

4 Meanwhile, heat the broiler. Run a fork through the rice, discard the bouquet garni and and adjust the salt and pepper to taste. Remove the zucchini from the plastic wrap and turn hollow-side down on a clean dish towel to drain. Turn them the right way up in a baking dish and season with salt and pepper. Fill with the rice, pressing down lightly, then put a large spoonful of tomato coulis on top of the rice and sprinkle with the cheese. Put the dish under the broiler 2 to 3 minutes until the cheese melts. Top with the lids and serve with extra tomato coulis.

Caramelized Pineapple and Rum with Vanilla and Szechuan Peppercorns

This is such a lovely dessert, full of an exotic mix of flavors. The pineapple is caramelized with rum—just imagine the aromas rising from the pan. There's also the delicate vanilla flavor and, to finish, the dry-roasted Szechuan pepper, my favorite of all the spices, with its slightly lemony overtones. Only the husks are used, because the seed is discarded. You will find it used a lot in traditional Chinese cuisine, and here I use it to enhance the dish and raise the pineapple to new heights.

SERVES 4
PREPARATION TIME 15 minutes
COOKING TIME 25 minutes

1 large pineapple, peeled, cored, quartered lengthwise and halved widthwise
1 cup light soft brown sugar
2 small vanilla beans, cut in half widthwise, then lengthwise and seeds scraped out, beans reserved
1¼ cups dark rum
3 tablespoons unsalted butter
¼ cup golden raisins
½ teaspoon Szechuan peppercorns, lightly toasted and gently crushed (see page 69)
1 red chili, seeded and finely chopped
coconut ice cream, coconut cake or Pistachio Madeleines (see page 75), to serve

1 Roll the pineapple pieces in the brown sugar to coat all sides. Add the vanilla seeds to the rum and mix well.

2 Melt the butter in a large, nonstick skillet over medium heat. Add the pineapple and cook a few minutes on each side. Add the vanilla beans and cook 8 to 10 minutes longer until the pineapple is golden brown. Add 7 tablespoons of the rum and the golden raisins, turn the heat down to low and leave for a few minutes to reduce, basting the pineapple continuously, until the mixture just forms a light syrup and starts to caramelize. Repeat this three more times, adding one-quarter of the remaining rum each time.

3 Add the the last of the rum with the Szechuan peppercorns and repeat basting one final until you have a lovely thick, light caramel-brown syrup that coats the pineapple. Finally, add the chilli and baste a few more times to fully coat the pineapple. Serve with coconut ice cream, coconut cake or madeleines.

Caramelized Apricots, Pistachios and Peach Sauce

If there is a season I wait for with impatience, it is spring. Why? Well, one of the reasons is the start of the apricot season. I love this fruit so much. When they are very fresh and ripe, they smell like fresh girolles—sweet, with a hint of dry leaf scent and a touch of flower blossom—and are simply gorgeous! So imagine what they are like when pan-fried and then served with crushed pistachios and a lemony peach syrup. You know what, I think I should stop talking about them now—let's just make and enjoy them! By the way, fruit always cook best when it has either been brought back to room temperature before cooking or has been stored at room temperature. Never cook fruit straight from the refrigerator, as the shock of the heat will often make the fruit split or stick to the pan.

SERVES 4
PREPARATION TIME 10 minutes
COOKING TIME 25 minutes

½ cup superfine sugar
2 large, ripe peaches, pits removed and roughly chopped
juice of 1 lemon
1 tablespoon chopped pistachios
2 tablespoons honey
8 large, firm apricots, halved and pits removed
2½ tablespoons unsalted butter
Pain de Gênes (see page 146), to serve

1 Heat a nonstick skillet over medium heat. Add the sugar and 1¼ cups water and heat until the sugar dissolves and the liquid just starts to simmer. Add the peaches and lemon juice, return the water to a simmer and poach the peaches 8 to 10 minutes until very soft and almost pureed, but still holding a little shape. Strain them through a strainer, catching the syrup in a clean bowl, then leave the bowl and strainer to one side so the juices can drip into the syrup.

2 Put the pan you've just used for the peaches back over medium heat. Add the pistachios and cook gently a few minutes until they are golden and slightly sticky. Drain them on a clean dish towel, then fold the towel over and gently crush the nuts using a rolling pin until they are just partially crushed.

3 Put the same skillet back onto the heat again. Add the honey and when it is just foaming, add the apricots, cut-side down, and instantly start gently swirling the pan around so the apricots don't stick or burn. Add the butter and when it is foaming, turn the apricots over and cook a few minutes until they are nicely caramelized. Add about ½ cup of the syrupy peach juices and cook 3 to 4 minutes longer until the apricots are lovely and tender, but are still holding their shape.

4 Spoon the apricots over the peaches and drizzle with the last of the peach syrup. Sprinkle with the crushed pistachio pieces and serve with *pain de gênes*.

Cinnamon and Honey-baked Figs with Sweet Ginger Slices

When I lived in the Algarve, in Portugal, I used to eat figs all the time, because it is such a favourable climate, the *figier* grew everywhere. As a result of a particularly bad drive on the golf course one day, I found myself off the fairway surrounded by fig trees loaded with fruit ... so ripe, so good, that I ate one fig, then another and another until I completely forgot the game! Meanwhile, my friend, still totally intent on the game, marched ahead. That shows you how much I like figs. The best ones for me are the purple-black ones, with their succulent flavor that is perfect in this gratin. The spiced crisp cake is just what you need to complement the dish, while the smooth yogurt with honey—well, imagine how good that is.

SERVES 4
PREPARATION TIME 10 minutes, plus freezing
COOKING TIME 40 minutes

3½-inch piece ginger cake, or other spice cake, frozen until almost hard
12 firm purple-black figs, cut into quarters from top to bottom but not all the way through, so the figs are held together
2 tablespoons honey
½ teaspoon ground cinnamon
5 tablespoons plain Greek yogurt
2 egg yolks

1 Cut the cake into 8 thin slices. Freezing the cake until it is almost hard makes it easier to slice thinly and also gives a much better crisp finish. Heat the oven 275°F, line a baking sheet with parchment paper and have another sheet of parchment paper and a second baking sheet ready.

2 Put the cake slices on the prepared baking sheet, cover with the second sheet of paper, then the second baking sheet so the slices are held flat, then bake 6 to 8 minutes. Carefully lift off the top sheet and paper, checking the cake is not too colored, then put the first baking sheet back in the oven 3 to 4 minutes longer so the slices dry out. Remove from the oven and leave the cake slices to cool. Turn the oven up to 350°F.

3 Put the figs in a baking sheet, cut-side up, drizzle the honey and 4 tablespoons water over and sprinkle with 2 pinches of the cinnamon. Bake 12 to 15 minutes until they are soft; there will be lovely liquid left in the baking sheet. Pour half the liquid into a large, heatproof bowl and leave to one side. Pour the remaining half into a serving bowl with the yogurt and mix well. Heat the broiler to medium.

4 Add the egg yolks to the juices in the heatproof bowl and mix together. Rest the bowl over a saucepan of gently simmering water, making sure the bottom of the bottom of the bowl does not touch the water. Beat the mixture 8 to 10 minutes, using an electric mixer, until it turns pale, becomes thicker and forms ribbonlike shapes when you lift the whisks out of the mixture. Spoon straight over the figs, then put the baking sheet under the broiler a few minutes until they are just brown. You don't want it too close to the broiler, or to leave it too long, just until it is light golden brown.

5 Sprinkle the yogurt with the remaining cinnamon. Serve the figs hot with the spiced crisp slices to dip into the yogurt.

Pan-fried Plums and **Almond Biscotti** with **Amaretto Cream**

Pan-fried plums are always flavorsome, with their touch of acidity and appealing, delicate texture, so I thought a cookie would be good with these— and a biscotti seemed just the right choice. It's unusual, perhaps not often baked at home, and the almonds give it a good nutty crunch. For a change, try serving the fruit with silky Greek-style yogurt with a sprinkling of cinnamon.

SERVES 4
PREPARATION TIME 30 minutes
COOKING TIME 40 minutes

FOR THE ALMOND BISCOTTI
7 tablespoons unsalted butter, soft
⅓ cup sugar
3 eggs
½ vanilla bean, halved lengthwise
   and seeds scraped out
2 cups all-purpose flour, plus extra
   for dusting
grated zest of ½ lemon
a pinch ground star anise
¼ cup very fnely ground blanched
   almonds
½ teaspoon baking powder
4 tablespoons whole blanched
   almonds, toasted
a pinch of salt

FOR THE PLUMS
½ cup sugar
10 plums at room temperature,
   halved and pitted, then each cut
   into 8 segments
1 tablespoon amaretto

FOR THE AMARETTO CREAM
¼ cup confectioner's sugar
1 egg
½ cup mascarpone,
   at room temperature
½ cup double cream
2 tablespoons amaretto

1 Heat the oven to 350°F and line a cookie sheet with parchment paper. To make the biscotti, beat together the butter and sugar, using an electric mixer, until very pale and fluffy. Add 2 of the eggs, one at a time, beating in between each addition, then add all the vanilla seeds and all the remaining biscotti ingredients, except the remaining egg and the salt. Continue to mix on slow speed until the dough just comes together. Scoop the dough onto a lightly floured countertop and form into a log about 8 inches long and 3 inches wide. Using the palms of your hands, roll the log until it is 1 inch thick, then put it on the prepared baking sheet; it should just fit.

2 Whisk the remaining egg with the salt and 1 tablespoon water. Brush this mixture over the top of the loaf, then bake 8 minutes. Turn the baking sheet around, front to back, turn the oven down to 300°F and bake 20 to 25 minutes longer until pale golden.

3 Meanwhile, to cook the plums, put a skillet over low heat. Add the sugar and cook slowly a few minutes until it turns to a light golden caramel. Add the plums, a few pieces at a time, mix them into the caramel and cook 5 minutes, or until they are soft. Drizzle the amaretto over and stir gently. Leave the plums to cool to room temperature.

4 To make the amaretto cream, whisk the confectioner's sugar and egg in a large bowl until very light and pale. Mix the mascarpone and cream in a separate bowl, then whisk in the amaretto. Whisk the mixtures together until smooth, silky and very soft but just holding soft peaks.

5 Remove the biscotti from the oven, transfer to a cutting board and cut off both ends of the loaf, then cut the rest into ½-inch slices. Put them flat on the cookie sheet and bake 5 to 8 minutes longer until they are just dry and a light golden color. Crumble the cut-off ends of the biscotti into ¼-inch pieces in a small bowl.

6 Sprinkle half the plums with the crumble and half the amaretto cream, then spoon some more plums on top and finish with the rest of the amaretto cream. Balance a biscotti on top and serve the rest separately.

Apple, Raspberry and **Thyme Puffs**

Depending on whether I had time to pop into the local bakery, I used to eat these *chaussons*—literally "slippers"—on the way to or from school, but we used to make them at home, too. You might call these apple turnovers—the idea is the same, but I make them in a slightly different way. The puff pastry gives them a beautifully warm, buttery crunch just before you reach the fruit, full of sweet acidity. There should be more fruit than pastry, so make sure the mix is not too runny or they can be tricky to close. And, I can assure you apple, raspberry and freshly picked thyme leaves are fabulous together!

SERVES 6
PREPARATION TIME 30 minutes, plus cooling
COOKING TIME 15 minutes

5 tablespoons sugar
4 large cooking apples, peeled, halved, cored and roughly chopped
a little all-purpose flour, for dusting
1 pound 10 ounces rolled all-butter puff pastry dough, thawed if frozen, cut into 12 fluted 3-inch circles
1 egg
a pinch salt
1 cup fresh raspberries
leaves from 1 thyme sprig

1 Heat a large, nonstick skillet over medium heat. Add the sugar, all the apples and 2 tablespoons water, cover and cook gently 8 to 10 minutes until the apples are cooked but not completely pureed. Remove the lid, then turn the heat up slightly so the liquid just starts to evaporate. Keep moving the apple around the pan with a spatula to help drive off the moisture and dry out the apple until you have a dry puree. Transfer the puree to a bowl and leave to cool completely. (The puree must be dry and cold before you start to make your *chaussons*, otherwise the dough will just melt and collapse.)

2 Heat the oven to 350°F and line a cookie sheet with parchment paper. Dust a countertop with a very little flour, then lay a dough circle on the dusted surface and roll with a rolling pin just once to the top and the bottom; you want the circle to become elongated into a slight oval shape. Repeat with the remaining circles. Lay all the ovals vertically out in front of you on the countertop. Mix the egg and salt with 1 tablespoon water in a small bowl to make an egg wash.

3 Put a spoonful of apple puree on the bottom one-third of a dough oval, ¾ inch from the side. Put 4 raspberries on top of the purée and a little sprinkle of the thyme, then brush the egg wash around the bottom edge of the oval—nothing so far has come above the halfway mark. Fold the top half of the pastry over to cover the filling, then gently press the edges together to seal. Brush the top of the dough with the egg wash, taking care not to get any on the back of the folded pastry, which would run down and make the pastry stick to the cookie sheet. Using a spatula, carefully lift each one onto the prepared cookie sheet. Use the back of a fork to make a crisscross pattern on top.

4 Bake 12 minutes, or until the pastry is golden brown. If not, return them to the oven 2 to 3 minutes longer. Remove from the oven and serve warm with a cup of coffee or Earl Grey tea.

Cherry and **Almond Cream Tartlets**

Kirsch was originally made from Morello cherries, grown in the Black Forest, in Germany, although it is now made from many varieties of cherry. Where I come from in eastern France, kirsch is a specialty of a town called Fougerolles. It is a clear fruit brandy made with a double-distillation of whole cherries, hence the slight taste of bitter almond. That hint of bitterness is just what we are looking for in this tart, for which we are using almonds, cherries, of course, and a lovely sabayon made with this beautiful *eaux de vie*. On top of the nutty crunchiness of the pastry, all these elements are from the same note—the almond! This dessert is best enjoyed warm as it releases all those wonderful flavors. But when I finished I thought something was missing, and it was a spoonful of creamy vanilla or almond ice cream!

SERVES 8
PREPARATION TIME 40 minutes, plus
  50 minutes chilling
COOKING TIME 20 minutes

FOR THE SWEET PASTRY DOUGH
grated zest of ½ blood orange
6 tablespoons unsalted butter, soft,
  plus extra for greasing (optional)
a pinch salt
½ cup plus 2 teaspoons
  confectioner's sugar
¼ cup very finely ground
  blanched almonds
1 egg
1⅓ cups plus 1 tablespoon
  all-purpose flour

FOR THE ALMOND CREAM
7 tablespoons unsalted butter, soft
½ cup plus 1 tablespoon
  confectioner's sugar
¾ cup ground blanched almonds
3 eggs
1 tablespoon kirsch

FOR THE TOPPING
1½ cups cherries, pitted and halved
  or quartered, depending on size
⅓ cup slivered almonds

Real Vanilla Ice Cream (see page
  23), to serve

1 To make the dough, beat the orange zest, butter, salt, sugar, ground almonds and egg in a bowl until light and fluffy. Sift in the flour and fold through just until the dough forms, then stop! You don't want to work this dough at all. Wrap it in plastic wrap and chill 20 minutes.

2 Grease eight 3½-inch loose-bottomed individual tartlet pans, about 1½ inches deep, with a little butter if they are not nonstick. Roll the dough between two sheets of wax paper until it is ⅛ inch thick, then cut out eight circles, each about 7 inches in diameter. One at a time, roll each pastry circle over the rolling pin and lift over a tartlet pan. With one hand, lift the dough edge and with the other, gently tuck the dough into the bottom and side of the pan so it fits tightly. Don't overstretch the dough or it'll break; just gently push out any bubbles. Trim off any excess dough by rolling the pin over the top edge of the pan. Prick the bottoms with a fork and chill 30 minutes to prevent the dough shrinking during baking.

3 Heat the oven to 315°F. To make the almond cream, beat together the butter, sugar and ground almonds in a large bowl, using an electric mixer, or in a food mixer, until light and fluffy. Add the eggs one at a time so the mixture doesn't split. Add the kirsch, then mix 8 to 10 minutes until very light and smooth. Divide the mixture into the dough cases, taking care to leave a good ½ inch clear from the top of the dough. Cover the mixture with the cherry pieces (if you really feel like it, you can arrange them perfectly, but random is fine!) and sprinkle slivered almonds on top of each. Place the tartlet pans on a cookie sheet.

4 Bake 20 minutes, or until a skewer inserted through the deepest part comes out clean. If not, return the tartlets it to the oven 3 to 5 minutes longer and check again. Serve warm with vanilla ice cream.

Earl Grey Rice Pudding with Blackberry Marmalade

Most of my childhood memories are great, except for rice pudding. My mom used to make it so often I did not want to eat it any more for a long time. But this recipe somehow brings it back to life. In the restaurant, we use carnaroli rice, which I think it is the perfect grain for it—strong enough, nutty enough, too. So cook the pudding very gently with all the other ingredients and it will taste delicious, but take note that I said gently. It must be cooked that way otherwise the grain will explode and the mixture burn if you have the heat too high. Then, of course, the lovely blackberry marmalade is perfect drizzled over the top to finish the dish.

SERVES 4
PREPARATION TIME 5 minutes
COOKING TIME 40 minutes

FOR THE BLACKBERRY MARMALADE
1⅔ cups blackberries
¼ cup plus 1 tablespoon sugar

FOR THE RICE PUDDING
½ cup carnaroli risotto rice
2 cups whole milk
¾ cup plus 2 tablespoons whipping cream
4 Earl Grey teabags
2 tablespoons sugar, or to taste

1 Start by making the blackberry marmalade. Put the blackberries and sugar in a nonstick skillet or sauté pan over low heat and cook 30 to 40 minutes, depending on how soft the berries are, stirring occasionally, until there is not any juice left and the blackberries are fully cooked. You want the blackberries to release their juices as they cook so don't be tempted to increase the heat. Eventually, they will dehydrate and turn into a marmalade.

2 Meanwhile, make the rice pudding. Put the rice, milk, cream and teabags in a saucepan, stir once to make sure all the rice is dispersed through the liquid, then bring to a boil. Turn the heat down to low and simmer 18 minutes, or until the rice is tender. You shouldn't need to stir, but just check a couple of times.

3 Remove the pan from the heat. There should be a little liquid left in the pan. Remove the teabags and squeeze them over the saucepan so the liquid goes into the rice, but be careful not to tear the teabags. Only then do you add the sugar and fold it delicately into the cooked rice, adding a little more to taste. Keep turning the rice very gently about 5 minutes to cool it down.

4 Serve the rice topped with a spoonful of the fresh blackberry marmalade.

Rosemary-infused Crêpes Suzette with Pink Grapefruit and Rosemary Syrup

Created in the late nineteenth century, both the name and origin of this dish are disputed, although everyone does agree a girl called Suzette was involved! In my new twist on this classic, we will make a syrup with grapefruit juice infused with rosemary, and you will see how different and delicious it is.

SERVES 4
PREPARATION TIME 20 minutes, plus 45 minutes infusing
COOKING TIME 25 minutes

FOR THE CRÊPES
1¼ cups milk
2 rosemary sprigs
1 cup all-purpose flour
2 tablespoons sugar
a pinch salt
2 eggs
2 tablespoons unsalted butter, melted, plus extra for frying (optional)

FOR THE SYRUP
½ cup sugar
7 tablespoons unsalted butter
grated zest of 1 and juice of 2 pink grapefruit (⅔ cup juice)
leaves from 1 small rosemary sprig, finely chopped

1 To begin the crepes, bring the milk to a boil in a saucepan over medium heat. Add the rosemary sprigs, then remove the pan from the heat, cover with plastic wrap and leave to infuse 45 minutes, or until just cool. Discard the rosemary.

2 While the milk infuses, make the syrup in a skillet over low heat. Add the sugar and cook slowly for a few minutes until it turns to a light golden caramel, then add the butter. When it is foaming, add the grapefruit zest and juice, mix well and bring to a simmer. Cook about 3 minutes until it forms a syrup, then remove the pan from the heat, toss in the chopped rosemary and leave to infuse in a warm place.

3 To finish the crepes, put the flour, sugar, salt, eggs and ½ cup of the rosemary-infused milk in a bowl. Add the melted butter and beat, using an electric mixer, until smooth, then whisk in the remaining milk until smooth, runny and lump-free. Adding the milk gradually means there is not any need to rest the batter before cooking.

4 Heat a 6- to 7-inch nonstick crepe pan or skillet over medium heat. If you use a nonstick pan, you won't have to add butter, although it does make flipping easier if you do. If you are not using a nonstick pan, add a little butter first to keep the crepe from sticking.

5 Using a ladle, pour enough batter into the pan to cover the bottom thinly, swirling the pan around to spread the batter, then cook 1 to 1½ minutes until the underside is golden. Now comes the fun part: try to flip it over, or turn it with a metal spatula. Cook 1 to 2 minutes longer until the other side is golden brown. Remove the crepe from the pan and keep it warm, then repeat with the remaining batter, adding more butter to the pan if necessary.

6 Fold the warm crepes in half one at a time, then pick them up with tongs and dip them into the syrup, swirling them around to make sure the crepe is coated, then fold over into quarters and serve immediately. Repeat with the remaining crepes and syrup. If you're really lucky the last one will be for you!

Gluten-free Chocolate and Ginger Fondant

Chocolate fondant is often served in restaurants in many different ways with many different flavors or spices added to it or infused into it. The main idea, however, is always the same—when the fondant is baked and turned out, the warm chocolate in the middle must find its way out, running slowly like lava coming down the slope of a volcano. That is a must, but there is also not any compromising when it comes to the chocolate you are using. It must be good quality, not too sweet, not too bitter, and it must be dark, not semisweet. In this recipe I've scented the chocolate with ginger, which I love. If that is not to your taste, try it with star anise, cinnamon, cardamom or even Szechuan pepper. Whatever the spice, however, you just want a hint of it, so use it sparingly.

SERVES 4
PREPARATION TIME 25 minutes, plus 30 minutes resting
COOKING TIME 8 minutes

7 tablespoons unsalted butter, plus extra for greasing
a little good-quality, unsweetened dark cocoa powder, for dusting
3½ ounces dark chocolate, 70% cocoa solids, broken into pieces
3 eggs
4 tablespoons sugar
4 tablespoons cornstem
1 ball preserved ginger, finely chopped
Chili Crème Anglaise (see page 23), to serve

1 Butter four 3½-ounce ramekins or ovenproof molds and dust with cocoa powder. Put the chocolate and butter in a heatproof bowl and rest it over a pan of simmering water, making sure the bottom of the bowl does not touch the water. Heat, stirring occasionally, until the chocolate melts. (Alternatively, melt very gently in short bursts in the microwave, stirring regularly.) Remove the pan from the heat and leave to one side.

2 Beat together the eggs and sugar, using an electric mixer, for at least 15 minutes until they are almost white in color, very shiny and almost forming soft peaks. This will give a really light, crusty outside to the fondant, with a meltingly soft inside. Pour the melted chocolate and butter into the batter and beat to combine. Sift the cornstarch over the top and fold it in, then finally fold in the preserved ginger, taking care not to overmix the batter at this point. Divide the batter into the prepared ramekins, filling them only three-quarters full. Put them on a cookie sheet in a cool place and leave to rest 30 minutes.

3 Heat the oven to 425°F. Bake the chocolate fondants 5 to 6 minutes until the fondant rises above the rim of the ramekins and forms a light crust on top and around the edges. Remove the cookie sheet from the oven and turn out the fondants straight onto serving plates. Serve immediately with chili crème anglaise.

Chocolate, Chili and **Lemongrass Tart**

Infused with lemongrass and chili and made with the finest cocoa, this superb chocolate tart has a rich texture, a silky silhouette and a wonderfully crisp pastry, a combination bound to make you happy. I almost decided not to give any of the details away, but this is was just too good to keep to myself!

SERVES 4 to 6
PREPARATION TIME 15 minutes, plus 50 minutes chilling and 1½ hours setting
COOKING TIME 15 minutes

FOR THE CHOCOLATE PIECRUST DOUGH
⅔ cup plus 1 tablespoon all-purpose flour
1 tablespoon unsweetened dark cocoa powder
4 tablespoons unsalted butter, softened, plus extra for greasing (optional)
¼ cup confectioner's sugar
a pinch salt
1 extra-large egg yolk

FOR THE CHOCOLATE FILLING
1 cup plus 2 tablespoons whipping cream
1 large really fresh lemongrass stalk, cut in half lengthwise and bruised
2 small red chilies, seeded and roughly chopped
7 ounces dark chocolate, 70% cocoa solids, roughly chopped
1½ tablespoons unsalted butter, soft

Orange, Cardamom and Thyme Salad (see page 214), made with ordinary oranges, to serve

1 To make the chocolate piecrust dough, sift the flour and cocoa powder into a bowl. In a separate bowl, beat together the butter, sugar, salt and egg yolk until light and fluffy. Sift in the flour mixture and fold it through gently until it just begins to form a dough, then stop! You don't want to work this dough at all. Wrap it in plastic wrap and chill 20 minutes.

2 Grease a 7-inch nonstick, loose-bottomed tart pan with a little butter, if necessary. Roll out the dough between two sheets of wax paper until it is ⅛ inch thick. Roll the dough over the rolling pin and lift it over the tart pan. With one hand, lift the dough edge and with the other, gently tuck the dough into the bottom and side of the pan so it fits tightly. Don't overstretch it or it will break, and press down gently to push out any bubbles. Trim off any excess dough by rolling the pin over the top edge of the pan. Prick the bottom with a fork and chill 25 to 30 minutes to prevent the dough shrinking during baking.

3 Meanwhile to make the filling, put the cream in a saucepan over medium heat and bring just to a simmer. Remove the pan from the heat, add the lemongrass and chili, cover with plastic wrap and leave in a warm place to infuse 30 minutes.

4 Toward the end of the chilling and infusing time, heat the oven to 350°F. Line the tart case with parchment paper and cover with baking beans. Bake 6 minutes, then remove the paper and baking beans, turn the oven down to 315°F and bake 3 to 4 minutes longer until the pastry is baked through and light brown.

5 Put the chocolate and butter in a heatproof bowl over a saucepan of simmering water, making sure the bottom of the bowl does not touch the water. Heat, stirring, until the chocolate melts. Remove the plastic wrap from the cream and strain to discard the lemongrass and chilies. Pour the cream slowly into the chocolate mix, whisking all the time until you have a soft, shiny, chocolate ribbon. Pour it into the pastry case and leave to one side in a cool place 1½ hours, or until just set. Do not put it in the refrigerator, because this will take the shine off the chocolate. Serve sliced with the orange salad.

Raspberry Tart with **Crème Pâtissière** and **Rosemary**

SERVES 4
PREPARATION TIME 25 minutes,
   plus 20 minutes infusing
COOKING TIME 30 minutes

36 raspberries (about 2⅓ cups)
confectioner's sugar, to decorate
grated zest of ½ lime
1 teaspoon chopped rosemary
   leaves
2 tablespoons crème fraîche

FOR THE SABLÉ PASTRY DOUGH

⅔ cup plus 1 tablespoon
   all-purpose flour
1 teaspoon baking powder
½ cup plus 2 teaspoons
   confectioner's sugar
4 tablespoons unsalted butter, soft
a pinch salt
2 egg yolks
grated zest of ½ lime

FOR THE CRÈME PÂTISSIÈRE

1 cup plus 2 tablesooons whole milk
½ vanilla bean, split lengthwise
3 egg yolks
¼ cup sugar
¼ cup cornstarch
1 tablespoon unsalted butter
juice of ½ lime

I have included a few recipes with raspberries in this chapter, and with herbs too, but I can assure you they are totally different. Here, for example, the touch of grated lime, the crème fraîche and rosemary bring a unique balance to the dessert with its crunchy Breton *sablé* crust.

1 Heat the oven to 325°C. To make the *sablé* pastry dough, sift together the flour and baking powder in a bowl. Beat together the sugar, butter, salt and egg yolks, using an electric mixer, until light and fluffy. Fold in the flour mixture and lime zest to make a soft dough. Flatten the dough between two sheets of wax paper to about ½ inch thick, then transfer to a cookie sheet, lifting off the top sheet of paper. Bake 12 to 18 minutes until it is light golden brown. Remove the cookie sheet from the oven and cut the pastry immediately into a 7-inch square while it is still pliable, but then leave it to cool completely before lifting it off the cookie sheet.

2 To make the crème pâtissière, put the milk in a saucepan over low heat. Use a sharp knife to scrape the vanilla seeds into the milk, then whisk the milk and add the vanilla bean as well. Heat the milk until it is almost simmering, then remove the pan from the heat, cover with plastic wrap and leave the milk to infuse about 20 minutes. Remove the vanilla bean from the milk, rinse and dry on paper towels, as you can use it again.

3 Meanwhile, whisk the egg yolks and sugar until light, thick and creamy. Gradually add the cornstarch, a spoonful at a time, whisking well after each addition to avoid any lumps forming. Slowly pour half the infused milk into the egg mixture, whisking as you pour, then transfer the mixture back to the pan with the remaining milk. Put over medium-low heat and stir continuously and quickly 10 minutes, or until the mixture begins to thicken. Remove the pan from the heat, whisk in the butter and lime juice and continue whisking until the mixture cools down and is smooth, thick and slightly trembling.

4 Spread the crème pâtissière about ¼ inch thick over the pastry, leaving a small margin clear around the edges. Arrange the raspberries in rows over the top of the crème pâtissière to cover it completely. Dust with a little sifted confectioner's sugar and sprinkle with the lime zest and a little of the chopped rosemary. Mix the remaining rosemary with the crème fraîche and spoon into a pastry bag, then pipe a small dot of crème fraîche on top of every other raspberry all over the tart. Add a small piece of rosemary to each crème fraîche dot, then it's ready to serve,

Thyme-infused Chocolate Pots

I love the subtle hint of thyme in this rich chocolate dessert. It adds an elegant and unexpected touch that should surprise your guests. Serving the chocolate with a crisp cookie provides a welcome contrast.

SERVES 8
PREPARATION TIME 15 minutes, plus
    10 minutes infusing and
    3 hours chilling
COOKING TIME 1 hour

1 cup plus 2 tablespoons whole milk
1 cup 2 tablespoons whipping cream
1 thyme sprig
5 tablespoons honey
4 egg yolks
9 ounces dark chocolate, 70% cocoa
    solids, roughly chopped
Almond Biscotti (see page 200),
    Pain de Gênes (see page 146)
    or Pistachio Madeleines (see page
    75), to serve

1 Heat the oven to 300°F and line a deep baking dish with parchment paper to direct the bubbles away from the chocolate pots, making the cooking process more gentle so the custard doesn't curdle. Have ready eight ⅔-cup ovenproof glasses or pots. Bring the milk and cream to a simmer in a small saucepan over medium heat. Remove the pan from the heat, add the thyme, cover with plastic wrap and leave to infuse 10 minutes.

2 Whisk together the honey and eggs in a bowl 1 to 2 minutes until the sugar dissolves. Put the chopped chocolate in a separate heatproof bowl. Remove the thyme from the cream mixture, return the pan to low heat and bring to a simmer. Pour the hot, infused milk over the chocolate, whisking all the time until the chocolate melts, then add the egg mixture to the chocolate and whisk together.

3 Divide the mixture into the glasses and put them in the prepared baking dish. Pour enough warm water into the dish to come halfway up the sides of the glasses to create a bain marie. Bake the chocolate pots 10 to 12 minutes until they are just trembling. If necessary, return the dish to the oven and bake 5 to 10 minutes longer.

4 Remove the baking dish from the oven, then transfer the glasses to a wire rack to cool completely. Cover with plastic wrap, then chill in the refrigerator 2 to 3 hours. Serve the chocolate pots with biscotti, *pain de gênes* or warm madeleines.

Crushed Strawberries and **Tarragon Crème Fraîche**

This recipe is so French and holds great childhood memories for me. I must have picked strawberries in my garden hundreds of times, and every time with the same enthusiasm. I was always the first to answer when Mom said, "Who wants to go to pick some strawberries?" I was also often the last to come back, because I had been too busy eating them! We'd enjoy a big bowl with a slice of toasted brioche spread with lovely fresh farm butter—so good! But here is a new way to serve them with crème fraîche and freshly chopped tarragon.

SERVES 4 to 6
PREPARATION TIME 20 minutes,
  plus 20 minutes macerating

5⅓ cups strawberries, hulled and
  roughly chopped
½ cup sugar
juice of 1 small lemon
1 cup crème fraîche
1 tablespoon chopped tarragon
  leaves
10 ounces fresh brioche loaf,
  thickly sliced

1 Mix the strawberries with the sugar and lemon juice in a nonmetallic bowl, cover and leave to macerate in the refrigerator 15 to 20 minutes.

2 Remove the strawberries from the refrigerator, add the crème fraîche and mix together, lightly crushing the fruit with the back of a fork. Add the tarragon and stir once more.

3 Toast the brioche, then serve it hot with the strawberries and tarragon cream.

Orange, Cardamom and **Thyme Salad**

I love to make this refreshing salad with blood oranges when they are in season. Oranges combine so well with so many desserts, especially chocolate, as the soft, sweet acidity cuts through that rich texture. Try this with my Chocolate, Chili and Lemongrass Tart (see page 208). The hint of thyme adds an elegant and unexpected touch.

SERVES 4
PREPARATION TIME 15 minutes,
  plus 30 minutes macerating
  and 30 minutes cooling

2 small blood oranges or ordinary
  oranges
2 cardamom pods, lightly crushed
2 tablespoons sugar
½ teaspoon freshly picked thyme
  leaves

1 Finely pare the orange zest, then peel and segment the oranges over a bowl to catch the juices. Put the cardamom into the juice and leave 30 minutes. Pat the orange segments dry on a clean dish towel.

2 Put the zest in a saucepan, cover with cold water and bring to a boil. Remove the pan from the heat, drain the zest and refresh under cold water, then drain again; repeat the process. Return the zest to the pan, add the sugar and 3 tablespoons water and stir to dissolve. Bring to a boil and cook 5 minutes, or until the zest is transparent, then leave to cool.

3 Strain the flavored juice into a small pan over medium heat and cook a few minutes until it reduces by half and is syrupy. Stir in the zest and syrup, then leave to cool. Toss with the orange segments in a bowl, then add the thyme leaves to serve.

Caramelized Pear and Rosemary Cake

I love the flavor of just-ripe fall pears, roasted in a red wine syrup with slivered almonds, in a *tatin*, with chocolate and vanilla ice cream or simply on their own when they're juicy. You will never enjoy them more, however, than when they are caramelized, then folded into a cake batter with a hint of scented rosemary. Of course, I could have replaced that with spices, but somehow that did not seem right. I wanted some freshness to spread through the cake while it was baking, so I added the rosemary only after the pears were caramelized and cooling to let the scent infuse the cake.

SERVES 6 to 8
PREPARATION TIME 25 minutes
COOKING TIME 30 minutes

FOR THE PEARS
½ cup sugar
3 tablespoons unsalted butter
2 pears at room temperature,
   peeled, halved, cored and roughly
   chopped
leaves from 1 rosemary sprig,
   finely chopped

FOR THE CAKE
7 tablespoons unsalted butter, plus
   extra for greasing
a little all-purpose flour, for dusting
½ cup confectioner's sugar
3 eggs
¾ cup plus 2 tablespoons
   all-purpose flour
1 teaspoon baking powder

1 Heat the oven to 315°F and butter and flour a 12- x 5- x 3½-inch bread pan or silicone cake mold. To cook the pears, put a large skillet over low heat. Add the sugar and cook slowly a few minutes until it turns to a light golden caramel, then add the butter. When it is foaming, add the pears. (Once more, it is essential the pears are at room temperature, otherwise the caramel will form lumps of hardened caramel and then it's a matter of starting again!) Cook the pears about 10 minutes until they are soft and caramelized. Remove the pan from the heat, add the rosemary and toss gently to combine, then lay the pears on a clean dish towel to cool and dry slightly; you want the dish towel to absorb any juices.

2 To make the cake, the butter needs to be really light in texture and color so beat the confectioner's sugar and butter, using an electric mixer, until almost white in color and very, very light and fluffy. Only then, add the eggs, one at a time, beating well between each addition. Sift the flour and baking powder together into a bowl, then sift two-thirds into the batter. Add the pears to the reserved flour and toss to coat thoroughly, then fold the dusted pears gently into the batter.

3 Spoon the batter into the prepared pan and smooth the surface. Bake 25 minutes, or until a skewer inserted into the middle comes out clean. If it isn't baked, return it to the oven 5 minutes longer and check again.

4 Transfer the cake to a wire rack and leave to cool for as long as you can wait, then cut a slice and serve with a cup of tea. And, if I were you, I'd sneak a slice quickly before everyone else smells it and wants some, too.

Chocolate Marble Cake with Citrus Fruit Glaze

When I was younger, I always wondered how the pattern on a marble cake was created! It looked so pretty when it was sliced, and the chocolate aroma used to pervade the room. As always, quality ingredients are crucial, so do make sure the cocoa powder is of great quality, as the success of the final result depends on it. You might need a little practice to perfect the technique of folding and swirling the batter, but the chocolate aroma will make it all worthwhile. Don't forget to drizzle the citrus syrup over while the cake is still warm so the liquid gold can gently find its way down this beautiful cake.

SERVES 6 to 8
PREPARATION TIME 25 minutes, plus 5 minutes cooling
COOKING TIME 30 minutes

FOR THE MARBLE CAKE

1⅓ cups plus 1 tablespoon white bread flour, plus extra for dusting
½ teaspoon baking powder
4 eggs
1 cup sugar
a pinch salt
6 tablespoons heavy cream
4 tablespoons unsalted butter, melted, plus extra for greasing
2 tablespoons unsweetened, dark cocoa powder

FOR THE CITRUS SYRUP

juice of 1 orange
juice of 1 pink grapefruit
juice of 1 lime
2 tablespoons sugar

1 Heat the oven to 315°F and butter and flour a 12- x 5- x 3½-inch bread pan or a silicone cake mold, then leave to one side.

2 Sift the flour and baking powder into a bowl. Put the eggs, sugar and salt in another large bowl and beat, using an electric mixer, for a good 8 to 10 minutes until it is really light, thick and foaming. Fold in the cream, then add the sifted flour and baking powder and fold gently together. Finally fold in the melted butter. Transfer one-third of the batter to a small bowl. Sift the cocoa powder into the remaining batter and mix gently until all the cocoa is combined.

3 Put half the cocoa mixture into the bottom of the prepared cake pan, then add the reserved plain batter and finish with the remaining cocoa batter. Put the handle end of a spatula into the batter at the left-hand side of the pan at a 45-degree angle. Using a folding action, gently pull the handle around the edges of the batter, then down through the middle, making three "folds" while moving from left to right down the length of the pan. This will give you a great marbled effect.

4 Bake the cake 25 to 30 minutes until a skewer inserted into the middle comes out clean. If the cake is not quite baked, then slide it back into the oven and bake 5 minutes longer and check again.

5 Meanwhile, put all the syrup ingredients in a small saucepan over low heat and heat slowly until the sugar dissolves. Turn the heat up to medium and cook until there is about 2 tablespoons syrup, which is thick enough to coat the back of a spoon. Remove the pan from the heat and leave to one side.

6 Remove the cake from the oven and put the pan on a wire rack to cool 5 minutes. Turn the cake out of the pan and drizzle the citrus syrup over the top. Leave to cool a little before slicing and serving.

Kitchen Terminology

I hope you find this short glossary useful when you are using the recipes. Many of the terms might be familiar, others less so, and there are some you might take for granted, but not really know the precise details.

Bain marie: Literally a water bath. The food is cooked very gently, on the stovetop or in the oven, in a container surrounded by water in a larger container, be it a baking dish, baking sheet or roasting pan.

Bake blind: To bake a pastry case without the filling, lined with parchment paper and covered with baking beans to keep it flat, about 10 minutes. The paper and beans are then removed and the pastry case is returned to the oven a few minutes longer.

Beignet: A fritter.

Blanch: Briefly immersing food in a pan of boiling water to barely cook it, before lifting out the food and submerging it briefly in ice water to stop further cooking.

Bouillon: A broth or stock made with meat and vegetables.

Boulangère: A dish made with meat and of layers of sliced vegetables, usually potatoes.

Bourguignonne: Cook in the style of the Burgundy region, typically in a full-bodied red wine.

Bouquet garni: A small bunch of mixed herbs—usually made up of a bay leaf, thyme, parsley and celery leaves—used to flavor a soup, stew or sauce.

Braise: To roast or brown a piece of meat, poultry or vegetable in fat, then add a small amount of liquid and slowly simmer in a covered pot.

Bruise: To gently crush an ingredient, such as a lemongrass stalk, to release the flavor.

Caramel: A rich golden brown syrup made by heating sugar and water together.

Cartouche: A circle of parchment paper with a small hole in the middle used to cover foods while they cook.

Ceviche: Raw fish marinated in citrus juice to "cook" the fish without any heat.

Clarify: To heat butter so the solids separate and can be discarded.

Confit: The French word for "preserved," most usually pork, goose, duck or turkey cooked in its own fat and then stored in a covered pot, but it can also refer to fruit preserved in syrup.

Coulis: A thick puree or sauce, made from fruit or vegetables.

Cure: To preserve food, usually by salting, smoking or drying.

Deglaze: Adding liquid to a cooking pan and stirring to dissolve the caramelized brown bits stuck on the bottom of the pan, and then boiling to reduce the liquid.

Dehydrate: Dry out a food to preserve it.

Emulsify: Combine two ingredients that don't usually mix, like oil and water, by gradually whisking them together.

En cocotte: Eggs baked individually in cream or butter in ramekins.

En papillote: Food cooked in sealed parchment-paper or aluminum-foil packages.

Farci: The French word for "stuffed," often refering to stuffed vegetables, such as stuffed potatoes or zucchini.

Flambé: To pour a measure of alcohol, often brandy, over hot food in a pan and briefly set it alight to burn off the alcohol.

Fold in: To combine two mixtures with a large metal spoon in a figure-of-eight movement, knocking out as little air as possible.

Fricassee: Describes a dish of small pieces of meat, often chicken, served in a thick white sauce

Gratin: A topping browned under a hot broiler, often including cheese or bread crumbs.

Julienne: Cutting vegetables or fruit zest into very thin sticks, $\frac{1}{16}$ x $1\frac{1}{4}$ inch, using a knife or a mandolin.

Macerate: To soak and soften before cooking or serving.

Marinate: To soak in a spiced liquid to impart flavor before cooking.

Mandolin: A manual slicer with different blades so you can use it to very thinly slice, grate or cut into strips.

Pithivier: A round, double-crust pie made with puff pastry.

Poach: To cook food gently in a very hot, but not bubbling, liquid, keeping the water just below a simmer.

Ragout: A stew made from meat, poultry, game, fish or vegetables that is cooked with herbs and spices.

Reduce: To boil in an uncovered pan to evaporate some of the liquid and, by doing so, to reduce the quantity of liquid and, thereby, strengthen the flavors of the liquid.

Refresh: To quickly immerse cooked food in ice or very cold water to stop the cooking process and set the color.

Rémoulade: A mayonnaise-based sauce seasoned with various ingredients, which can include chili, capers or paprika.

Rillettes: Cooked, shredded meat preserved in fat.

Sabayon: A light, frothy sauce made by whisking egg yolks with liquid in a bowl set over a pan of simmering water.

Sauté: Cooking in a little fat in a shallow pan over medium to high heat to brown or cook ingredients, keeping the food constantly moving around the pan.

Sous-vide: To cook food in a vacuum pack, either by boiling or steaming.

Steam: To cook food in the heat from the steam from boiling water.

Tian: A dish made of alternate layers of various sliced vegetables and other ingredients, with herbs and seasoning.

Velouté: One of the basic sauces in classic French cuisine, made with the cooking liquid and thickened with a roux, a blend of butter and flour.

Index

Author Acknowledgments

I would like to thank the following people:
My entire family, for their support, friendship, patience and love.
The team at HHB, especially Heather Holden-Brown, for believing in me, for your valuable support and for setting up this second book.
My publishers, Duncan, and to Grace – you are a star. And the rest of the gang at DBP – you are brilliant.
Janet Brinkworth, for working so hard to help me put the book together.
The management and my team at The Vineyard for allowing me the time I needed to work on the book and to do the photoshoot. In particular, Anthony Millon, my pastry chef, for giving me lots of tips on my dessert ideas to help make them happen. And to Greig Young for your help in The Vineyard kitchen when I was testing recipes.
My supplier, Peter, at Aubrey Allen, for helping me with the gorgeous produce – thank you very much.
Also Wendy Hobson and Nicola Graimes for editing the recipes and trying to keep me on time (or not!) and for your everlasting patience.
Manisha, Yuki and Aya – you are all very talented in what you do. It is always a privilege to work with you and I could not have done this book without you. You are the team!
And finally, Heston Blumenthal – your foreword is a joy to read, and thank you for being my friend. It is always appreciated.